"Saeng shares our Lao culture and food beautifully. *The Lao Kitchen* has taken me back to a time when my life was a perfect place of family and food. I am so proud to be Lao and even more proud of Saeng for sharing his love of the Lao kitchen with the world."

—**Jujubee**

"As someone who's been following the work of Saeng and tasted his cooking personally, I know his passion for educating the world about the joy of Lao cuisine is simply unmatched. This book is a delight in learning about the untold beauty of Lao flavors, and whether you're an expert in cooking or a novice, it'll make you itch to cook and taste the culinary delights that Laos has to offer."

—**Kim Chi**, drag queen, author of *Kim Chi Eats the World*, and a beauty mogul

"I have been in love with Lao food since my first bite. I remember it like yesterday. It had a bite in the best kind of way: funky, sweet, spicy, bitter, sour, and a little something extra I couldn't quite put my finger on. I found myself wanting to know more, and then I found Saeng. The way he cooks is unapologetic and at the same time preserves history one bite, and one story, at a time. This book is a national treasure, and we will all be cooking like a Lao grandma because of Saeng."

—**Tiffany Derry**, chef, restaurateur, TV personality, and social justice advocate

"Saeng's cookbook is more than a collection of recipes, it's a love letter to every Lao American household that has bridged cultures through food. I see this work as a powerful extension of the Lao Food Movement's mission: to preserve, celebrate, and amplify the stories of our community through the lens of our kitchens. Saeng captures the resilience, creativity, and heritage of Lao cooking in each page, making this book an invaluable addition to every book collection, not only for Lao families but for anyone seeking connection through food and storytelling."

—**Aleena Inthaly**, creative director, Lao Food Movement

Saeng Douangdara

The Lao Kitchen

ເຮືອນຄົວລາວ

LAO FLAVORS & STORIES TOLD THROUGH FAMILY RECIPES

TEN SPEED PRESS
California | New York

Contents

6. Noodle Dishes 149

7. Soups & Stews 173

8. Desserts 197

9. Lao American Fusion 223

FOREWORD

BY KULAP VILAYSACK

I met Saeng in the spring of 2017 when he entered an event at my house for Legacies of War (LoW). LoW is a Lao American–led "educational and advocacy organization working to address the ongoing impact of the American wars in Laos, Cambodia, and Vietnam." From 1964 to 1973, the United States dropped more than two million tons of ordnance on Laos—most of it in the form of cluster bombs. That amounted to more than 270 million cluster bombies, 80 million of which did not explode on impact and are still in the ground. Laos remains the most-bombed country per capita in history. It's fitting that our story began on the day of that LoW event—two Lao Americans from the Midwest trying to bridge the gap between our war-refugee parents' definition of being Lao and our own.

Even though Saeng walks through life like a grandma who can operate her iPhone, I am technically older, so I am his Euay (big sister) and he is my Nong Sai (little brother). And thus I have forced him into a dynamic where I could loosely be called a mentor—basically, I offer him advice and support, and lovingly boss him around. I have had the pleasure of witnessing Saeng's professional evolution from a UCLA college counselor who moonlighted as a caterer, a cooking instructor at The Gourmandise School in Santa Monica, and a private chef for an NBA player, to a full-time content creator, cookbook author, and food photographer. Of course, as his Euay, I am so proud . . . and I humbly take my credit, thank you.

I've also had the privilege of watching Saeng's personal evolution, which is very tied to his professional one. There was a distinct turning point in his content creation when, on top of his delicious Lao food demonstrations, he began to share his full self with the viewer. He told the stories only he could tell, bravely being vulnerable in the lion's den that is social media. Very quickly it became clear that in doing so, he connected with a large audience who related to him—and for a '90s gay kid from conservative Wisconsin, I can't begin to tell you how meaningful that is. It's beautiful, because Saeng is very passionate about Lao food representation—I would say it's his life's mission. Perhaps this is overstepping (I don't know what that term is because I am his Euay), but I think that through giving his authentic self for the love of his mission he accomplished the greatest one of all, a love of self. This is what I am most proud of him for.

Our motherland is Laos and our home is the United States. To escape Laos, my father pulled my mom across the Mekong River in a tire, in the dead of night. I was conceived in a Thai refugee camp and Saeng was born in another. We stand on our parents' strong and traumatized shoulders, with the intimate knowledge that no one leaves home unless they have to. It's because of them that whenever I think about my Lao-ness, my Lao identity, I taste it first. I picture us sharing loud family meals: steaming sticky rice in a bamboo basket, a variety of pungent dips, soupspoons going into one single large bowl of stew, a big plate of laab, a colander of fresh herbs, and grilled fish with the head on. This is why I am so excited for this book, because food is the way I will always feel connected to my family.

The above is my abridged and incomplete version of how we got here: with you, dear reader, holding a Lao food cookbook from a major U.S. publisher in your hands. This book is an American dream, realized by my smart, sweet, sensitive, spicy, and very funny nong sai, Saengthong Douangdara.

INTRODUCTION

If Lao food were to be described in one word, it would be "funky." However, if you look a little deeper, you will discover a cuisine that uses its ingredients in a way that balances all of the five basic tastes: sweetness, sourness, bitterness, savoriness, and saltiness in perfect harmony. In Lao food, palm sugar is often used to add sweetness, while limes act as a sour counterpart, offsetting the intensity and bringing life to the dish. Plants like cassia leaves introduce a subtle bitterness, and a hint of MSG boosts the savoriness of anything it touches to an astronomical level of yum. Lastly, padaek (unfiltered fish sauce), the liquid gold unique to Lao cuisine, acts as the general, providing saltiness while keeping the other tastes in line. All the tastes and elements work together to create beautifully balanced dishes that showcase the pillars of Lao cuisine: sticky rice, padaek, hot peppers, fresh herbs, and aromatics.

The bold flavor profiles and rustic cooking techniques of Lao food have made significant impacts on other cultures' cuisines throughout history. Despite this, Lao food itself is still relatively unknown in the culinary world. Many people who claim that they have never heard of Lao food may not know that some of their favorite Asian dishes, like laab and papaya salad, actually originated in this landlocked country hidden in the jungles of Southeast Asia. Someone once told me that food has no borders, and Lao cuisine is the perfect example of the truth of this. The flavors of Laos have been expanding beyond its borders for centuries: historically throughout the northernmost part of the Kingdom of Siam (modern-day Thailand) and, more recently, across the globe as refugees fled and relocated, displaced by what we term the "American Secret War" of the 1960s and 1970s.

Laos has had a turbulent history of imperialism, colonization, and war. And for many, Lao food remained the only constant throughout. Beginning in the late nineteenth century, Laos was a colony of France, as part of French Indochina, but briefly gained independence in the mid-1950s. Internal conflict led the country into civil war shortly thereafter, furthering the chaos and uncertainty about the country's future. When the Vietnam War started in 1955, the conflict spilled over into neighboring countries, including Laos. Although the country officially remained neutral, this was far from the reality. The U.S. government trained the Royal Lao forces, along with fighters from ethnic minorities like the Hmong and Mien, in an effort to push back communist-backed forces and to destroy the Ho Chi Minh Trail, which passed through Laos.

While training the Lao forces, America was also relentlessly bombing the country, with a goal of disrupting the communists' supply chain on the Vietnam-Laos border. This campaign, known colloquially as the "American Secret War," led to Laos becoming the most bombed country in the world per capita, with 2.5 million tons of explosive ordnance dropped, the equivalent of a planeload of bombs dropping every eight minutes, twenty-four hours a day, for a total of nine years. In the aftermath of the Vietnam War, countless Lao people fled to refugee camps in neighboring Thailand in an effort to escape political persecution. Having left behind all of their material possessions and facing an uncertain future, many families, including mine, had only one way to re-create the comfort of the home they once knew: through cooking.

As refugees eventually moved out of camps and relocated to different countries, often traveling thousands of miles across the Pacific Ocean, and landing in every corner of the world, they took with them the flavors and culinary experience of Lao food. It was with this displacement that we truly began to see Lao food slowly introduce itself to the world. Many refugees opened restaurants in whatever city they ended up in, hoping to bring the comfort they found in their food to others in their new community. However, according to many long-time Lao restaurant owners, at the time people were intimidated by the boldness of Lao flavors. The food was often deemed "too funky" to enjoy, forcing restaurant owners to market the food as something else in order to make it feel like a safer option. Due to the popularity of Thai food, many Lao refugees who started restaurants sold their food under the guise of the more accepted cuisine. This gave rise to the phenomenon of the Lao/Thai restaurant, typically owned by a Lao person trying to find business success while quietly maintaining their identity. These restaurateurs tended to keep Lao options on the menu to a minimum, or only made them available to patrons ordering off the "secret menu."

In the 2000s, after decades of establishing a foothold in the restaurant world, these same owners were finally able to begin marketing their food as Lao, emboldened by growing demand for more authentic Lao eateries that embraced the power of the funk. In re-creating delicate, often intricate foods strictly from memory without the aid of written recipes, these chefs in the Lao diaspora achieved miracles. What they have been able to accomplish for Lao food worldwide deserves every praise.

Few cookbooks exist that are dedicated to Lao food. This is in large part because food culture in Laos is traditionally passed down orally and picked up through observing. Memorized recipes typically use measurements that are by nature inconsistent: The utensil used in "a spoonful" of something could be anything from a teaspoon to a soupspoon, setting the novice up for failure from the start. The Lao immigrant kitchen is also often home to mysterious sauces stored in repurposed gallon-sized ice cream tubs and spices in unmarked containers. To the uninitiated, these random containers may seem to exist only to cause disappointment as they never contain what they are meant to. However, the experienced cook knows how these ingredients can be transformed into drool-worthy food in feats that are nothing short of magical.

A lot of my childhood was spent watching my mae (mom) perform magic in the kitchen, turning common Midwest ingredients into a Lao feast. Looking back, I can only imagine how difficult it must have been for her to relocate to a foreign country that offered so little access to all the things that are at the core of Lao cuisine. Yet she persevered. She and my paw (dad) would drive over an hour each way to Madison, Wisconsin, to get a bag of sticky rice, a food so deeply ingrained in our culture that the Lao people refer to themselves as "the children of sticky rice." She made her own padaek from the fish Paw caught in a nearby river. And whatever herbs and peppers she could not find in the local market she grew in her garden. Her story is like that of so many other refugees, showcasing their imperative will to preserve culture, culinary know-how, and traditions using the resources available to them.

One unintended consequence of passing down recipes solely by word of mouth is that it has created a barrier to entry for those who would like to try cooking Lao food. Younger generations in the Lao diaspora not only have to overcome a language barrier if they don't speak Lao, but must also be brave enough to source and cook with ingredients that may be unfamiliar to them, such as beef bile or duck blood. It is also the case that, in an example of fully cooking from the heart, when Lao recipes are passed down, they are often tied to personal stories and experiences, sometimes traumatic ones, with the emotions manifesting themselves in the end product. As younger generations become

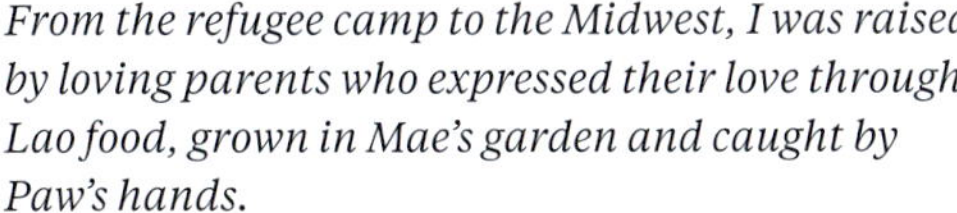

From the refugee camp to the Midwest, I was raised by loving parents who expressed their love through Lao food, grown in Mae's garden and caught by Paw's hands.

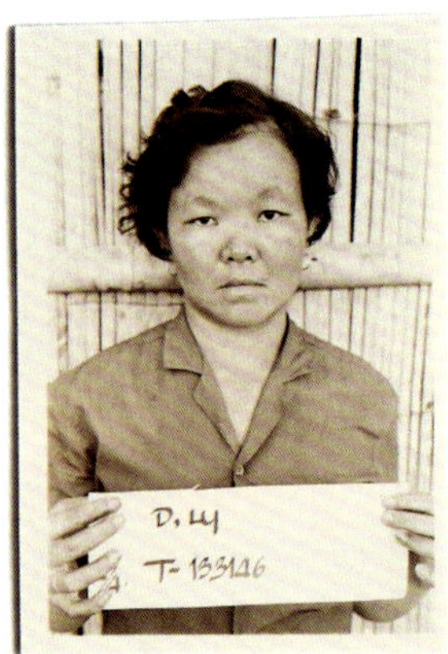

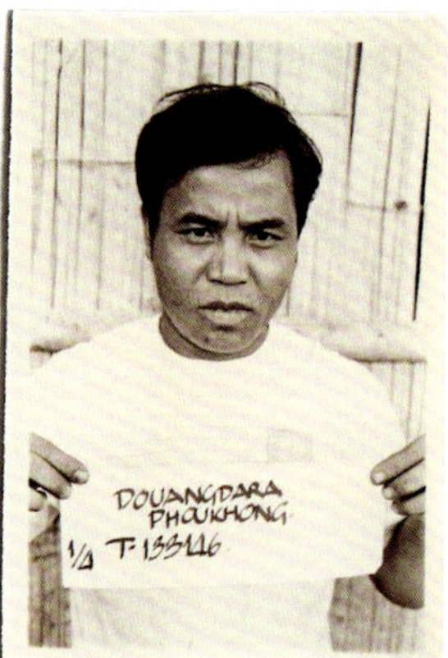

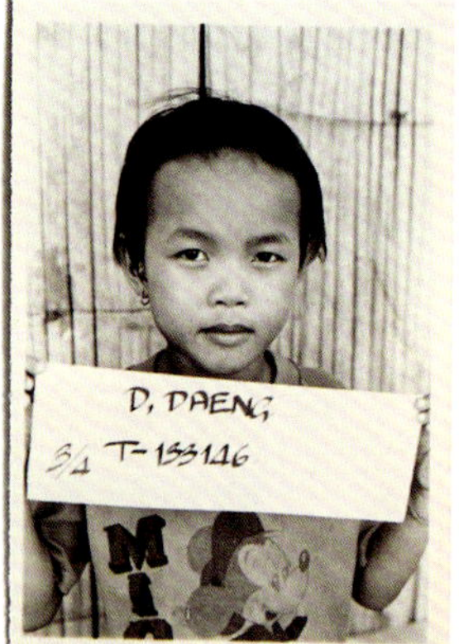

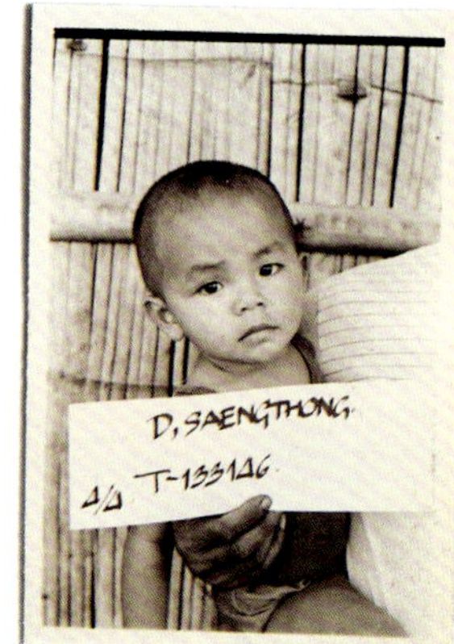

more removed from both the experiences and the culinary knowledge of those who came before them, they may find themselves unable to exactly replicate the flavors that live in their memories. And, perhaps, that's okay.

It's been almost fifty years since much of the Lao diaspora fled Laos. Ever since, our community has worked to find new ways of preserving our food traditions. Throughout this same time, there has been a large and growing interest in Southeast Asian cuisine, and in this context Lao food has started to gain more recognition. This in turn inspires new generations of Lao people to embrace and innovate within our culinary heritage. In the hope of expanding on what Lao cooking is to me as a member of the Lao diaspora, my contribution to that movement is this cookbook, which contains both traditional Lao recipes and reimagined classics, along with the stories that inspired them. I hope this book will help bridge gaps between generations and cultures and ensure that Lao culinary knowledge and traditions continue to be passed down and cherished. The stories I share are my own, but with them I hope to provide you with a starting point on your own journey to create new stories and memories that you can one day share with others.

By embracing the funk, we can each honor the culinary heritage of Lao cuisine and cook dishes that leave a lasting impression on both our taste buds and our hearts. So add the padaek and make it "Lao hot." Be as bold as the flavors of the masterpieces you are about to make. In fact, I challenge you to make it even Lao-der.

These refugee photos were a critical part of my family's resettlement process. They served not only as proof of our identity, but also as a lasting record of our journey and survival.

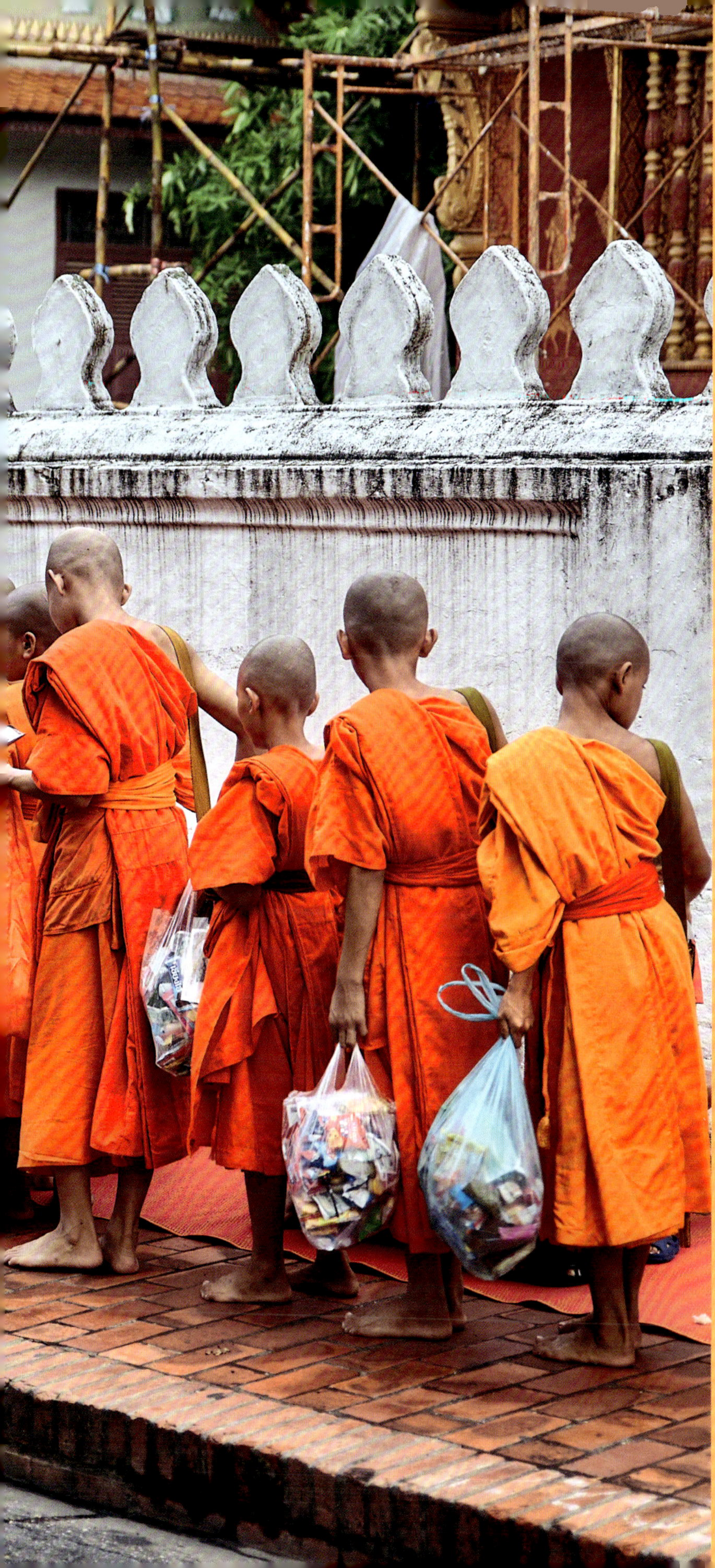

1

DIPS & OTHER KITCHEN STAPLES

ແຈ່ວບອງ
Chili Paste with Buffalo skin
30.000
Tel:77775155

The Diaspora of Laos Pantry

With the Lao diaspora spread across the globe, our ability to re-create traditional Lao dishes is both a challenge and a celebration of heritage. Through community gatherings, Lao families have found innovative ways to adapt their cooking to new environments, keeping our cuisine alive while embracing local ingredients.

This chapter provides a foundational guide to setting up a Lao kitchen, making it easy to re-create the recipes in this book no matter where you are. From selecting the right rice, peppers, fish sauce, and aromatics to finding suitable alternatives, I'll help you simplify your grocery shopping. After going through pantry staples, we'll explore dips, which are often used as ingredients in other recipes or served as accompaniments.

Lao Pantry Staples

This section is a primer on key ingredients and pantry staples used throughout the book, along with tips on how to prepare them and what to look for when buying them.

Rice

Sticky rice (also known as **glutinous rice**) comes in several varieties. Laos does not export its sticky rice, and Thailand supplies most sticky rice available worldwide. However, the varieties grown in Laos are unique. In Xieng Khouang Province, the rare khao gai noi sticky rice thrives due to the region's specific environmental conditions. This short-grain variety has a distinctive appearance and texture and is unlike the long-grain sticky rice commonly sold elsewhere. Traditionally, sticky rice is steamed, not boiled, requiring hours of soaking to achieve a soft, fluffy texture; it's eaten by hand. Once cooked, sticky rice is stored in a bamboo basket (thip khao) to keep it warm and aerated and to prevent sogginess. Leftover sticky rice doesn't need refrigeration; instead, it can be resteamed the next day, with the old rice layered on top of freshly cooked rice. This timeless method of preparation connects sticky rice to its roles as both a staple food and an essential utensil in Lao cuisine, a centerpiece of every meal.

Roasted sticky rice powder is used to add a smoky, nutty flavor to dishes. It is a common ingredient in laab, where it helps to absorb and bind the other ingredients, and is also used in soups, stews, and dips. To make roasted sticky rice powder, it's best to work outside, as the process can get very smoky. Start by heating a cast-iron skillet over high heat until a drop of water sizzles. Add 1 cup of uncooked sticky (glutinous) rice and toast it for about 8 minutes. Stir frequently and adjust the heat as needed to prevent burning. The rice should become evenly toasted, taking on an almost dark brown color. Once it's toasted, transfer the rice to a plate and let it cool completely. When it's cool, grind it into a fine powder using a mortar and pestle or a spice grinder. Store it in a zip-top bag, pressing out as much air as possible to keep it fresh; keep it in the pantry for two months or in the freezer for up to six months. It won't spoil, but it will start to lose its aroma and flavor after that time. Roasted sticky rice powder is available in some markets, but I've noticed that it's usually not roasted as dark as I prefer.

The recipes in this book will specify the type of **rice flour** needed. My preferred brand is Erawan. Their jasmine rice flour comes in a red bag, and their glutinous (sticky) rice flour is packaged in green bags. If you use other brands, choose a flour with a fine texture.

Fish Sauce

When you're making recipes that call for **padaek (unfiltered fish sauce),** I recommend making your own, though keep in mind it needs at least three months and up to a year to ferment; the recipe is on page 97. If your padaek isn't ready, you can use store-bought padaek. I suggest Pantai preserved fish sauce.

When "fish sauce" is called for in this book, I'm referring to a clear and **filtered fish sauce,** such as nam pa. There are many fish sauce brands available, so stick with one you like to get familiar with its flavor. Some fish sauces are saltier than others, so you may need to adjust a recipe's added salt accordingly. A few brands I enjoy are Three Crabs, Red Boat, and Squid.

Chile Peppers

Most of the hot peppers used in this cookbook are **bird's eye chile peppers,** also known as Thai chile peppers. If a recipe calls for "**fresh bird's eye chiles,**" it refers to the red ones, unless stated otherwise. "**Dried bird's eye chiles**" refers to the whole peppers that are typically sold at Southeast Asian markets. When a recipe calls for "**ground bird's eye chile,**" it means ground dried peppers.

Whether you're grinding them or using them whole, it's best to toast dried peppers to increase their spiciness and smokiness. To do so, set a medium pan over medium-low heat; when it's hot, lay whole dried chile peppers in it and dry-toast them for about 3 minutes, flipping frequently to ensure even toasting, until their color slightly darkens. Let them cool a bit and then grind them in a mortar and pestle or spice grinder. If a recipe calls for a tablespoon measurement of ground dried chile, it takes about six whole dried chiles to make 1 tablespoon of ground chile.

Oils and Coconut Milk

The most common oil I use in these recipes is **vegetable oil,** but other **neutral cooking oils** like peanut or avocado oil also work well, whether for sautéing or deep-frying. When deep-frying, it's best to use a neutral oil with a high smoke point: canola, peanut, avocado, grapeseed, and safflower (among others) work well.

When buying canned **coconut milk,** look for whole-fat, unsweetened varieties; reduced-fat coconut milk doesn't give the same results. My recommended brands include Chaokoh, Aroy-D, and Chef's Choice.

For homemade coconut milk, puree the meat of a mature coconut in a blender with 3 cups of warm water, then strain out the solids. Homemade coconut milk can be stored in the refrigerator for up to five days.

Pastes

Various pastes are essential ingredients for adding flavor and texture to many dishes. Black crab paste, firm shrimp paste, tamarind paste, red curry paste, and limestone paste can all be found at Southeast Asian markets. When buying **black crab paste,** make sure to get the jet-black paste, not crab paste in bean oil. Look for **shrimp paste** in a firm block; avoid the saucy version. **Tamarind paste** refers to the spoonable form that comes in jars, but if only the solid brick form (tamarind pulp) is available, you can make your own by mixing it with warm water until it reaches a ketchup-like consistency and then straining out the pulp. **Red curry paste** is often sold in single-serving cans, but fresh paste is always better (see page 21). **Limestone paste** comes in a white or red/pink form. The white form is preferred in cooking; its alkalinity is used to keep ingredients firm in some dishes and to help make fried pastry crispy in others.

Red Curry Paste

Makes 1½ cups

1½ cups loosely packed California chiles (dried Anaheim chiles), stemmed (about 1 ounce)

4 cups boiling water, for soaking

½ cup minced lemongrass (from the soft part of about 3 lemongrass stalks)

⅓ cup minced peeled galangal

2 tablespoons minced fresh makrut lime leaves (about 10 leaves)

3 tablespoons minced garlic

½ cup minced shallots (about 3 whole)

½ cup chopped cilantro root (see page 22), or use stems from 1 bunch cilantro

1 fresh bird's eye chile, stemmed and minced

1½ teaspoons coarse kosher salt

1 teaspoon MSG

Place the California chiles in a large bowl and add the boiling water to cover. Soak for 5 minutes. Remove the chiles from the water and cut them in half. Using a spoon, remove the seeds and discard them; chop the rehydrated chiles. In a food processor, combine the chopped chiles, lemongrass, galangal, lime leaves, garlic, shallots, cilantro, bird's eye chile, salt, and MSG. Process until all the ingredients form a rough paste. Transfer to a container with an airtight lid, using a silicone spatula to scrape down the sides of the food processor bowl. Store the curry paste for up to two weeks in the refrigerator or freeze it in ¼-cup blocks for up to 3 months and defrost in the refrigerator before using it.

Aromatics

Alliums like **shallots** and **garlic** are often used in these recipes. Raw shallots are commonly used in salads; yellow onion can substitute if needed. Cooked shallots help thicken dips and sauces. **Fried shallots** and **fried garlic** are used often as well; these can be bought in jars at Asian grocery stores. (See the Herbs and Produce section below for information about **scallions'** role.)

To make fried shallots, peel and thinly slice 3 shallots crosswise into rings (you should have about 1 cup). In a medium pan with enough oil to cover the shallots (about 1 cup), cook the shallots over medium heat, stirring occasionally, for 10 to 15 minutes, until the shallots turn light golden blond. Strain the shallots through a fine-mesh sieve, reserving the shallot oil in a bowl underneath, and let the shallots drain and become dry. Once dry, store the fried shallots in an airtight container lined with a paper towel.

To make fried garlic, place 1 cup of minced garlic in a medium pan and add enough oil to cover the garlic, about 1 cup. Cook over medium-low heat, stirring occasionally, for 8 minutes, until the garlic turns light golden blond. Strain the garlic through a fine-mesh sieve, reserving the garlic oil in a bowl underneath, and let the garlic drain and become dry. Once dry, store the fried garlic in an airtight container lined with a paper towel.

Galangal is commonly used in Lao cuisine, but **ginger** makes a good substitute if you can't find galangal. For laab and curries, galangal or ginger are often finely minced, while for broths, they are thinly sliced and boiled. Any extra can be chopped into pieces and stored in the freezer.

Fresh **lemongrass** is usually sold in bunches of six to ten stalks. The soft inner part of the lemongrass is used in pastes and to flavor salads, dips, and other dishes. Many broths are flavored by a **lemongrass bundle,** and some recipes in this book call for one. To make the bundle, remove the tough outer layers of 1 stalk of lemongrass, setting one layer aside. Fold the remaining layers, the central layers of the stalks, into thirds, then wrap the saved layer around the bundle, tucking the ends underneath to secure it.

Sauces

Like pastes, sauces are essential flavor components in many dishes; they're also often used as marinades. **Oyster sauce** is commonly used in meat-heavy dishes, both as a marinade and to add a slight sweetness.

Sriracha (hot sauce) adds spice and acidity to many noodle soups. In Laos, Shark brand sriracha is commonly used, while in the United States, Huy Fong sriracha is more popular. If neither is available, Jeow Bong (page 26) can be used to add both spice and sweetness.

Seasoning sauce is a versatile soybean-based condiment, used for dipping hard-boiled eggs, pairing with sticky rice, or as an additional marinade for proteins. Golden Mountain brand is preferred; if it's unavailable, Maggi brand can be substituted.

Sweet soy sauce is another common condiment that enhances sweetness in marinades and sauces. The preferred brand is Kwong Hung Seng; Lee Kum Kee is a suitable alternative.

Sweeteners, Spices, and Seasonings

Lao cuisine often relies on fresh herbs and vegetables to create its bold flavors but also uses dried spices like **white and black pepper.** To enhance the spice and depth of flavor in dishes, use freshly ground pepper. Coarse kosher salt is preferred because its large crystals offer better measurement control and are more forgiving when seasoning. It also contains no additives like anti-caking agents or iodine, making it ideal for ferments and dipping sauces.

Most recipes in this book that call for sugar use **granulated sugar.** However, if you have access to **palm sugar,** I recommend using it for its unique flavor. Palm sugar typically comes in half-circle blocks; break it into clumps to measure it accurately.

MSG (monosodium glutamate) has been unfairly villainized for decades, even though it's a natural compound found in cheese, tomatoes, seaweed, and mushrooms. It is also used as an added ingredient in products like potato chips, soups, and even some drinks. MSG powder is a seasoning (similar to salt) that enhances the umami flavors in dishes. This cookbook calls for MSG in various recipes, and I encourage you to try using it in other dishes as well: It can help balance the flavors in a dish without adding more salt.

Herbs, Produce, and Specialty Foods

Makrut lime leaves (available online or in Southeast Asian markets) are highly fragrant. Fresh makrut lime leaves are best because they release aromatic essential oils into the food during cooking. Dried leaves have very little oil left, so they're much less flavorful. If you can't find makrut lime leaves, you can substitute 1 teaspoon of lime zest for every 4 leaves. To fully release their flavor, the leaves should be finely minced. To do this, fold the leaf in half lengthwise and pull or slice out the thick central vein, then stack the leaves, roll them tightly into a tube shape, and thinly slice perpendicular to the roll to create ribbons. Finally, mince the ribbons for a fine, uniform texture. Whole leaves can be used to flavor broths; when you do so, lightly crush them in your hands to release their aroma. The leaves are left in the dish for visual appeal, but they aren't meant to be eaten. Extra leaves can be stored in the freezer.

Cilantro and scallions are a staple herb duo used to garnish many Lao dishes. Both the white part of the scallion and the roots or thick stems of cilantro are packed with flavor and can be used to enhance curries or add depth to soups. In fact, if you find cilantro with the roots still attached, snatch it up; cilantro root has a slightly earthy, peppery taste that's highly prized by many cooks.

Unripe papaya has a crisp texture that is key to dishes like papaya salad. Look for a firm fruit with a deep forest-green color. Press gently on the skin and if it gives, it's too ripe. You can find unripe papayas in the produce section of most Southeast Asian markets.

To prepare unripe (green) papaya, peel the fruit and rinse it under cold water. Pat it dry with paper towels and proceed to shred it into thin slices. For a traditional approach, employ a cleaver: Hold the papaya in your non-dominant hand, create small lengthwise indentations, then run the blade down the side to generate uneven, small strands (this can be achieved with a chef's knife if you don't have a cleaver). This technique enhances the dish's texture and adds a delightful crunch.

Pandan leaves are often referred to as "the vanilla of Laos." The leaves are available at Southeast Asian markets, typically frozen, and sometimes fresh, bundled in plastic wrap. To extract the most flavor, leaves are blended with water in a high-speed blender, which breaks them down and releases their aroma into the liquid (see page 201). Some recipes in this book call for tying a pandan leaf into a knot. To do this, use a leaf about 12 inches long. Fold it back and forth every 3 inches to form a zigzag pattern. Then take the last 4 inches of the leaf, wrap it around the center of the zigzag, and tuck the end into the wrap to secure the knot. If your leaf is too short, you can use two 6-inch pieces instead.

Banana blossoms are sold fresh and wrapped in plastic wrap in the produce section of Southeast Asian markets. These recipes are designed for fresh banana blossoms, not canned ones, which have a different texture. The tender leaves are often used as toppings, adding a mild bitterness, earthy flavor, and crunch. While the flavor isn't the same, finely shredded napa cabbage can be a good substitute for a similar texture. Fresh banana blossoms, or buds, are about 10 inches long. They have concentric layers of "petals" (actually these are modified leaves called bracts) enclosing flower buds inside; the layers of thin leaves might remind you of the layers of a leek. **To prepare fresh banana blossoms:** Fill a large bowl halfway with water and squeeze two lime halves into it, or add a slosh of vinegar. Remove and discard the first four outer layers of the blossom, then rinse it. Cut the blossom in half lengthwise and, using a sharp knife or a mandoline, thinly slice one blossom in half horizontally from the top; transfer the slices to the acidified water as you go to keep them from browning. When your slices start cutting off the top tips of the soft white flower parts, stop, and start peeling away the outer layers of the banana blossom, setting them aside. Depending on your plans for them, keep or discard the long pale flowers as you go. When you reach the tender inner layers of the blossom, stack the set-aside layers together and thinly slice them and the tender inner layers into long strands. Place all the sliced pieces in the acidified water. If you will be using the flowers, remove the pistils by pulling out the florets, then peeling them open to expose the pistils. Detach the pistil from the base of the floret and discard it, as it is tough and not pleasant to eat.

Morning glory, also known as water spinach in English, ong choy in Cantonese, and pak boong in Lao, is a versatile vegetable. It adds a crisp texture when eaten fresh with papaya salad, and it's often blanched for noodle soups or stir-fried as a side dish. It is commonly found in Asian markets, where it's sold in long, leafy bundles that resemble bunches of spinach.

Rice paddy herb is called pak kha yang in Lao, and it adds a distinct cumin-like, earthy flavor to soups and stews. It's typically added at the end of cooking to preserve its aroma. Look for it at Southeast Asian markets, pre-portioned on trays and wrapped in plastic.

Banana leaves are a natural and sustainable alternative to aluminum foil, and are commonly used for wrapping, steaming, and transporting food. They are widely available in the frozen section of Asian markets in various sizes; fresh ones can sometimes be found in large African, Latin American, and Caribbean markets. When preparing the leaves for use, gently wipe each with a wet paper towel. Since the banana leaves available in the West tend to be dense, they may need to be lightly heated over a flame to make them pliable enough to use.

Coagulated pork blood can be found at Asian markets, usually packaged on a plastic-wrapped tray. To use it in the recipes in this book, cut the pork blood into 1-inch cubes. To cook the cubes, add them to a medium pot with a bundle of lemongrass (see page 21) and cover with water. Bring to a boil, then simmer for 10 minutes. Drain and set aside to use in your dish.

Traditional Equipment

You can find this traditional equipment at Southeast Asian supermarkets and online.

The **sticky rice steamer** (huat khao) consists of two main parts: a woven bamboo basket on top to hold the rice and a metal pot below to hold the water (see page 73 for how to use it). (To make cleanup easier and prevent the bamboo from tearing, I recommend lining the basket with **cheesecloth** before placing the rice inside.) Once the rice is cooked, transfer it to a **woven bamboo rice platter**, and gently spread it apart to release excess heat. After it's cool to the touch, roll the rice into a ball and place it in a **sticky rice basket** (thip khao, or eap khao) for serving. These baskets come in various shapes and sizes, but their woven design is essential; it keeps the rice warm while allowing steam to escape, preventing the rice from becoming mushy. If you can't locate traditional items like a sticky rice steamer, you can use a bamboo dim sum steamer or a metal steam basket.

A deep clay **Lao mortar and wooden pestle** (khok and sahk) is ideal for making many Lao salads and pastes (though other kinds of mortars can be used if that is what you have). This particular type of mortar and pestle originated in Laos and later became common in Thailand as papaya salad spread to neighboring countries.

For breaking down dense, thick ingredients like whole chicken, a **cleaver** is the most efficient, effective tool. A cleaver is also commonly used for shredding papaya into strands, cutting through kabocha pumpkin with ease, and many other cutting and slicing tasks.

Once Lao food is ready to serve, the dishes are plated and arranged on a low, **circular bamboo table** called a pha khao. These tables come in various sizes to accommodate different family gatherings, ensuring everyone can share the meal. The phak hao is placed on a saht, a traditional **woven mat**, upon which everyone sits cross-legged, enjoying both the meal and, often, the shared experience of preparing it.

Jeows

Once you've stocked up on Lao pantry essentials, you'll be ready to dive into jeows, flavorful dips made by smashing aromatics into umami-rich pastes, perfect for pairing with sticky rice. Mastering the mortar and pestle for these dips is your first step into the rhythmic process of Lao cooking, preparing you for all the techniques used in the recipes in this book.

Jeow Bong ◆ Luang Prabang Fermented Pepper Dip

แจ่วบอง

Jeow bong is an irresistible introduction to the variety of jeows in Lao cuisine. When I was growing up, my mae kept a constant rotation of jeows in the fridge, and jeow bong was always front and center. When I visited Laos for the first time in 2019, I discovered a completely different type of jeow bong: mild in heat, luscious in texture, and chewy with ox skin. Jeow bong from northern Laos, specifically Luang Prabang, is dramatically less spicy than Mae's version, which was influenced by her upbringing in southern Laos. The dip stains every grain of sticky rice with its vibrant magenta hues, while garlic and galangal punctuate its sweet, salty, aromatic flavor. This recipe re-creates Luang Prabang jeow bong using Korean coarse pepper flakes, also known as gochugaru, to achieve the characteristic bright pepper color and mild spice level.

Makes 3 cups | Serves 8 to 10

¼ cup chopped peeled galangal

20 garlic cloves, lightly smashed

1⅓ cups gochugaru (Korean chile flakes)

3 tablespoons ground dried bird's eye chile (see page 18)

3 cups thinly sliced yellow onion

1½ teaspoons coarse kosher salt

¾ cup vegetable oil

1½ teaspoons MSG

⅓ cup sugar

⅓ cup fish sauce (see page 18)

¼ cup tamarind paste

Prepare the aromatic base: In a deep mortar, smash the galangal into a paste. Add the garlic and continue pounding into a rough paste. Transfer the paste to a large bowl. Add the gochugaru, ground chile, onion, and salt. Toss until all ingredients are combined and the onion is evenly coated.

Cook the aromatic base: Heat the oil in a medium nonstick soup pot over high heat until it reaches 375°F on a kitchen thermometer. Add the aromatic base to the hot oil and sauté for 5 minutes, stirring constantly with a silicone spatula. Reduce the heat to medium and continue stirring for 10 more minutes, occasionally scraping the bottom of the pot to prevent burning. The mixture will become vibrant red and aromatic.

Strain and cool: Set a fine-mesh sieve over a bowl and pour the base into it. Let the paste rest and cool in the strainer for about 30 minutes, gently pressing the mixture with a spatula from time to time to remove excess oil. Pour the chile oil from the bowl into a separate small container, and use to season other dishes (it will keep for 2 weeks in the fridge).

Season and blend to finish: In a large bowl, stir together the MSG, sugar, fish sauce, and tamarind paste until well combined. Add the cooled pepper paste to the bowl and stir until it's fully incorporated. Transfer the mixture to a food processor and blend until it's smooth. Use immediately, or refrigerate in an airtight container for up to 2 weeks.

Jeow Mak Len ◆ Spicy Tomato Dip

ແຈ່ວໝາກເລັ່ນ

When I was growing up, tomatoes were not a food I sought out unless they were on a pizza with extra mozzarella or in the simple cheese-and-tomato burritos that lived in our freezer next to Mae's cherry tomatoes from the summer's harvest. However, some foods are completely transformed when paired with fish sauce, and tomatoes are one of them. In this recipe, they are pulverized in the mortar and pestle, and all their bright acids swirl into the salty fish sauce to create an irresistible jeow. I always try to scoop up the biggest amount I can with my ball of sticky rice, even though I know I'll regret it if I randomly get a chunk of chile with all its seeds. It's a risk I'm willing to take. This spicy jeow is always brought out for Paw's summer barbecues, and it tastes even better when the ingredients are charred on the grill. Jeow mak len is a dip made for sticky rice, but it can also be spread on those once-frozen pizzas, enhancing every bite of them with magical flavors.

Serves 3 or 4

- 2 cups whole cherry tomatoes
- ⅔ cup peeled shallot halves
- 15 peeled garlic cloves
- 10 fresh bird's eye chiles, stemmed
- 2 tablespoons padaek (see page 97)
- 1 tablespoon fish sauce (see page 18)
- ½ teaspoon MSG
- 3 tablespoons minced cilantro

Preheat the oven to 400°F.

Prepare the ingredients for roasting: Cut four 18-inch squares of aluminum foil. Arrange the tomatoes, shallots, garlic, and chiles separately on the foil sheets. Fold each sheet into a flat parcel, sealing the edges tightly. Place all the parcels on a baking tray.

Roast the ingredients: Place the tray on the middle rack of the oven and bake until slightly charred and softened, about 30 minutes.

Make the paste: Remove the tray from the oven and carefully open the parcels. Transfer the shallots, garlic, and chiles to a mortar and pound them into a rough paste using a pestle. Add the tomatoes, leaving most of the juices behind in the foil. Gently smash the tomatoes into the mixture, forming a slightly chunky paste.

Season the dip and serve: Mix in the padaek, fish sauce, MSG, and cilantro. Taste and adjust seasoning if needed, then transfer the paste to a serving bowl. Serve the dip warm with sticky rice, barbecued spareribs, or your preferred protein.

Jeow Padaek ◆ Unfiltered Fish Sauce Dip

แจ่วปาแดก

Jeow padaek could be the farthest dip from you on the table, and its pungent aroma would still reach you. It's a mixture of smashed fermented fish and aromatics that brings out the best in the most intense ingredients. It's also one of Mae and Paw's favorite jeows, and I suppose their enjoyment comes in part from knowing the work it took to catch the fish and the patience required for it to ferment. There are certain Lao foods I didn't appreciate until later in life, when I had developed both a more refined palate and an understanding of how, for example, an unassuming paste earned its place on the table. This is one of those foods. If you are making padaek, and your sauce is in the sweet spot between 6 months and a year of fermentation, you can substitute ⅓ cup of padaek chunks, which are the fish fillet parts that have softened in the sauce. Enjoy jeow padaek with boiled bamboo shoots and sticky rice.

Serves 2 to 4

25 fresh bird's eye chiles, stemmed (about ½ loosely packed cup)

1 cup chopped shallots

4 garlic cloves, chopped

¼ cup padaek (see page 97), or ⅓ cup padaek chunks

3 scallions, green parts only, minced

⅓ cup minced cilantro stems

½ teaspoon MSG

1 tablespoon lime juice

Salt, to taste

Make the paste: In a small nonstick pan, dry-sauté the chiles, shallots, and garlic over medium-high heat until charred and softened, 5 to 8 minutes. Transfer the charred aromatics to a deep mortar and pound them into a rough paste using a pestle.

Prepare the padaek: If you're using homemade padaek, remove any fish pieces and discard any bones. Depending on the age of the padaek, the fish meat may have dissolved, leaving only skin; if this is the case, pound the skin thoroughly in the mortar to create a smooth paste. If the skin does not become a paste, use kitchen shears to assist. Add the padaek to the mortar and mix it with the aromatics until well combined.

Add fresh herbs and season: Add the minced scallions and cilantro stems, pounding lightly to incorporate them into the paste. Stir in the MSG and lime juice. Add salt to taste and serve.

Jeow Hua Sikhai ◆ Fragrant Lemongrass Dip

ແຈ່ວຫົວສີໄຄ

A bowl of smashed lemongrass is one of those food memories that is connected to both my past and my present. When I first went to visit my aunt's village in Laos, an hour outside Savannakhet, I was presented with a celebratory meal featuring a mystery feast of Lao foods. I remember taking the sticky rice and dipping it into this green, chunky jeow. Once it touched my tongue, I immediately recognized the strong, fragrant flavors mixed with the pungent brine of the padaek. I was sitting on a mat in Laos, overlooking the farm: the pigs, chickens, and oxen near the rice fields, and the fire pit that had just been used to boil the chicken to make laab nearby. But tasting the jeow, I was instantly back in our Wisconsin kitchen with Mae as she hovered over the mortar and pestle, pounding each ingredient until the fresh lemongrass she had just harvested turned a bright hue of green. It was a powerful reflection of the food knowledge Mae had brought to the United States and a revelation of how food has no boundaries. I'd often wondered if Lao food tasted the same in Laos and in other places around the world, and I found my answer in this jeow. Enjoy it with sticky rice, barbecued chicken, or grilled fish.

Serves 4 to 6

⅔ cup minced lemongrass (from the soft part of about 4 lemongrass stalks)

4 fresh bird's eye chiles, stemmed

¼ cup chopped scallions, green parts only

¼ cup chopped cilantro, tender stems and leaves

8 cherry tomatoes, halved

1 teaspoon MSG

2 tablespoons padaek (see page 97)

In a mortar, combine the minced lemongrass and chiles and use the pestle to pound into a rough paste. (If a mortar and pestle is unavailable, use a small food processor.) Add the chopped scallions and cilantro to the mortar, and pound until the herbs are well incorporated into the paste. Add the halved cherry tomatoes, MSG, and padaek to the mixture. Lightly smash the tomatoes to release their juices, and gently mix until all the ingredients are well combined.

Jeow Mak Kua ◆ Charred Eggplant Dip

ແຈ່ວໝາກເຂືອ

I didn't like this dip as a kid because my eight-year-old mind didn't understand how cooked eggplants melted into a custardy consistency as they were sloshed back and forth in the mortar and pestle. My child brain thought the dip was made from Mae's sometimes strange ingredients, not the eggplant we routinely ate raw with everything. Looking at this dip, I thought it was made with too many peppers, but it was the seeds of the eggplants mimicking the look of pepper seeds. Like baba ghanoush, this creamy dip pairs perfectly with fresh vegetables, although it also always goes well with sticky rice.

Serves 6 to 8

- 5 large round green Thai eggplants, halved
- 1 large yellow onion, quartered
- 4 fresh bird's eye chiles, stemmed
- 10 garlic cloves
- ½ cup water
- 1 tablespoon padaek (see page 97)
- 1 tablespoon fish sauce (see page 18)
- ½ teaspoon MSG
- 2 tablespoons chopped cilantro leaves

Cook the vegetables: In a 10-inch cast-iron skillet over high heat, arrange the eggplant and onion pieces flat side down, then add the chiles and garlic evenly around them. Cook until the vegetables are slightly charred, 6 to 8 minutes. Reduce the heat to low, pour in the water, and cover the skillet. Let the vegetables simmer until tender about 10 minutes.

Drain and cool: Transfer the cooked vegetables to a plate lined with paper towels to absorb the excess moisture; allow them to cool slightly.

Make the dip and serve: In a deep mortar, mash the chiles and garlic into a paste. Add the eggplants and onion and mash them into a coarse paste, leaving some texture. Add the padaek, fish sauce, MSG, and cilantro and mix well. Serve the dip warm.

Jeow Som ◆ Fiery Lime Dip

แจ่วสົ້ມ

At my parents' house, this jeow was a thicker, pepper-forward dip. My version has evolved over time to a more liquid consistency, ideal for drizzling over oysters, shrimp, and other seafood. It's an instant classic, even for those new to Lao cuisine. For me, jeow som is essential when eating balut. The acidity of the dip cuts through the rich, fatty yolk of the egg, balancing its flavors. It's also the perfect complement to sticky rice and an addictive dipping sauce for grilled meats and vegetables.

Serves 4 to 6

- 10 garlic cloves
- 10 fresh bird's eye chiles, stemmed
- 2 tablespoons minced cilantro stems
- 2½ tablespoons sugar
- ½ teaspoon MSG
- ½ cup fish sauce (see page 18)
- 3 tablespoons lime juice
- 2 tablespoons cilantro leaves, for garnish

Make the paste and season: In a deep mortar, combine the garlic, chiles, and minced cilantro stems. Pound the ingredients together until they form a rough paste. Add the sugar, MSG, fish sauce, and lime juice to the mortar. Mix until all the ingredients are well combined.

Garnish and serve: Transfer the sauce to a serving bowl. Garnish with the cilantro leaves and serve.

Alternative Method

For a quicker preparation, blend all the ingredients (including the cilantro garnish) in a blender. This will produce a smoother texture than the rustic, chunky consistency achieved with a mortar and pestle.

Jeow Bee ◆ Tangy Bitter Steak Sauce

ແຈ່ວຂົມ

On select weekends, Mae and Paw would join others in our Lao diaspora community in slaughtering a cow and dividing the parts among themselves. For my parents and their friends, this was a familiar practice, something they had done regularly in their villages. One of the most distinctive parts of this process was extracting beef bile from the gallbladder. It was an intricate and not-for-the-faint-of-heart process, requiring gentle handling of the digestive organs, and simmering to ensure the bile was safe to use. They stored enough to last for months, until the next farm visit, using it to flavor soups, laab, and jeow bee, a tangy, bitter dip that pairs perfectly with sticky rice and barbecued steak.

Serves 3 or 4

- 2 tablespoons crushed dried bird's eye chile (see page 18)
- 2 tablespoons roasted sticky rice powder (see page 17)
- 1 teaspoon MSG
- 2 tablespoons padaek (see page 97)
- ¼ cup fish sauce (see page 18)
- 1 tablespoon beef bile (see Note)
- 1 tablespoon minced scallions, green parts only
- 1 tablespoon minced cilantro leaves
- 2 tablespoons water, as needed

In a bowl, combine the crushed chile, roasted sticky rice powder, and MSG; mix thoroughly. Stir in the padaek, fish sauce, and beef bile until fully incorporated, then mix in the scallions and cilantro. Add water to achieve a thin consistency; taste and adjust the fish sauce as needed. Serve fresh for the best flavor. Keep in mind that if the sauce sits overnight, the rice powder will absorb the liquid and become chunky. Add more water to smooth it out.

Note

Using beef bile may seem intimidating, but it's a widely available product in the frozen section of Southeast Asian markets. If you're adventurous (and well connected), source it from a knowledgeable Lao auntie who works with local butchers. If you're unsure about the sourcing and want to ensure safety, you can pasteurize it using the sous vide method. Vacuum seal the bile in a food-grade bag, place it in a 165°F sous vide bath for 30 minutes, then immediately cool it in an ice bath. This step ensures safety from potential foodborne illness while preserving the integrity of the bile.

Jeow Kapi ◆ Bold Shrimp Paste Dip

ແຈ່ວກະປິ

This sauce is intensely salty and incredibly spicy; paired with bamboo shoots, as it is here, it was my eleven-year-old self's ideal cartoon-watching snack. Looking back, I'd say this jeow played a big role in shaping my taste for Lao cuisine early on. It's meant to be bold and unapologetic, with flavors that are "too much" on their own but that balance perfectly with the bamboo shoots, which mellow out the saltiness and heat. This isn't a mild dip by any means; the fermented shrimp paste brings strong, pungent aromas and flavors that demand your attention. It's as intense as it is unforgettable!

Serves 4 to 6

- 4 garlic cloves
- 20 fresh bird's eye chiles, stemmed
- 2 tablespoons shrimp paste
- 1 teaspoon MSG
- 1 teaspoon sugar
- ¼ cup fish sauce (see page 18)
- 2 tablespoons lime juice
- 10 ounces canned bamboo shoots

Prepare the dip: In a deep mortar, pound the garlic and chiles into a rough paste. Add the shrimp paste, MSG, and sugar. Continue pounding until the mixture forms a smooth, evenly combined paste. Stir in the fish sauce and lime juice and mix until well combined. Set the dip aside.

Prepare the bamboo shoots: Drain the canned bamboo shoots and rinse them under cold water. Cut the shoots in half lengthwise. Place them in a small pot and add enough water to cover them by at least 1 inch. Bring to a boil over high heat, and boil for 10 minutes (this removes any impurities and reduces bitterness). Drain the shoots and let them cool completely. Once they're cooled, slice them into ¼-inch-thick strips. Arrange the strips on a plate and serve with the spicy shrimp paste dip.

Jeow Mak Phet Hang ◆ Smoky Pepper Dip

ແຈ່ວໝາກເຜັດແຫ້ງ

By the end of the summer, Mae's bird's eye chile plants always flourished, producing dozens of vibrant red peppers ready for harvest. The yield was so abundant that she could have set up a stand at the farmers' market. Instead, she kept the entire crop for herself, carefully dividing it for different uses throughout the year. She allocated a quarter to be eaten fresh, adding crunch and heat to every slurp of noodles. Another quarter went into the second freezer, reserved to meet our weekly cravings for papaya salad. A third quarter was gifted to friends, sparing them the trouble of hunting for extra-spicy peppers. The final quarter was spread out to dry under the sun. In just a few days, the peppers shriveled, their skins wrinkling as their red hue deepened further. Mae stored these dried chiles in a bamboo basket, ready to spice up curries, add depth to the next batch of padaek fermentation, or create her fiery dip, jeow mak phet hang. This dip showcases the dried chiles, transforming their sun-dried and roasted flavors into layers of smoky heat and complexity. Use this spicy herb paste as a dip with sticky rice, grilled meats, or vegetables.

Serves 4 to 6

1 cup dried bird's eye chiles, stemmed

2 small shallots, peeled and chopped

1 tablespoon peeled, minced galangal

½ cup chopped cilantro, tender stems and leaves

½ cup chopped scallions, green parts only

¼ cup padaek (see page 97)

1 tablespoon fish sauce (see page 18)

1½ teaspoons sugar

½ teaspoon MSG

¼ cup lime juice

Roast the chile peppers: Heat a medium pan over low heat. Add the dried chiles and dry-roast, stirring occasionally to prevent burning, until the chiles are fragrant and slightly darkened, 7 to 10 minutes. Transfer the roasted chiles to a deep mortar and pound them into a rough powder.

Make the herb paste and serve: Add the shallots, galangal, cilantro, and scallions to the mortar. Pound the mixture until it forms a coarse paste. Add the padaek, fish sauce, sugar, MSG, and lime juice to the mortar. Mix thoroughly to combine, and serve.

Jeow Khao Khua ◆ Roasted Sticky Rice Dip

ແຈ່ວເຂົ້າຂົ້ວ

In many refugee families, the oldest child often becomes a part-time adult, helping care for younger siblings, translating during hospital visits, and managing tasks like reading mail and keeping track of bills. My older sister, Daeng, had to step into this role early on, shouldering these duties while navigating her formative years in a new country. Daeng was just seven years old when we arrived in the United States, yet she still reminisces about riding elephants in Laos. Her responsibilities extended to the kitchen, where she created moments of care and connection. One of my favorite memories is of her making and sharing jeow khao khua with me. This dip, with its signature bold Lao flavors of sweet, spicy, sour, and funky, was our perennial childhood snack, especially as we sat together doing homework after dinner. We typically paired it with tart unripe mango from the Southeast Asian market in Madison, but a Granny Smith apple works just as well, as do passion fruit, unripe guavas, and crab apples. This dip perfectly balances sour fruits. Much like the Mexican Tajín spice blend, each bite makes your mouth water and pucker, leaving you wanting more. Jeow khao khua remains a recipe of comfort and care passed down through generations. Watching my niece enjoy her mom's early lessons in food brings everything full circle, connecting each of us to those uncertain but loving times.

Serves 4 to 6

- 3 unripe mangoes, peeled
- 2 teaspoons shrimp paste
- 2 tablespoons fish sauce (see page 18)
- 2 tablespoons ground bird's eye chile (see page 18)
- ¼ cup roasted sticky rice powder (see page 17)
- ¼ cup sugar
- 2 teaspoons MSG
- ½ cup padaek (see page 97)
- ¼ cup minced shallot
- 2 tablespoons minced fresh bird's eye chile

Cut the mango flesh into thin strips, lengthwise. Place the mango slices in an ice-cold water bath and set aside while you prepare the dip.

In a medium bowl, combine the shrimp paste and fish sauce, stirring until the shrimp paste is fully dissolved. Add the ground chile, roasted sticky rice powder, sugar, MSG, padaek, minced shallots, and fresh chile. Mix thoroughly until well combined. Drain the mango slices from the ice bath and pat them dry. Serve with the spicy dip.

Jeow Nam Som Pak ◆ Fermented Mustard Greens Dip

ແຈ່ວນ້ຳສົ້ມຜັກ

On my first trip to Ban Chan, a historic village in Luang Prabang famous for its pottery, I stumbled upon a modest home that doubled as a food stall. Many homes in Laos serve as small shops, feeding travelers and locals alike. As I explored the stall, a dark paste wrapped in plastic and secured with a red rubber band caught my eye. The packaging was a telltale sign of homemade food, the kind I knew would be special. The vendor told me it was jeow som pak, a dip made from fermented greens and aromatics cooked down into a dark paste. After the first bite with sticky rice, I was mesmerized. The spicy, sour flavor was both familiar and entirely new, a balance that left me wanting more. True to the generous spirit of Lao people, the vendor eagerly shared how it was made. I was fascinated and tucked the recipe into my memory. This dip, jeow nam som pak, reminds me of the hospitality and kindness I experienced during that visit. It's more than just a recipe to me; it's a way to share that same warmth and connection with others. Enjoy it with sticky rice and cooked bamboo shoots.

Serves 2 to 4

2 cups fermented mustard greens (see Note)

1 cup dried bird's eye chiles, stemmed

⅔ cup chopped shallots

⅓ cup peeled, thinly sliced galangal

½ cup water

¼ cup minced cilantro stems

1 teaspoon MSG

¼ teaspoon sugar

Prepare the greens and toast the chiles: Squeeze the liquid from the mustard greens and set 3 tablespoons of it aside. Chop the greens and set them aside; you should have about 1¼ cups of greens. In a small pan over medium-high heat, dry-sauté the chiles for 2 minutes, stirring constantly. Transfer to a bowl.

Cook the aromatics and greens: In the same pan, dry-sauté the shallots and galangal for 5 minutes over medium-high heat, stirring constantly. Remove the galangal from the pan and set it aside. Keep the shallots in the pan and add the chopped mustard greens and ½ cup water; stir to combine. Bring the mixture to a simmer, cover the pan, and reduce the heat to low. Cook for 3 minutes. Remove the lid and cook, stirring, until the liquid evaporates and the mustard greens are dry, about 4 minutes. Remove from the heat.

Make the paste and season the dip: In a deep mortar, pound the toasted galangal into a rough paste. Add the toasted chiles and pound until the paste is smooth. Add the shallot mixture and cilantro stems and pound to incorporate, then mix in the MSG and sugar, and stir in the mustard green juice, 1 tablespoon at a time, until you reach your desired saltiness; serve.

Note

Fermented mustard greens can be found in Southeast Asian markets; make sure the greens you buy are fermented with salt-based brine and not with vinegar. If you're using store-bought fermented mustard greens, taste the dip as you add it since the saltiness of the brine can vary.

Jeow Tua Nao ◆ Fermented Bean Dip

ແຈ່ວຖົ່ວເນົ່າ

The star ingredient of this dip is mak tua nao, a fermented soybean commonly used in Northern Lao dishes like khao soi (see page 171). While it's similar to other fermented soy products like Japan's natto or China's fermented bean curd, mak tua nao stands out due to the extra spicy flavors incorporated during fermentation. It is often sold in blocks or dried discs, and it adds a unique funk to dishes. If you're looking for a plant-based alternative to padaek, mak tua nao is an excellent choice. In Laos, families specialize in fermenting these soybeans, which they sell at morning markets. If you aren't able to find mak tua nao, you can substitute with doenjang, a Korean fermented soybean paste, and add some crushed dried bird's eye chiles for the extra kick of heat. Serve this dip with barbecued meats or use it as a spicy bean paste for Khao Leng Feun (page 160).

Serves 4 to 6

15 fresh bird's eye chiles, stemmed

10 garlic cloves

¼ cup thinly sliced peeled ginger

1½ cups halved shallots (about 6 shallots)

⅔ cup mak tua nao (fermented bean paste)

½ teaspoon sugar

2 tablespoons minced cilantro stems

Roast the ingredients: Preheat the oven to 400°F. Cut three 18-inch squares of aluminum foil. Place the chiles, garlic, and ginger in the center of one foil sheet and fold it into a flat parcel with all the sides sealed up. Make separate foil parcels for the shallots and the fermented bean paste (ending up with three parcels).

Arrange the parcels on a baking tray and place the tray on the middle rack of the oven. Roast until the ingredients soften and develop a slightly smoky aroma, about 30 minutes. Remove the parcels from the oven, and open them to allow the ingredients to cool a bit on the foil.

Make the paste and serve: Transfer the roasted ginger to a deep mortar and pound it into a paste. Add the roasted chiles and garlic, and pound them until well combined, then add the roasted shallots and pound into a smooth, chunky paste.

Add the roasted fermented bean paste, sugar, and minced cilantro stems to the mortar. Mix thoroughly to combine and enjoy.

๖

2

SMALL PLATES

A Snack Can Be a Feast

Laos, like the United States, is a land of incredible diversity, home to hundreds of ethnic groups that bring their unique languages, traditions, and flavors to the table. This rich cultural mosaic is evident everywhere, from the vibrant traditional clothing worn daily to the variety of ceremonies celebrated year-round. Nowhere is this diversity more beautifully expressed than in the snack food culture of Laos, in which food serves as both a bridge between communities and a celebration of shared identity.

Many snacks and drinks not typically labeled as Lao are, in fact, Lao, originating within the country's borders. However, the depth and richness of Lao food culture would not exist without the invaluable contributions of the many ethnic groups that make up the population and whose distinct culinary practices have shaped the flavors of the nation. For instance, the Mien people are known for their fermented soybean pastes, which add complexity to dishes like Lao khao soi. The Hmong people living in the mountains enjoy a simple yet comforting meal of cooked jasmine rice mixed with extra water, creating a rice soup. This is typically served with a spicy pepper dip and grilled meat. The Khmu, indigenous to northern Laos, craft Lao hai, a robust rice whiskey enjoyed during countless festivities throughout the country. These contributions are threads woven into the larger fabric of Lao food culture, enriching it immeasurably.

Lao snacks, such as sakoo yat sai (tapioca dumplings) or seen savanh (heavenly beef jerky), are often simple. But in the presence of good company, these humble bites transform into something extraordinary. The blend of casual food and heartfelt connection epitomizes Lao hospitality and supports the belief that food is a unifying force. In Laos, the line between a snack and a meal often blurs, as a modest bite grows into a long, shared feast. Families, friends, and even strangers gather around baskets of warm sticky rice, vibrant fresh herbs, and fiery jeow, sharing stories, laughter, and companionship for hours.

For those who have left Laos, food remains a powerful link to the homeland. It is both a way for us to reclaim identity and a tangible connection to our heritage. Understanding the terms *Laos, Lao,* and *Laotian* provides insight into this identity: *Laos* refers to the nation, officially the Lao People's Democratic Republic, while *Lao* denotes both an ethnic and a cultural identity. The term *Laotian,* introduced during French colonization, is widely used in the West, but is often associated with the painful history of displacement and loss.

In this book, I choose to use *Lao* as an identification, as a way of honoring and celebrating our culture. For those of us in the diaspora, embracing *Lao* reflects a journey of resilience and pride. Growing up in Wisconsin, I experienced our cultural connections firsthand. My family worked long hours on farms alongside other refugee families, including Hmong and Mien. Our shared meals of sticky rice, Mien fermented soybean paste, and Hmong vegetable soup became moments of connection, tying us to one another and to the lives we had left behind.

When Lao families visited, my mother would always say, "Ma soom gun." This phrase, which roughly translates to "Come gather," is an invitation to

snack, share, and connect. These gatherings often stretched for hours, and our meals featured fresh herbs, garden vegetables, and a spread of appetizers served alongside Beerlao. These moments were never just about eating; they were about catching up on one another's lives, sharing stories, and just being together.

This chapter invites you to embrace the spirit of soom gun in your own home. Prepare these recipes, gather your loved ones, and experience the joy of connecting over food. Lao snacks, whether simple or elaborate, embody the heart of the culture: a celebration of diversity, community, and the enduring power of food to bring people together.

Yaw Khao ◆ Fresh Spring Rolls

ຍໍ່ຂາວ

Serves 4 to 6

This recipe is a twist on the popular fresh Lao spring rolls. The combination of fresh vegetables, pork skin, and roasted sticky rice powder brings a distinctive roasted, nutty flavor to every bite. One of the highlights of this recipe is the tangy-sweet dipping sauce, infused with fish sauce, which pairs beautifully with these spring rolls among many other dishes. Yaw khao are perfect for a gathering or party where everyone can customize their rolls with their preferred fillings. Feel free to experiment with seasonal herbs and produce to make these your own!

Filling

1½ teaspoons vegetable oil

1 tablespoon minced garlic

1 pound ground pork

1 tablespoon oyster sauce

1 teaspoon coarse kosher salt

½ teaspoon freshly ground black pepper

4 ounces cooked pork skin, roughly chopped (see Note)

2 tablespoons roasted sticky rice powder (see page 17)

Dipping Sauce

½ cup sugar

1½ cups water

1 garlic clove

2 fresh bird's eye chiles, stemmed

¼ cup roasted peanuts

¼ cup fish sauce (see page 18)

2 tablespoons lime juice

Assembly

12 large (10-inch) rice paper sheets

12 whole romaine lettuce leaves, tender parts and center ribs removed

1 (14-ounce) package of vermicelli rice noodles, cooked according to the package directions and cooled

1 cup crushed Khao Kope (page 79)

2 medium cucumbers, thinly sliced

½ cup chopped scallions

½ cup chopped cilantro

½ cup chopped fresh mint

Make the filling: Heat the vegetable oil in a medium pan over medium-high heat. Sauté the garlic for 20 to 30 seconds, until fragrant. Add the pork, oyster sauce, salt, and black pepper. Break up the pork and stir until it's fully cooked (no longer pink), 5 minutes. Transfer the pork mixture to a large bowl and let it cool to room temperature, about 15 minutes. Stir the chopped pork skin and roasted sticky rice powder into the cooled pork.

Caramelize the sugar: In a small pan over medium-high heat, gently stir the sugar as it melts and caramelizes, 4 to 5 minutes; it should turn golden brown and liquefy. Immediately add the water, stirring to dissolve all the caramel. Simmer for 3 minutes, then remove from the heat.

Make the sauce: In a mortar, combine the garlic and chiles and pound into a rough paste. Add the roasted peanuts and lightly crush them. Pour the caramel into the mortar and mix well. Stir in the fish sauce and lime juice and set aside.

Assemble the spring rolls: Fill a large bowl with room-temperature water. Submerge one sheet of rice paper for 2 to 3 seconds, then place it on a plate. Make sure the paper is softened but not saturated, as the rice paper will become too fragile to work with.

Layer ingredients on the rice paper: Start with lettuce, then add a twelfth-portion of the vermicelli, 2 tablespoons of the pork mixture, some crushed khao kope, and a few cucumber slices. Add a pinching portion each of scallions, cilantro, and mint.

Roll the rice paper away from you until it's halfway rolled, then fold the sides inward to enclose the filling. Continue rolling tightly to seal the roll. Repeat with the remaining rice paper and filling. Serve the spring rolls with the dipping sauce on the side.

Note

Packaged cooked pork skin is available at Asian markets.

Serves 4 to 6

Yum Salat ◆ Egg Dressing Salad

ຍຳສະລັດ

Dressing

8 eggs

1 garlic clove, minced

2 tablespoons fish sauce (see page 18)

2 tablespoons lime juice

2 tablespoons sugar

½ cup water

Chicken

2 tablespoons vegetable oil

1 tablespoon minced garlic

10 ounces minced chicken thigh meat

1 tablespoon oyster sauce

¼ teaspoon MSG

¼ teaspoon freshly ground black pepper

Salad

6 cups romaine lettuce cut into 2-inch pieces

2 cups watercress with thick stems removed

1 cup chopped cilantro, leaves and tender stems

⅓ cup chopped scallions, green parts only

1 cup thinly sliced Persian cucumber

1 cup thinly sliced radish

1 cup thinly sliced Roma tomatoes

4 cups radicchio cut into 2-inch pieces

Toppings

⅓ cup crushed roasted peanuts

⅓ cup fried garlic (see page 21)

⅓ cup fried shallots (see page 21)

Many times, Mae would say an English word with her heavy Lao accent, and I would assume it was a Lao word. One memorable example was her telling me to throw the trash in the "gabet." It wasn't until I was thirty-three that I realized she was saying "garbage." These funny moments of language blending and getting lost in translation were a regular part of my growing up, and they even applied to dishes like yum salat. Yum salat is a Lao take on an American salad, and its name reflects that, borrowing the English word *salad* and adding a Lao accent with a pronounced "t" sound. Over time, dish names like this have become traditional in Lao cuisine, and have even helped Lao people learn some English words. Unlike typical Western salads, this recipe doesn't use oil in its dressing. Instead, the richness comes from egg yolks, with lime juice and fish sauce balancing the flavors. I encourage cooks to embrace the spirit of Lao food by experimenting with the salad ingredients and using what's in season. It's a versatile dish that, like the Lao language, adapts beautifully to what's fresh and available.

Make the dressing: Place the eggs in a medium pot and cover them with water by at least 1 inch. Bring the water to a simmer on medium heat and cook, uncovered, for 10 minutes. Drain the water and transfer the eggs to an ice bath for 5 minutes. Peel the eggs and cut them in half lengthwise. Separate the yolks from the whites. Slice each half of the egg whites into thirds and set aside.

In a blender, combine the egg yolks, garlic, fish sauce, lime juice, sugar, and water. Blend until the mixture is smooth and well combined.

Cook the chicken: Heat a medium pan over high heat for 1 minute. Add the vegetable oil and garlic, lower the heat to medium, and sauté for 1 minute. Add the minced chicken, oyster sauce, MSG, and black pepper. Sauté for 5 minutes, stirring to ensure even cooking.

Assemble the salad and serve: In a large bowl, combine the lettuce, watercress, cilantro, scallions, cucumber, radish, tomatoes, radicchio, cooked chicken, and cooked egg whites. Pour the dressing over the salad and gently toss to coat all ingredients evenly. Sprinkle the salad with the roasted peanuts, fried garlic, and fried shallots. Serve immediately.

Khai Ping ◆ Baked Green Eggs

ໄຂ່ປີ້ງ

Makes 20 eggs | Serves 6 to 8

Every time Mae made these eggs, I could hear the pride in her voice as she admired how well they turned out. The eggs took on a light green hue from the cilantro and scallions and had the texture of a hard-boiled egg. She was always experimenting with different techniques. One day, she used a turkey baster to fill the eggshells; another time she tried a mini funnel to get the liquid through the small opening. Mae is a natural recipe developer, and I like to think I inherited some of that curiosity and creativity from her. I often find myself in the kitchen experimenting with traditional recipes, using the techniques Mae taught me. I still call her to this day, asking if she's discovered any new tricks for making khai ping. Serve these eggs with sticky rice and Jeow Som (see page 31).

- 20 extra-large eggs
- 2 teaspoons coarse kosher salt
- 2 teaspoons MSG
- 2 teaspoons freshly ground black pepper
- 2 tablespoons minced garlic
- ½ cup diced scallions, white and green parts
- ½ cup diced cilantro leaves and tender stems

Prepare the eggshells: All 20 eggs should be in their cardboard (not Styrofoam or plastic) cartons, narrow ends up. About 1 inch from the top of the narrow end of an egg, gently tap the shell with a small spoon to crack the top of the shell, removing it to create an opening about ½ inch in diameter. Discard the top portion of the shell, and use a chopstick to poke the yolk and lightly mix it into the egg white inside the shell. Pour the egg into a large bowl, and replace the intact shell back in the cardboard carton. Repeat with each of the remaining 19 eggs.

Season the eggs: Transfer the eggs from the bowl into a blender. Add the salt, MSG, black pepper, garlic, scallions, and cilantro. Blend until well combined, about 30 seconds. Strain the blended egg mixture through a fine-mesh strainer into a large bowl, pressing the solids to extract as much liquid as possible. Skim the foam off the top of the mixture, transfer it to a separate bowl, and set it aside to liquefy. Pour the strained egg mixture into a pitcher with a narrow spout (or use a funnel). Carefully fill the empty eggshells with the liquid, leaving ¼ inch of space at the top unfilled. Once all the shells are filled, use the liquefied foam to top them off.

Bake the eggs: Preheat the oven to 175°F. Carefully set the cartons of filled eggshells on a large baking tray. Bake for 1 hour, then increase the oven temperature to 200°F, rotate the cartons, and bake for an additional 2½ hours. Test the eggs by inserting a toothpick; if it comes out clean, they are done. If the eggs are not fully set, bake for an additional 30 minutes. Let the baked eggs cool for 30 minutes. Peel off the shells and serve.

Serves 4 to 6

Seen Savanh ◆ Heavenly Beef Jerky
ຊີ້ນສະຫວັນ

1 pound top round steak

5 garlic cloves, minced

1 teaspoon peeled, minced galangal

3 tablespoons water

1½ teaspoons seasoning sauce (see page 22)

½ teaspoon MSG

1½ teaspoons coarse kosher salt

1½ tablespoons sugar

2 tablespoons sesame seeds

½ teaspoon ground white pepper

Vegetable oil, for frying

When I was young, I never thought twice when I saw beef jerky drying outside next to my underwear. It was in the backyard, out of anyone's sight, so it didn't seem like a big deal. While the jerky dried under the sun for several hours, Mae did other tasks. Once the beef was dried sufficiently, she pan-fried it to perfection, each bite so flavorful and satisfying that it earned its heavenly name. At the time, these moments were just ordinary parts of our day, but as I got older, I recognized the humor, and maybe the oddity, of drying underwear and jerky side by side. Yet, I also realized that it taught me Mae's sabai sabai (laid-back) mentality: As long as the job got done and effort was made, that was what mattered. Making this recipe gives you plenty of time to tackle some household chores while your jerky dries. Enjoy the fried jerky with warm sticky rice and your favorite jeow.

Prepare the meat and marinade: Cutting against the grain, slice the steak into strips about ¼-inch thick. Place the meat in a large bowl and set aside. In a deep mortar, combine the garlic and galangal and smash them into a fine paste. Add the water, seasoning sauce, MSG, salt, sugar, sesame seeds, and white pepper to the paste and mix until fully combined.

Pour the marinade over the beef slices. Using your hands, mix the beef thoroughly to ensure all the pieces are evenly coated with marinade. Cover and let the beef marinate for at least 1 hour, or refrigerate overnight for deeper flavor.

Dry the beef: Arrange the beef slices in a single layer on a dehydrator tray or a drying rack. Set outside in sunny weather, or in a 165°F oven. In the oven, the jerky should be ready in about 4 hours. In the last half-hour or so, check frequently to ensure the jerky dries evenly: It should feel dry on the surface but remain slightly pliable, not brittle. If you're drying the jerky outdoors, allow 6 hours in sunny weather (more if it's overcast).

Fry the jerky and serve: In a large, shallow pan over medium-high heat, heat ½ inch of vegetable oil to 350°F. Add the dried beef slices to the oil in small batches and fry for about 30 seconds per side. The jerky should float when it's cooked. Be careful not to overcook it. It should remain tender and not turn crispy. Remove the jerky from the oil and drain it on paper towels. Serve warm or at room temperature.

Sai Oua ◆ Lao Sausage

Makes about 2 pounds | 8 to 10 sausage links

An increasing number of restaurants are embracing and showcasing Lao cuisine, with Lao sausage taking center stage. In the United States, the term "Lao sausage" has become a universal standard and, by compelling people to say and read the word "Lao," it provides a vital cultural reference point. Lao food has often been labeled generically as "Southeast Asian" on menus, out of belief that people wouldn't recognize or understand the term "Lao." Over time, Lao sausage paved the way for restaurants to more confidently label their food as "Lao." As more regular restaurant diners returned and specifically asked for it, thanks to its unique and aromatic flavors, it became a top seller and its reputation for deliciousness spread through word of mouth. This is all to say: When you're introducing people to Lao cuisine for the first time, this sausage tops my list of recommendations. Its distinctiveness lies in its explosion of flavors derived from aromatic ingredients common in Lao cuisine. This recipe gives a method for stuffing the sausage filling into hog casings, followed by an alternative method of forming the filling into meatballs (see Notes).

¼ cup uncooked sticky rice

2 tablespoons peeled, minced galangal

3 tablespoons minced lemongrass (from the soft part of about 1 stalk)

½ cup minced shallot

½ cup minced scallions, white and green parts

⅓ cup minced cilantro leaves and tender stems

1½ teaspoons minced fresh makrut lime leaves (about 4 leaves)

1 tablespoon minced garlic

2 fresh bird's eye chiles, stemmed

½ pound roughly chopped pork belly

1½ pounds ground pork

1 tablespoon oyster sauce

1 teaspoon coarse kosher salt

½ teaspoon sugar

½ teaspoon freshly ground black pepper

1 tablespoon padaek (see page 97)

1½ teaspoons fish sauce (see page 18)

4 ounces salted hog casings (see Notes)

To Serve

1 head romaine lettuce

½ cup julienned ginger

½ cup roasted peanuts

2 cups cooked sticky rice (see page 73), for serving

Prepare the sticky rice: Rinse the sticky rice in a medium bowl, repeating three times, until the water runs clear. Drain. Combine the rice and ½ cup of water in a medium nonstick pot. Bring to a boil, then reduce the heat to low, cover, and simmer for 10 minutes. Transfer the cooked rice to a small bowl, rinse it under cool water, then strain.

Make the filling: In a food processor, combine the galangal, lemongrass, shallots, scallions, cilantro, lime leaves, garlic, and chiles. Pulse until everything is evenly minced. In a large bowl, combine this aromatic mixture with the pork belly, ground pork, ½ cup cooked sticky rice, oyster sauce, salt, sugar, black pepper, padaek, and fish sauce. Mix thoroughly with your hands until the mixture becomes sticky, 3 to 5 minutes. Cover the bowl with plastic wrap and refrigerate while you prepare the hog casings.

Prepare and fill the casings: Prepare the hog casings according to the instructions on the package. When they are ready, take the pork mixture out of the refrigerator. Attach the hog casing to a sausage stuffer (or use a funnel made from a 20-ounce plastic soda bottle;

Continued

see Notes). Leaving 3 inches of casing at the end for tying, slowly fill the casing with the pork mixture, pushing it through the funnel with a spoon or cranking the sausage machine. As you work, hold and guide the casing to ensure even filling. Once the casing is filled, form 6-inch links and slice through the casing 3 inches from the filling, and tie off both ends of the casing with kitchen string. Use a clean thin needle to poke one hole along every inch of the string of sausages to prevent them splitting as they cook.

Cook the Sausages and Serve: Preheat the oven to 400°F. Line a baking sheet with aluminum foil. Arrange the sausage links on the sheet and bake on the middle rack for 20 to 30 minutes. Switch the oven to the broil setting and broil the sausages on the top rack, flipping halfway, until lightly charred on both sides, 4 to 5 minutes. To serve, slice the sausages into ½-inch lengths. Wrap sausage slices in lettuce leaves along with julienned ginger and roasted peanuts, and serve with the sticky rice.

Notes

If hog casings are unavailable, roll about 2 tablespoons of filling into balls. As you form the meatballs, place them on an aluminum foil–lined baking sheet. Bake on the middle rack of a 400°F oven for 20 minutes, turning the meatballs halfway through. Turn the broiler on and move the baking sheet to the top rack and broil the meatballs until lightly charred, 2 to 3 minutes.

To make a soda bottle funnel, cut the bottom off of a 20-ounce plastic soda bottle 5 inches from the opening, and remove the cap (including the plastic tab around the cap). Attach the sausage casing to the bottle opening, securing it tightly with kitchen string. Using a wide spoon, fill the funnel with filling, pushing it through into the casing. As the casing fills, gently squeeze and guide the mixture down to ensure an even distribution. When all of the filling is used, tie off, pierce, and cook the sausages as described above.

Oua Sikhai ◆ Pork-Stuffed Lemongrass
ອົ່ວສີໄຄ

Makes 7 | Serves 3 or 4

There are very few cookbooks dedicated to Lao cuisine, but one stands out as a cornerstone of Lao culinary heritage: *Traditional Recipes of Laos*, by the late chef of the royal palace in Luang Prabang, Chaleunsilp Phia Sing. This cookbook is considered a treasure of Lao culture, not only because it was the first of its kind available to the public, but also because of its remarkable journey to publication. Chef Phia Sing was a man of many talents: a skilled architect, sculptor, painter, and poet. In the late 1960s, as his health began to decline, he meticulously documented his recipes, hoping to preserve them for future generations. His efforts might have remained obscure if not for a chance encounter between the Crown Prince of Laos and Alan Davidson, a British ambassador to Laos and a passionate gastronomy enthusiast. During the time of political upheaval in Laos that followed the establishment of the new government in 1975, the Crown Prince shared Chef Phia Sing's handwritten recipes with Davidson. Deeply moved, Davidson contacted the late chef's wife, who revealed that her husband's dying wish was to have his recipes published for the world to enjoy. Honoring this wish, Davidson ensured the cookbook's publication, with proceeds going to support Lao refugees starting new lives around the world. The following recipe for pork-stuffed lemongrass is inspired by and honors Chef Phia Sing's work, continuing his legacy and celebrating the spirit of Lao cuisine.

7 whole lemongrass stalks

1 pound ground pork

½ cup minced scallions

¼ cup minced shallot

1 tablespoon minced garlic

1 tablespoon oyster sauce

1½ teaspoons cornstarch

1 tablespoon fish sauce (see page 18)

½ teaspoon coarse kosher salt

1 teaspoon freshly ground black pepper

Vegetable oil, for frying

3 eggs

Prepare the lemongrass: Remove the first three tough outer layers of each lemongrass stalk. Cut each stalk into 7-inch segments, starting from the base. Bring a large pot of water to boil. Steam the stalks for 5 minutes in a steamer basket, or cover them with a damp paper towel and microwave them for 2 minutes. Let the stalks cool, then cut four slits lengthwise down the middle of each, leaving about 1 inch intact at both the top and bottom and creating a pocket in the center of the stalk that is surrounded by four strips of lemongrass.

Make the pork filling: In a large bowl, combine the ground pork, scallions, shallots, garlic, oyster sauce, cornstarch, fish sauce, salt, and black pepper. Mix with a spoon or your hands until the filling is well blended and homogeneous. Divide the mixture into seven portions and roll each into a cylindrical shape that is slightly smaller than the length of the lemongrass pockets.

Continued

Oua Sikhai ◆ Pork-Stuffed Lemongrass
continued

Stuff the lemongrass: Gently open a slit between two strips in a lemongrass stalk and stuff the stalk with a cylinder of pork filling. Carefully press the strips of the lemongrass stalks into the meat filling to secure it. If any strip rips, press it onto the filling so it sticks. If the filling portion is too large to fit in the space between the strips, remove some filling until it fits snugly inside the stalk. Repeat until all the stalks are filled.

Deep-fry the stuffed lemongrass: In a wide pan over medium heat, heat at least 3 inches of oil to 350°F. Crack the eggs into a wide bowl and whisk them until smooth. Dip each stuffed lemongrass stalk into the eggs, ensuring it's evenly coated. Fry the stalks in two batches (of three or four) until golden brown, 8 to 10 minutes. Remove the stalks from the oil and place them on a paper towel–lined plate to drain. Enjoy!

Galabao ◆ Pork Steamed Buns

ກາລະເປົາ

Makes 8 buns

My baby cousin is named Galabao, after Lao steamed buns. The first time I met him was the day I arrived in Savannakhet, the city where my parents grew up. Growing up, it was always just me, Mae, Paw, and my two sisters. Extended family felt like strangers, people we only knew through old photographs around the house or late-night phone calls from Laos that Mae would answer. Meeting Galabao for the first time was like looking into a mirror. He was the cutest two-year-old boy, with big, curious eyes. My cousins' rural village was unlike anything I'd known. The roads were unpaved, and the community functioned as one big family, everyone helping to care for one another. While my cousins prepared a homecoming dinner in my honor, Galabao and I spent the day exploring his world: catching playful puppies, chasing chickens that would later become dinner, and swinging beneath the raised house. Despite his young age, Galabao left a profound impression on me. When I returned to the U.S., I wanted to celebrate his joyful spirit, though I wasn't sure how. Fortunately, life had its own plans: A friend of ours mentioned their dog had just given birth to puppies and asked if we wanted to adopt one. The puppy that came into our lives was small, white, as soft as a freshly steamed bun, and just as cute as my little cousin Galabao. Life has a magical way of connecting you to what your heart desires, often in unexpected ways. For me, the story of Galabao and Galabao is a reminder to remain rooted in my community and cherish the ties that bring us closer to our origins.

Dough

1 cup warm unsweetened soy milk (or warm water)

1½ teaspoons instant dry yeast

2 tablespoons sugar

2⅓ cups soft white wheat flour, preferably Red Lotus Brand

1 teaspoon coarse kosher salt

Filling

1 pound ground pork

⅔ cup cooked bean thread noodles cut into 1-inch pieces

3 garlic cloves, minced

¼ cup minced scallions, white and green parts

¼ cup minced yellow onion

¼ cup chopped (thin strips) wood ear mushroom

1 tablespoon oyster sauce

1 teaspoon fish sauce (see page 18)

1 teaspoon sugar

1 teaspoon coarse kosher salt

¼ teaspoon MSG

¼ teaspoon freshly ground black pepper

2 hard-boiled eggs, quartered

1 Chinese-style sausage, sliced into eight ¼-inch thick pieces

Preheat the oven to 200°F, then turn it off right before making the dough.

Make the dough: In a large bowl, combine the soy milk, yeast, and sugar. Mix well. Add the flour and salt to the bowl and mix with a silicone spoon until clumps form. Transfer to a lightly floured work surface and knead for about 1 minute, until a rough dough comes together. Place the dough in a clean bowl, cover with plastic wrap, and place it in the preheated oven for 45 minutes to proof.

Make the filling: In a large bowl, combine the ground pork, cooked noodles, garlic, scallions, onion, mushrooms, oyster sauce, fish sauce, sugar, salt, MSG, and black pepper. Mix until the filling

Continued

Galabao ◆ Pork Steamed Buns
continued

is well combined and homogeneous. Cover with plastic wrap and refrigerate until ready to use.

Shape the buns: Cut eight 2-inch squares of parchment paper and set aside. Remove the dough from the oven; it should have doubled in size. Knead the dough in the bowl until smooth. Divide the dough into 8 equal pieces. Lightly flour a work surface, and roll one piece of dough into a 6-inch circle. Place ¼ cup of the filling in the center of the circle, then top with a quarter of an egg and a sausage slice.

To fold the bun, pinch a corner of the dough to create a pleat. Continue pleating and gathering the edges toward the center, covering the filling; twist the top to seal the bun and place it on a parchment paper square. Repeat with the remaining dough and filling until you have 8 buns. Let the buns rest for 10 minutes before steaming.

Steam the buns: Bring water in a large pot to a boil. Arrange the buns in a steamer basket, keeping at least 1 inch between them to allow for expansion. Steam over high heat for 25 to 30 minutes. Remove the buns from the steamer and let them cool slightly before serving.

Notes

Wrap any leftover buns in plastic wrap and store them in the refrigerator. To reheat, place a bun on a plate, cover with a wet paper towel and microwave for 1 to 2 minutes.

Chinese sausage, also known as lap cheong, adds a sweet bite to galabaos. These thin, red sausages are found at Asian grocery stores in vacuum-sealed packages.

Sakoo Yat Sai ◆ Tapioca Dumplings

ສາຄູຍັດໄສ້

Makes 30 dumplings | Serves 5

These dumplings were the highlight of my "fat boy" days. I was the kid who lived in stretchy pants (I refused to wear jeans) and always ate like I hadn't had food in days, even though I'd probably devoured a doughnut a few hours earlier. Maybe it was a lingering refugee hunger from my family's past that followed me into adolescence. When my parents dragged me to Lao parties so they could catch up with friends, I made the most of it. For me, the main event wasn't the conversations, it was the platters of food on the table. No matter how full my plate was, I always found room for these dumplings. Though a savory dish, these dumplings lean heavily toward the sweet side, and I think that's where my sweet tooth began. Each bite ignited my taste buds with the perfect balance of sweet and savory, complemented by the chewy, satisfying texture. When I finally tried making these treats myself, I realized how much love and effort goes into creating the perfect tapioca dumpling. It gave me a new appreciation for this dish that had been such a delicious centerpiece of my childhood.

¼ cup (1½ ounces) salted whole turnips (see Note)

1¼ cups mini tapioca pearls

Filling

1½ teaspoons vegetable oil

½ cup sugar

⅓ cup minced shallots

4 garlic cloves, minced

½ pound ground lean pork

⅓ cup lightly salted roasted peanuts, ground or chopped fine

¼ teaspoon freshly ground black pepper

2 tablespoons fish sauce (see page 18)

To Serve

1 head butter lettuce

1 cup chopped cilantro leaves

1 cup whole mint leaves

½ cup fried garlic (see page 21)

½ cup fried shallots (see page 21)

½ cup sliced fresh bird's eye chile

Prepare the turnip and tapioca pearls: Finely mince the salted turnip and soak it in a bowl of warm water for 30 minutes. Place the tapioca pearls in a large bowl. Rinse them with room temperature water three times. After the final rinse, drain in a strainer for 30 minutes to remove most of the water. When the salted turnips have soaked for 30 minutes, drain them and squeeze out the water. Set aside.

Make the filling: Heat a medium pan over medium-high heat and add the vegetable oil and sugar. Let the sugar melt, stirring occasionally, until it turns lightly golden, about 3 minutes. Add the minced shallots and garlic and sauté for 1 minute, until fragrant and lightly golden. Stir in the ground pork and cook for 5 to 6 minutes, breaking it up and mixing it with the aromatics. Add the minced turnip, ground peanuts, black pepper, and fish sauce. Stir well and cook until most of the liquid evaporates, 1 to 2 minutes. Transfer the pork mixture to a bowl and place it in the freezer for 30 minutes to cool completely.

Continued

Sakoo Yat Sai ◆ Tapioca Dumplings

continued

Make the dumplings: Line a plate with parchment paper. Once the filling has cooled, scoop out heaping 1½ teaspoon portions and roll them into small balls; press firmly with your hands to ensure that they hold together. Set the balls on the parchment-lined plate. Take 1 tablespoon of the tapioca pearls and flatten them into a disk in your palm. Place a pork ball in the center, then wrap the tapioca around the filling, rolling it around your hand until the pork is fully enclosed. Repeat with the remaining filling and tapioca.

Bring a large pot of water to a boil. Line a steamer basket with lightly oiled parchment paper. Arrange the dumplings in the basket about 1 inch apart to prevent sticking. Cover and steam in batches until the dumplings turn translucent, about 5 minutes. Carefully remove the steamer basket from the heat. Lightly spray the dumplings with oil to prevent them from sticking to one another and set them on a plate while you steam the rest of the dumplings.

To serve, wrap the dumplings in butter lettuce with chopped cilantro, mint leaves, fried garlic, fried shallots, and bird's eye chile peppers.

Note

Packaged salted whole turnips are available in Asian markets.

Pun Pa ◆ Fish Lettuce Wraps

พัນປາ

Serves 2 to 4

The Rock River in south central Wisconsin always provided our family with a bounty of freshly caught fish. When I was a boy, Paw tried taking me fishing with him, but I quickly realized it wasn't for me. I was impatient, restless, and hesitant to touch (or kill) worms for bait. While Paw quietly waited for the fish to bite, I spent my time playing near the water until it was time to go home. By the time we left, Paw had caught dozens of fish. Together, he and Mae would scale and gut the fish, deciding whether to ferment them for padaek, freeze them for later meals, or deep-fry them to enjoy in lettuce wraps with pineapple dip. Of all the preparations, I loved the fish best when it was deep-fried and wrapped in lettuce. The skin was irresistibly crispy, and the pineapple jeow perfectly cut through the richness of the fish.

Fish

1 (1-pound) whole tilapia, gutted and scaled

1 teaspoon coarse kosher salt

2 tablespoons sticky rice flour (see page 18)

Vegetable oil, for frying

Pineapple Jeow

1½ cups chopped fresh pineapple

2 tablespoons chopped fresh ginger

2 garlic cloves, smashed

3 fresh bird's eye chiles, stemmed and chopped

½ teaspoon MSG

1 teaspoon sugar

1½ tablespoons fish sauce (see page 18)

1½ tablespoons padaek (see page 97)

Toppings and Wraps

1 head butter lettuce

1 cup chopped pork rinds

1 cup halved cherry tomatoes

1 shallot, minced

1 cup chopped cilantro leaves and tender stems

1 cup chopped dill

½ cup roasted peanuts

¼ cup thin matchsticks fresh ginger

10 ounces vermicelli rice noodles, cooked

Prepare the fish: Place the fish on a cutting board and pat it dry with paper towels. Using a sharp knife, make diagonal cuts across the fish from the top fin to the belly, spaced about 1-inch apart. Repeat on the other side. Lightly season both sides of the fish with salt, then sprinkle a thin layer of sticky rice flour over the fish and tap gently to remove any excess.

In a large wok or deep pan, heat 3 inches of oil to 350°F. Carefully lower the whole fish into the hot oil. Fry for 6 minutes on each side to ensure even cooking. Remove the fish with two spatulas and place it on a paper towel–lined plate to drain.

Make the pineapple jeow: In a food processor, combine the pineapple, ginger, garlic, and bird's eye chiles. Pulse until finely chopped. Transfer the mixture to a bowl and add the MSG, sugar, fish sauce, and padaek. Mix thoroughly to combine.

Assemble the wraps: Arrange the lettuce, pork rinds, cherry tomatoes, shallot, cilantro, dill, peanuts, ginger, and vermicelli noodles on a large serving plate. Serve the fried fish alongside the toppings and the pineapple jeow. Wrap a piece of fish, toppings, and a drizzle of pineapple jeow in a lettuce leaf for a flavorful bite.

Serves 6 to 8

Mok Pa Ling ◆ Steamed Catfish in Banana Leaves

ໝົກປາລີ່ງ

Rice Paste

¼ cup uncooked sticky rice

2½ cups water

2 tablespoons minced lemongrass (from the soft part of 1 lemongrass stalk)

2 tablespoons minced cilantro root (see page 22), or use 4 cilantro stems

2 tablespoons peeled, minced galangal

3 fresh bird's eye chiles, stemmed and minced, plus more for garnish

⅓ cup minced shallots

3 tablespoons padaek (see page 97)

1 tablespoon fish sauce (see page 18)

½ teaspoon MSG

Fish Mixture

1½ pounds catfish, boned and cut into ½-inch cubes

2 scallions, green and white parts, chopped, plus extra for garnish

1 tablespoon minced fresh makrut lime leaves (about 4 leaves)

1 cup minced dill leaves and tender stems, plus extra for garnish

To Wrap and Serve

12 banana leaves, each 10 inches in length (or use aluminum foil)

8 toothpicks

Cooked sticky rice (see page 73), for serving

Banana leaves are a sustainable and versatile alternative to conventional wrapping materials, and using them to wrap foods is one of my favorite aspects of Lao cooking. This technique not only adds stunning visual appeal but also imparts a distinct earthy aroma to the dish. Depending on the type and source of the banana leaves, they may be too stiff initially and need to be warmed to soften the fibers, making them easier to fold (see page 25 for guidance). Once they're warmed, the leaves become pliable, much like parchment paper, and can be folded into various shapes. In Lao cuisine, they're folded into cups to hold desserts, crafted into beautiful centerpieces for baci ceremonies, and used to wrap savory dishes like mok pa ling. This banana leaf–wrapped catfish is a classic Lao dish, packed with bold, aromatic flavors and held together with a fragrant sticky rice paste. The banana leaves here showcase the deep connection between Lao culture and nature, emphasizing the Lao affinity for harmony and resourcefulness in everyday life.

Prepare the rice paste: Rinse the sticky rice three times, then place it in a small bowl. Bring 2 cups of water to a boil. Cover the rice with the boiling water, and let soak for 10 minutes. Drain the rice and, using a deep mortar and pestle, pound it until it forms a paste. Add the lemongrass, cilantro root, galangal, chiles, and shallots to the mortar, and continue pounding until a rough paste forms. Season the paste with the padaek, fish sauce, remaining water, and MSG. Mix well to combine.

Prepare the fish mixture: In a large bowl, combine the cubed catfish with the rice paste and mix well using a spoon. Add the scallions, makrut lime leaves, and dill and gently toss to ensure the fish is evenly coated with rice paste and aromatics.

Fold and steam the parcels: For each parcel, layer two banana leaves on top of each other. Place ½ cup of the fish mixture in the center of the leaves. Fold the package lengthwise, then fold the sides inward, creasing the top down securely. Use a toothpick (or chopped wooden skewer) to hold the parcel together. Bring a large pot of water to a boil. Place the parcels in a steamer basket, ensuring they're arranged in a single layer with space between them. Steam for 30 minutes over high heat.

To serve, garnish with additional chopped scallions, dill, and extra bird's eye chiles for added heat. Enjoy with sticky rice.

Ping Gai Ta Padaek ◆ Roasted Chicken with Padaek

ປີ້ງໄກ່ທາປາແດກ

Serves 4 to 6

Lao barbecue is a true art, with a mastery of the flame so universal that it guarantees incredible flavor in every dish you find on the streets of Laos. The meats are always perfectly seared and bursting with smoky, savory goodness. A hallmark of Lao barbecue is the use of bamboo sticks to hold meats together securely, making it easy to rotate them and roast them evenly over the fire. If you pass by a Lao barbecue stand, don't miss the chance to grab a piece of grilled meat paired with sticky rice and jeow. This recipe is my take on Lao barbecue, adapted for the convenience and easy cleanup of an oven. While it may skip the open flame, it doesn't compromise on flavor: Each drumstick is generously coated in padaek to capture the essence of Lao street food. Pair this chicken with sticky rice or fresh vegetables for a complete meal.

¼ cup minced lemongrass (from the soft part of about 2 lemongrass stalks)

8 garlic cloves, minced

¼ cup cilantro stems and leaves

Marinade

¼ cup chili garlic sauce (sambal)

¼ cup oyster sauce

1 tablespoon dark soy sauce

1 tablespoon fish sauce (see page 18)

2 tablespoons seasoning sauce (see page 22)

1½ teaspoons freshly ground black pepper

1 teaspoon MSG

1 tablespoon lime juice

Chicken

2½ pounds chicken drumsticks

1 tablespoon sugar

2 tablespoons padaek (see page 97)

Make the lemongrass paste: In a deep mortar, combine the minced lemongrass, garlic, and cilantro. Pound into a coarse paste.

Prepare the marinade: In a medium bowl, combine the chili garlic sauce, oyster sauce, dark soy sauce, fish sauce, seasoning sauce, black pepper, MSG, and lime juice. Mix well. Add the lemongrass paste from the mortar to the bowl and stir until fully incorporated.

Prepare the chicken: Place the chicken drumsticks into a large zip-top bag. Add the marinade, then seal the bag and massage it to coat the chicken evenly with marinade. Refrigerate for at least 1 hour, and preferably overnight, to allow the flavors to develop.

When you're ready to cook the chicken, preheat the oven to 400°F. Line a baking tray with aluminum foil. Arrange the marinated chicken drumsticks in a single layer on the baking tray. Cook for 30 minutes, flipping the drumsticks halfway through for even cooking. Meanwhile, prepare a glaze by mixing the sugar and padaek in a small bowl. Remove the drumsticks from the oven and brush a thin layer of the padaek glaze on each drumstick, then return the chicken to the oven to cook for another 10 minutes. Serve hot.

3

RICE DISHES

Children of Sticky Rice

Sticky rice, known as khao niew in Lao, is the cornerstone of Lao cuisine and culture, transcending its role as sustenance to become a symbol of identity and resilience. Often called glutinous rice, sticky rice is grown more extensively in Laos than anywhere else in the world, with over 3,200 distinct varieties. The Lao people consume the most sticky rice per capita, averaging an astonishing 377 pounds per person each year. It is a staple woven into the daily lives of Lao families, holding an equivalent cultural significance in Lao cuisine as the baguette does to the French. Showcasing its unmatched versatility, it forms the base of nearly every meal, whether dipped in spicy jeows, used to soak up the flavors of a rich soup, or paired with meat from dishes like laab.

Due to its high starch content, sticky rice has a chewy, clumping texture, which is only achievable through steaming. Though the cooking process may seem simple, the key to perfectly steamed rice that is soft but not sticky to the touch lies in mastering all of the little details. These include the method of washing and soaking the grains, knowing how long to steam the rice, and handling the rice gently and quickly after it's cooked. In a traditional Lao household, the process of preparing sticky rice actually begins the day before consumption, when the grains are rinsed and then soaked overnight. In the morning, the rice is transferred into a conical bamboo basket and steamed over a metal pot of boiling water. Once the rice is done, it is spread out onto a bamboo platter to cool and aerate before finally being molded into a ball. The signature ball shape symbolizes unity and togetherness, an idea that is reflected when the rice is placed at the center of the table to be shared and eaten by hand.

Community also plays an important role in the cultivation of sticky rice in Laos: The entire process is deeply tied to the land and to the people's agricultural heritage. Rice is grown and harvested in a labor-intensive process that requires the cooperation of the entire village. Though the fields are sometimes prepared with the help of water buffalo, most of the process is done by hand, starting with the planting of rice seeds from the previous year's harvest in a small plot of land. Villagers then work relentlessly under the sun, replanting seedlings in the muddy paddies until dusk. After a few months, the stalks mature and turn golden, signaling they are ready to be hand-harvested with a sickle and then processed.

Bundles of rice stalks are laid out to dry in the sun and then beaten to release the grains from the stalk. The grains are sorted using a bamboo fan, which winnows away the underdeveloped grains, leaving behind only those that are suitable for consumption. The final step is removing the husks to reveal the naked rice grains, the product of months of hard work now in its final raw form. In village life, rice is not just food, it is shared and treasured, and every part of the plant is utilized. Rice stalks become brooms and animal feed; husks contribute to making padaek and rice wine; and the water used to rinse the rice grains before cooking is repurposed for shampoo. Sticky rice is not just a food but a way of life based on minimizing waste and maximizing utility.

Sticky rice also holds a sacred place in Lao spiritual traditions. It plays a vital role in tak bat, the daily alms-giving ritual in Theravada Buddhist practice,

where monks receive sticky rice and other offerings from villagers at dawn. This act of giving connects people to their faith and reinforces communal bonds. Even in the Lao diaspora, these traditions persist, with families preparing sticky rice as part of offerings made during temple ceremonies and religious holidays.

Mae, like many Lao mothers, was the keeper of the rice-based traditions in our home. She always insisted we eat sticky rice with our meals, reminding us that without sticky rice, we wouldn't feel truly full, a sentiment that echoes across generations; sticky rice connecting us to our roots. Each morning before heading to work, she would steam the day's sticky rice, ensuring it was ready for us to eat with every meal. She and I shared a special mother-son tradition: When the daily rice was ready, she would place a clump of hot rice in my hand, and I would immediately toss it hand to hand like a hot potato. She would remind me to blow on it to cool it down, but I was invariably impatient. By the time she warned me, I had already stuffed the steaming rice into my mouth and was heaving from the heat.

Sticky rice's versatility in Lao cuisine is endless. It is deep-fried into crispy rice puffs, grilled with an egg and fish sauce marinade, and turned into sweet desserts like stuffed rice wrapped in banana leaves. Its presence elevates every meal, whether it's there as a vessel for bold flavors or as the star of the dish. Sticky rice exemplifies Lao ingenuity, how every day we transform a simple grain into an integral part of our culinary and cultural identity. The recipes in this chapter will help you become a master at preparing sticky rice and also show you many of the traditional dishes where it's the star. By the end, you'll understand why it holds such a profound place in Lao hearts and homes, why we are dubbed "the children of sticky rice," and why, for us, no meal feels complete without it.

Khao Niew ◆ Lao Sticky Rice

ເຂົ້າໜຽວ

What's that one food your mom makes that always brings you comfort? For me, it's khao niew, or sticky rice. Mae cooks it perfectly every time. When I was a kid, she always knew I wanted it straight from the steamer with a little salt sprinkled on top. If any rice was left over after meals, she saved it for the next day, crumbling it on top of the new uncooked rice so it would warm up and not overcook. She never let anything go to waste. Although I don't live with Mae now, wherever I go, I make sticky rice and share a handful with new friends and family, always feeling at home with its warmth and comfort.

Makes 8 cups | Serves 6

Special Tools

Mao khao: An aluminum pot for steaming sticky rice

Huat khao: A woven bamboo sticky rice steamer

Thip khao: A traditional bamboo basket for serving and storing sticky rice

Rice

4 cups sticky rice (glutinous rice)

Room-temperature water, to rinse, soak, and cook

Rinse and soak the rice: Place the sticky rice in a large bowl and cover with room-temperature water. Gently agitate the rice with your hands to release its excess starch, which will turn the water cloudy. Carefully pour out most of the water, then rinse and repeat three more times, until the water is clear. Add enough water to the rinsed rice to submerge it by at least 2 inches. Soak the rice for at least 12 hours (usually overnight). For a quicker preparation method, see the Notes.

Steam the rice: Fill the aluminum pot with at least 5 inches of water and bring it to a boil over high heat. Drain the soaked rice and transfer it into the bamboo steamer; give the rice a quick rinse within the steamer to ensure it settles evenly at the bottom. Position the steamer over the boiling pot and cover it with a lid. Steam over high heat for 15 minutes. Remove the steamer from the pot and gently flip the rice so the top layer moves to the bottom. Place the steamer back on the pot, cover, and steam for another 15 minutes.

Cool and shape the rice: Remove the steamer from the pot and transfer the hot sticky rice to a nonstick surface like a baking sheet lined with parchment paper. Use a wooden spoon to gently break apart the rice, allowing steam to escape. Let it cool until it can be handled with your bare hands, then shape the rice back into a ball and place it in a bamboo basket (thip khao).

Serve immediately or wrap the basket in a towel to keep the rice warm for later meals.

Notes

If you're short on time, you can soak the rice for 1 hour in hot water (instead of overnight). Longer soaking results in fluffier rice, but avoid soaking for less than an hour to prevent hard granules.

As an alternative to the traditional bamboo steamer, you can use a regular steamer lined with cheesecloth.

Khao Jee ◆ Grilled Sticky Rice

Serves 8

Sticky rice never goes to waste in our household, and this recipe is perfect for giving day-old sticky rice a second life. Once it's re-steamed, the rice becomes bouncier and stickier, ideal for making khao jee, a popular Lao street food. These rice patties, coated in a rich egg batter with padaek, offer a burst of umami with every bite. Best enjoyed hot off the grill or skillet, they have an almost cheesy stretch that makes them irresistible.

4 cups day-old cooked sticky rice (see page 73)

1 teaspoon coarse kosher salt

Oil, for spraying

2 large eggs

1 tablespoon padaek (see page 97)

1 tablespoon seasoning sauce (see page 22)

½ teaspoon MSG

½ teaspoon freshly ground black pepper

1 tablespoon vegetable oil

Jeow bong (see page 26), for serving

Prepare the rice patties and egg mixture: Bring a large pot of water to a boil. Crumble the day-old cooked sticky rice into a steamer basket. Steam for 7 minutes, then flip the rice and steam for another 7 minutes to ensure it's fully reheated.

Transfer the hot sticky rice to a bowl and sprinkle with the kosher salt. Mix thoroughly while the rice is still warm. Lightly spray a cutting board with oil. Measure ¼ cup of sticky rice and shape it into a ½-inch-thick patty on the board, or in your hands. To achieve uniform patties, you can lightly spray a musubi press or tortilla press with oil. Place the rice in the center and press firmly to shape a patty. Once the patties are formed, cut them into shapes, such as squares or rounds.

In a small bowl, whisk together the eggs, padaek, seasoning sauce, MSG, and black pepper until fully combined. Set aside.

Cook the patties: Heat a large sauté pan over medium heat and add the vegetable oil. Cook the rice patties in batches for 2 minutes on each side, until they're crispy and golden brown, moving them to a paper towel–lined plate until they're all cooked. Lower the heat to low. Still working in batches to fit into your pan, brush the egg mixture onto one side of each patty and cook egg-side down for 30 seconds. Brush the top of the patty with egg mixture, flip it, and cook for another 30 seconds. Repeat this process twice to fully coat each patty with the egg mixture. Place the finished patties on a baking sheet in a 200°F oven to keep them warm before serving.

Serve the crispy, egg-coated patties immediately with jeow bong.

Khao Tom ◆ Coconut Sticky Rice Parcels

ເຂົ້າຕົ້ມ

Serves 13, 1 bundle per person

Thirteen (10½-inch) rectangular frozen banana leaves

¾ cup sugar

½ teaspoon coarse kosher salt

1 (13½-ounce) can coconut milk

2 cups uncooked sticky rice

7 ripe baby bananas, peeled and halved lengthwise

Before big events like baci ceremonies and other cultural celebrations, I often entered the kitchen to see Mae and her friends sitting on the floor, gossiping while they rolled bundles of khao tom in big batches. During a baci ceremony, khao tom are often held in one hand, palm up, while the other hand is raised toward the sky. This gesture symbolizes positivity and acceptance as an elder chants blessings and well wishes, and ties a white blessing string around the person's wrist. This treat is not only flavorful but, since it's wrapped in banana leaves, it's also easy to take on the go. Once the sweetened coconut sticky rice is cooled to room temperature, it becomes delightfully chewy, while the banana, nestled within it, adds an extra touch of sweetness. You can replace the banana with sweetened black beans or taro for a different flavor profile. Prepare these sticky rice bundles for your next celebration as a meaningful way to share well wishes with your loved ones.

Defrost the banana leaves at room temperature for 30 minutes. Wipe both sides of each leaf with a damp paper towel to remove any dirt or debris. Set aside.

Make the coconut sauce: In a small pot over low heat, combine the sugar, salt, and coconut milk. Stir well, and let the mixture simmer for 8 minutes. Remove the pot from the heat and set it aside.

Cook the sticky rice and combine with the sauce: Cook the sticky rice using your preferred method (see page 73). While the rice is still hot, transfer it to a large bowl, pour the coconut sauce over it, and mix thoroughly. Let the mixture cool for 15 minutes to allow the rice to absorb the liquid.

Assemble the wraps: On a work surface, lay one banana leaf flat with the veins running horizontally. Scoop ¼ cup of the sticky rice mixture onto the bottom part of the banana leaf. Place a slice of banana on top of the rice. Roll the banana leaf away from you to form a tight tube. Fold and tuck both ends under the wrap to seal it securely. Repeat with the remaining wraps and leaves.

Steam the wraps and serve: Bring a large pot of water to a boil. Place the wraps in a steamer basket, cover, and steam for 30 minutes. Remove the parcels to a plate and allow them to cool for at least 1 hour before serving. Serve at room temperature, enjoying the delicate sweetness and chewy texture of khao tom.

Khao Kope ◆ Sticky Rice Puffs

Makes 15 puffs | Serves 6

Every Lao family in my hometown had their own specialty dish that we would trade with one another. My childhood best friend's family were experts at making khao kope, sweet and savory circular rice patties drizzled with caramel sauce. Every time I played at his house, his family greeted me with these crispy, sticky rice puffs. For me, khao kope weren't just a snack; they were a symbol of friendship, something I could share with new neighbors or use to introduce people to the flavors of Lao snacks. You can eat these puffs as is or lightly crush them into noodle soup, where they add a satisfying crunch to every slurp. Steam the rice in a traditional sticky rice steamer (huat khao; see page 73) if you have one.

Rice Puffs

2 cups uncooked sticky rice

⅓ cup coconut milk or water

Pinch of coarse kosher salt

Vegetable oil, for spraying and for deep-frying

Palm Sugar Glaze

½ cup palm sugar

Pinch of kosher salt

3 tablespoons coconut milk

Prepare the sticky rice: In a large bowl, rinse the sticky rice three times in warm water to remove excess starch. Cover the rice with hot water and let it soak for at least 1 hour. Steam the rice in a rice steamer for 30 minutes, flipping it halfway through to ensure even cooking. Transfer the cooked sticky rice to a rice cooker set to the "warm" setting. Gently mix in the ⅓ cup coconut milk and salt, taking care not to pack the rice.

Shape and dry the rice disks: Lightly spray a 3½-inch mason jar lid and a ¼-cup measuring cup with oil. Place ¼ cup of the rice mixture into the lid and lightly flatten it into an even disk (do not overpack). Invert the rice disk onto a baking sheet. Repeat until all the rice is used. Place the shaped rice disks in a food dehydrator or an oven set to 165°F, and dry for 2 hours; alternatively, place them in a sunny spot to dry all day. The disks are ready to fry when they are completely dry but not brittle.

Fry the rice puffs: Add at least 4 inches of oil to a deep-fryer or pot and heat it to 350°F. Set a tray lined with paper towels next to the fryer. Fry each disk for about 60 seconds, turning every 20 seconds, until they puff up and turn golden. Remove and place the fried rice puffs on the paper towel–lined tray to drain excess oil.

Make the palm sugar glaze: Roughly crush the palm sugar blocks in a mortar and pestle or with a rolling pin. In a small saucepan over medium-low heat, melt the sugar and salt, stirring until it turns into a golden-brown syrup, about 5 minutes. Reduce the heat to low, add the coconut milk, and stir until smooth.

Drizzle the palm sugar glaze over the fried rice puffs while they are still warm. Allow the glaze to set slightly before serving.

Serves 4 to 6

Mieng Muang Luang ◆ Sticky Rice Paste Wraps

ໝ້ຽງເມືອງຫຼວງ

2 tablespoons sugar

2 cups water

1 cup halved cherry tomatoes

2 tablespoons fish sauce (see page 18)

1 teaspoon padaek (see page 97)

½ teaspoon MSG

12 sticky rice puffs (see page 79)

¼ cup fried shallots (see page 21)

¼ cup fried garlic (see page 21)

To Serve

2 heads butter lettuce

1 thinly sliced lemongrass stalk, soft part only

1 cup chopped cilantro leaves and soft stems

¼ cup thinly sliced ginger matchsticks

½ cup roasted peanuts

1 cup chopped cherry tomatoes

2 tablespoons thinly sliced fresh makrut lime leaves (about 10 leaves)

1 cup thinly sliced purple cabbage

In this dish, sticky rice undergoes an epic transformation, from a dry grain to fluffy, bouncy rice that's sun-dried and puffed into a chip and then, finally, becoming a flavorful paste used as the centerpiece of a meal. This versatility highlights why the people of Laos are often called the "children of sticky rice": They have perfected every form and variation of the staple ingredient. This is one of the most customizable ways to enjoy sticky rice: Simply pair a scoop of the paste with seasonal toppings for a unique and satisfying experience.

Prepare the tomato water: Heat a small pot over medium-high heat and add the sugar. Cook for 2 to 3 minutes, stirring, until the sugar caramelizes and turns golden. Add the water and stir until the sugar fully dissolves. Add the halved cherry tomatoes, bring to a simmer, cover the pot, and reduce the heat to low. Simmer for 15 minutes, then season the tomato water with the fish sauce, padaek, and MSG. Mix well and remove from the heat.

Process the sticky rice puffs: Place the sticky rice puffs in a food processor and process until they are finely ground (or crush them in a deep mortar with a pestle); you should end up with about 3 cups of ground puffed rice. Add the ground puffed rice to the warm tomato water and mix until the liquid is fully absorbed into the rice. Return the tomato-rice mixture to the food processor and add the fried shallots and fried garlic. Blend until the mixture has a sticky, cohesive texture.

Assemble the lettuce wraps: Flatten a large leaf of lettuce on a work surface. Add a scoop of the sticky rice mixture to the center. Top with your choice of lemongrass, cilantro, ginger, roasted peanuts, chopped cherry tomatoes, lime leaves, and purple cabbage. Fold the lettuce around the filling to create a wrap and enjoy.

Khao Jee Taut ◆ Savory Sticky Rice Pancake

Serves 4 to 6

Leftover sticky rice is incredibly versatile, often transformed into something completely new and unrecognizable. One of my favorite ways to repurpose it is by turning it into a savory "what's left in the fridge" pancake. This recipe is a version of that. It's packed with flavors from herbs and fish sauce, making it a perfect hands-on dish. It can be made heartier with additions like pieces of Chinese sausage, mushrooms, or Som Moo (page 115) cooked together with the rice. It's a fun and satisfying way to breathe new life into leftover rice. Serve it warm with Jeow Som (page 31) for dipping.

2 cups leftover sticky rice (see page 73)

2 eggs

1 tablespoon padaek (see page 97)

1½ teaspoons fish sauce (see page 18)

½ cup chicken broth

½ teaspoon MSG

¼ cup minced cilantro tender stems and leaves, plus more for garnish

¼ cup minced scallions, green parts only, plus more for garnish

¼ cup sticky rice flour (see page 18)

2 tablespoons vegetable oil

Prepare the pancake: In a large bowl, combine the leftover sticky rice, eggs, padaek, fish sauce, chicken broth, and MSG. Break up the sticky rice with your hands or a spoon and mix well until evenly combined. Add the cilantro, scallions, and sticky rice flour. Mix until fully incorporated.

Heat a large sauté pan over medium heat and add the vegetable oil. Once the oil is warm, pour all the pancake mixture into the pan and spread it out evenly. Let it cook until the bottom becomes crispy and golden brown, 5 to 6 minutes. Carefully flip the pancake using a wide spatula. Cook until the other side is crispy and golden brown, about 3 minutes.

To serve, transfer the pancake to a cutting board and cut it into 12 pieces, like pizza slices. Garnish with additional cilantro and scallions if desired. Serve warm.

Serves 4 to 6

Khao Piek Khao ◆ Rice Porridge

ເຂົ້າປຽກເຂົ້າ

Meatballs

½ pound ground pork

1 teaspoon minced ginger

½ teaspoon freshly ground black pepper

½ teaspoon coarse kosher salt

Broth

2 tablespoons vegetable oil

1 tablespoon minced garlic

¼ cup ¼-inch-thick slices of ginger

4 whole fresh makrut lime leaves

9 cups water, plus more as needed

½ pound spareribs with soft bone, cut into 2-inch pieces

1 cup uncooked jasmine rice

¼ cup uncooked sticky rice

1 tablespoon fish sauce (see page 18)

½ teaspoon coarse kosher salt

1 teaspoon MSG

To Serve

1 cup thinly chopped scallions

1 cup roughly chopped cilantro leaves and soft stems

½ cup fried shallots (see page 21)

Freshly ground black pepper

6 Chinese doughnuts, for dipping (see Note)

Optional Toppings

Fish sauce (see page 18)

Chile oil

Seasoning sauce (see page 22)

6 Poached Eggs with Vinegar (recipe follows)

Every Saturday morning, the house filled with the rich aroma of fried garlic as Mae prepared her signature breakfast dish, khao piek khao. The scent wafting through the air acted as my weekend alarm clock: I'd wake up to the smell of garlic sizzling in the kitchen and make my way to the living room to watch morning cartoons. Soon, Mae's voice called out, "Khao piek law le, ma gin der" ("The rice porridge is ready, come eat"). My two sisters and I would rush into the kitchen, stomachs rumbling and faces lit with excitement, ready to devour this comforting and hearty meal. Mae knew exactly how each of us liked our porridge. I always got extra dried peppers and pork, Daeng's bowl overflowed with herbs and veggies, and Amy preferred hers plain and simple. In the center of the table, Mae laid out fresh vegetables from the garden and an assortment of sauces so everyone could customize their bowls. Paw amazed me with how many raw peppers he could eat with every spoonful of porridge. Mae, ever selfless, was the last to sit down. She made sure we were all fed and happy before serving herself. This act of putting others first is a lesson that has stayed with me, resonating both in and outside the kitchen.

Prepare the meatballs: In a small bowl, combine the ground pork, minced ginger, black pepper, and salt. Mix until well combined, then roll the mixture into meatballs, using 1 tablespoon of meat per ball. Arrange the meatballs on a plate and set aside.

Prepare the broth: Heat the vegetable oil in a large stockpot over high heat for 30 seconds. Add the minced garlic, sliced ginger, and lime leaves. Sauté for 30 seconds, until aromatic. Add the water and bring it to a boil.

Carefully drop the meatballs into the boiling broth, followed by the spareribs. Bring the broth back to a boil, then reduce to a low simmer for 10 to 15 minutes. Skim any impurities that rise to the surface.

Prepare the rice: While the meatballs and spareribs are simmering, combine the jasmine rice and sticky rice in a large bowl. Rinse the rice three times with warm water to remove excess starch. Strain the rice and set it aside.

Continued

Finish the porridge: When the meatballs are plump and fully cooked, season the broth with the fish sauce, salt, and MSG. Add the rinsed jasmine and sticky rice and stir to combine. Cover the pot and simmer on low for 20 minutes, stirring occasionally. Check the consistency, and if a thicker porridge is desired, let it simmer for an additional 5 minutes.

To serve, ladle the porridge into bowls and garnish with scallions, cilantro, fried shallots, and a sprinkle of black pepper. Serve with Chinese doughnuts for dipping, and, if you like, add optional toppings: fish sauce, chile oil, seasoning sauce (page 22), and a poached egg.

Note

Premade Chinese doughnuts can be bought fresh or found in the frozen section of Asian markets.

Poached Eggs with Vinegar

2 cups water

1 cup distilled vinegar

4 to 6 eggs

Prepare the vinegar mixture: In a medium bowl, combine the water and vinegar. Stir to mix well.

Soak the eggs: Gently crack the eggs into the vinegar mixture, ensuring they are fully submerged. Let sit for 15 minutes.

Poach the eggs: Heat a small pot of water over medium heat until hot, but not simmering (160° to 180°F). Using a slotted spoon, carefully remove an egg from the vinegar mixture and gently slide it into the hot water. Repeat with the remaining eggs. Let the eggs poach in the hot water until the whites are set and the yolks remain soft, about 6 minutes.

Drain and serve: Remove the eggs from the water with the slotted spoon and place them on a paper towel to drain. Serve as is, or add to porridge, salads, or other dishes.

Serves 3 or 4

Nam Khao Tod ◆ Crispy Rice Salad

ແໜມເຂົ້າທອດ

Rice Patties

2 cups jasmine rice

2½ cups water

1 teaspoon vegetable oil plus more for deep frying

1 tablespoon minced garlic

8 ounces ground pork

1 egg

3 tablespoons Red Curry Paste (see page 21; or use store-bought)

1 tablespoon sugar

1 cup dried shredded coconut

2 tablespoons minced fresh makrut lime leaves (about 10 leaves)

Salad

2 tablespoons fish sauce (see page 18)

2 tablespoons lime juice

Pinch of coarse kosher salt

Pinch of MSG

1 cup diced cured pork (Som Moo, store-bought or homemade; page 115)

¼ cup diced shallots

½ cup chopped cilantro leaves and tender stems

½ cup sliced scallions, white and light green parts only

¼ cup roasted peanuts

To Serve

1 cup dried bird's eye chiles, fried (see page 18)

1 cup thinly sliced banana blossom (see page 23)

1 cup whole mint leaves

1 head butter lettuce

Nam khao tod has become one of the more famous Lao dishes, almost as recognizable as laab. Some call it nam khao for short, or nam thadeau, based on where it originated. It has gained international adoration over the years and there is no doubt this recipe will get anyone hooked on Lao food. Every bite of this fried rice salad offers a delightful combination of crunch, spice, and umami, making it an absolute hit at parties. Nam khao tod has long been a staple at Lao celebrations, and it's no wonder: everyone loves deep-fried rice—in this case, fragrant jasmine rice.

Cook the rice: Rinse the jasmine rice in a large bowl, repeating three times until the water runs clear; drain. Combine the rice and the 2½ cups of water in a medium pot, and bring to a boil over high heat.

Once the water is boiling, cover the pot, reduce the heat to low, and cook for 15 minutes, until the rice is fluffy and the water is absorbed. Remove the pot from the heat and transfer the cooked rice to a parchment-lined tray. Spread it out evenly and let it cool for 30 minutes.

Make the curried rice mixture: In a medium pot, warm 1 teaspoon of the vegetable oil over medium heat. Sauté the minced garlic until fragrant, then add the ground pork. Cook until browned, about 5 minutes, and set aside. In a large bowl, whisk together the egg, red curry paste, and sugar until smooth. Add the cooled rice, cooked pork, coconut, and minced lime leaves, and mix thoroughly.

Make the rice patties: Wet your hands lightly and scoop up a handful of the rice mixture; press it firmly into a disk-shaped patty, and place on a plate. Repeat with the remaining mixture.

In a pan over medium-high heat, heat 1 inch of vegetable oil to 340°F. Fry the patties in batches of four, cooking until golden brown on both sides, 4 to 6 minutes per side. Remove the patties to drain on a paper towel–lined basket or plate.

Assemble the salad and serve: In a large bowl, crumble the fried rice patties into small pieces. In a small bowl, mix the fish sauce, lime juice, salt, and MSG. Pour this mixture over the crumbled rice and gently toss to coat. Add the cured pork, shallots, cilantro, scallions, and roasted peanuts. Mix everything together gently. Arrange the crispy rice salad in a large serving bowl. Garnish with the fried bird's eye chiles, sliced banana blossom, and mint. Serve with lettuce leaves for wrapping.

Naem Pa ◆ Puffed Rice Fish Salad

แหนมปา

Serves 3 or 4

In Lao cuisine, salads are much more than simple combinations of lettuce and dressing: They're celebrations of bold aromatics, intricate techniques, and carefully layered flavors. This recipe relies on one technique that is a key element in many Lao dishes, including fish laab: ensuring the cooked fish fillet is thoroughly dried. To do this, use your hands to squeeze as much water as possible from the cooked fish. This step is crucial in this recipe because the well-dried fish crumbled and evenly distributed throughout the salad adds a unique texture and flavor.

10 ounces skinless tilapia fillet

Sauce

½ teaspoon coarse kosher salt

½ teaspoon MSG

2 teaspoons fish sauce (see page 18)

2 tablespoons lime juice

1 tablespoon minced peeled galangal

2 tablespoons minced lemongrass (from the soft parts of 1 stalk)

1 shallot, thinly sliced crosswise

⅓ cup chopped long beans (¼-inch pieces)

⅓ cup chopped cilantro leaves and tender stems

⅓ cup thinly crosswise scallion slices

1 cup thinly sliced banana blossom (see page 23)

Fish Salad

8 sticky rice puffs (see page 79)

½ cup sugar

1½ cups water

1 garlic clove

2 fresh bird's eye chiles (see page 18), stemmed

¼ cup roasted peanuts

¼ cup fish sauce

2 tablespoons lime juice

To Serve

1 head green leaf lettuce, for wrapping

1 cup purple mint or peppermint, for garnish

Prepare the fish: Fill a large pot with enough water to cover the fish, and bring it to a boil. Add the tilapia fillet and cook over medium-high heat for 5 minutes. Remove the fish from the pot and let it cool. Shred the fish into small pieces, ensuring that no bones remain. Squeeze some of the shredded fish in your hands to remove excess water; transfer to a bowl. Repeat until you have squeezed dry all the fish. Set aside.

Make the sauce: Heat a small pan over medium-high heat and add the sugar. Allow it to melt and caramelize, stirring occasionally, for 3 to 4 minutes. Add the water to the pan and simmer for 3 minutes, stirring until the sugar fully dissolves. Remove the pan from the heat.

Smash the garlic and bird's eye chiles in a deep mortar. Add the roasted peanuts and crush them into small pieces. Add the caramelized water, fish sauce, and lime juice to the mortar and mix well. Set this sauce aside.

Assemble the fish salad: Into a small bowl, hand-crush the sticky rice puffs into coarse pieces (not powdered); you should have about 2 cups; set aside. In a large salad bowl, combine the shredded fish, salt, MSG, fish sauce, and lime juice. Mix thoroughly. Add the galangal, lemongrass, shallot, long beans, cilantro, scallion, and banana blossom. Mix until evenly combined. Toss in the crushed sticky rice puffs and mix gently to incorporate.

To serve, scoop the fish salad into lettuce leaves to create wraps. Drizzle the sauce over each wrap and garnish with purple mint.

4

FERMENTED FOODS & SALADS

The Foundation Is Fermented

Preserving food through fermentation has always been essential to Lao cuisine. Throughout human history, fermentation techniques have been created out of necessity, allowing us to stretch the longevity of common foods and ensure that sustenance is available in times when meat and vegetables are scarce. Fermentation extends the shelf life of food through the production of acids, alcohol, and other compounds that create an environment inhospitable to spoilage-causing microorganisms, thus allowing for longer storage time without refrigeration. The process also develops complex flavors and aromas that are often more intense and rich than the original foods, enhancing their taste and making them more savory, tangy, or umami-rich. Even after the introduction of refrigerators and other modern technologies, Lao food has continued to embrace fermentation: It adds depth and funk that cannot otherwise be replicated. With some help from aromatics and grains like sticky rice, Lao foods and drinks such as laolao (sticky rice whisky), som moo (sour pork sausage), and padaek (unfiltered fish sauce) are all created using different iterations of this natural process.

Lao people excel at fermenting foods because the process is deeply intertwined with their foraging and farming expertise. Laos is, by any standard, an agricultural country, with over three quarters of the population engaged in farming. Sticky rice accounts for nearly 90 percent of its crops, truly living up to the people's moniker "the children of sticky rice." With the abundance of this particular crop, the Lao people have found creative ways to utilize the fruits of their labor in an effort to minimize waste, and this includes using various fermentation methods for any harvest surplus.

In addition to farming, Lao people have a long tradition of fishing, particularly in communities along the Mekong River. The Mekong serves as Laos's lifeline (it's the world's largest inland fishery), and it's one of the most biologically diverse rivers in the world. The Lao people's fishing skills and knowledge have been honed over centuries, making them particularly adept freshwater fishermen. However, fishing in Laos is highly seasonal, peaking during the rainy summer months, when water levels rise and attract migrating fish. So as not to waste the yield of bountiful months, people ferment extra fish, creating the liquid gold central to Lao cuisine: padaek.

Padaek is one of the most important ingredients in Lao dishes, and it holds a polarized reputation due to its pungent smell and appearance. Compared to the clear fish sauces commonly found in other Southeast Asian cuisines, padaek is thicker, chunkier, and has a more intense flavor. Creating high-quality padaek requires at least a year of fermentation, with some batches aged for five years or more, like fine wine or some vinegars. The process begins with gutting and scaling the fish and cutting it into large chunks, which are then cleaned with rice powder and soaked in salt overnight. Roasted sticky rice powder (see page 17) and water are added to create a fermentation medium, along with ingredients like pineapple rinds, garlic husks, and dried chiles to build flavor. Over time, the mixture transforms from light brown to a rich, dark liquid that enhances dishes from papaya salad to stews.

Padaek is to Lao cuisine what salt is to any home kitchen: It's a staple, and one that adds not just

saltiness but a deep, layered complexity. Most Lao families keep a variety of padaek jars, using different blends depending on the dish being prepared. The aroma of padaek can fill a kitchen in seconds, signaling that a Lao meal is being served, ready to reward adventurous eaters with its bold and funky flavors. In the past, eating padaek and sticky rice has been seen as a marker of lower-class status, particularly in neighboring Southeast Asian countries. But the winds of change have steered the Lao food movement in the right direction. As a result, there is a growing appreciation for padaek and other fermented foods, and ingredients that were once used in secret are now proudly highlighted on menus around the world.

My admiration for padaek has also grown as I've come to understand the immense care, patience, and skill required to produce high-quality versions. The profound transformation of simple ingredients into something new feels almost magical as the microbes perform their alchemical acts unseen. Though fermentation demands careful control, patience, and an understanding of biological processes, it rewards with deep, flavorful, nutritious, and culturally significant foods. In this chapter, I hope to demystify the process of fermentation, allowing you to celebrate one of nature's wonders and, more importantly, preserve your own foods and learn how to use them in recipes that fully embody Lao ingenuity and tradition.

Padaek ◆ Unfiltered Fish Sauce

ປາແດກ

Makes about 7 cups

Padaek is the golden child of Lao cuisine, a kitchen staple that has traveled with Lao families as they moved across the globe. While each family's padaek may share common traits, the sauce also takes on unique characteristics depending on the local environment. When I was growing up in Wisconsin, Paw would go to the Rock River every morning to meditate and catch fish. Mae would fry the catfish, fillet and air-dry the bass, and ferment the excess fish in five-gallon buckets she got from the local hardware store. She rotated the buckets regularly, bringing the ones whose contents had fermented longest to the front and tucking the newly filled ones away until the next snowfall in Wisconsin. She became known for her spicy, dark papaya salad, which others could never quite replicate: Her homemade padaek was unique, and a world apart from the store-bought variety. Eventually, she began selling her padaek to other families, becoming the go-to source for funky Lao cuisine in our city. This is Mae's perfected padaek recipe, refined over the years. The process is slow and intentional, but in six months, you'll have flavorful padaek ready to use. This recipe yields approximately 60 fluid ounces of padaek, so be sure to use a sterilized glass or food-grade plastic fermenting jar. The jar should have an opening large enough for your hands to fit through easily when adding the fish pieces.

- 5½ pounds gutted and scaled whole striped bass
- 1 cup coarse kosher salt, divided, plus more as needed
- ⅓ cup sticky rice flour (see page 18)
- 3⅓ cups water, divided, plus more to rinse and/or submerge fish
- ½ cup roasted sticky rice powder (see page 17; see also Notes)
- 3 ounces pineapple rind, rinsed and chopped into 1-inch pieces
- Husks from 6 garlic cloves
- 1 small yellow onion, quartered
- 12 dried bird's eye chiles (see page 18), stemmed and halved

Prepare the fish: Using kitchen shears, trim the fins from the bass. With a sharp knife, cut behind the gill plate (the sides of the head) down to the bone. Make a thin incision along one side of the spine, running from head to tail. Glide the knife against the bone to separate the fillet. Repeat on the other side of the spine. Slice the fillets into 3-inch pieces. Use kitchen shears to cut the fish carcass, including the head into 3-inch sections as well.

In a large bowl, combine all the fish pieces with ⅓ cup of the salt, the sticky rice flour, and ⅓ cup water. Mix thoroughly, rubbing the salt and flour mixture onto the fish to clean it well. Swirl the fish in the bowl with 4 or 5 changes of fresh water, until the water is clear; drain.

Ferment the fish: For the first fermentation (day 1), mix the cleaned fish pieces with the remaining ⅔ cup of salt, ensuring all the fish is

Continued

Padaek ◆ Unfiltered Fish Sauce
continued

evenly coated. Transfer the fish to a fermenting jar or tub, cover the top of the jar with plastic wrap, and let it sit at room temperature for 24 hours.

For the second fermentation (day 2), uncover the fermenting jar. The fish pieces should feel firm. Transfer the fish and any liquid it has released to a large bowl; add the roasted sticky rice powder and the 3 cups of water. Transfer everything back into the fermenting jar or tub, making sure all the fish is fully submerged. Add more salted water (at a ratio of 1 cup water to 4 tablespoons salt; see Notes) to cover the fish if needed, then put a lid on the jar. Label and date the jar, and store in a cool, dark place, such as a closed cabinet, for three months.

Add optional aromatics: After three months, there will be a white film on top of the padaek; this is a type of yeast that is harmless. Skim it off. To deepen the flavor and funkiness, add the pineapple rind, garlic husks, onion, and dried bird's eye chiles to the fermenting jar. Mix well and cover. Continue fermenting for another three months. The padaek can be used after a total of six months of fermenting although it won't yet be fully developed. At this point, the liquid and fish pieces should be tan and the fish pieces slightly dissolved.

After one year, the padaek will be fully developed and ready for optimal use. It should be dark brown, with most of the fish flesh dissolved, the bones and skin remaining. Skim off the white film of yeast and mix the padaek well before using. Leave it in the covered jar in a dark cabinet to let it continue fermenting. Padaek has a long shelf-life if properly stored and sealed, and the flavor will only become more complex with time.

Notes

Use freshly prepared roasted sticky rice powder for optimal flavor.

If you need to add liquid during fermentation, always maintain the water-to-salt ratio of 1 cup water to 4 tablespoons salt. Add the salted water to make sure the fish is covered at all times while it's fermenting. Fermentation times can vary slightly depending on the environment, so monitor your padaek's progress from time to time.

Thum Mak Hoong ◆ Lao Papaya Salad

ຕຳໝາກຮຸ່ງ

Serves 2 to 4

Whenever I eat papaya salad from other Southeast Asian countries, it always feels like something is missing. Papaya salad originated in Laos, and as it spread to neighboring countries, different versions emerged. What sets Lao papaya salad apart are its heavy pour of padaek and the extra funky flavors from crab and shrimp pastes. Lao papaya salad has a distinct look, dark and overflowing with padaek, and it's renowned for its rich colors, bold flavors, and vibrant zestiness. It's an integral part of the Lao meal trifecta that includes sticky rice and laab. Lao papaya salad is probably where Lao kids build up their spice tolerance. At Lao restaurants, spice levels are often toned down for those unaccustomed to the cuisine. However, if you dare, requesting "Lao hot" will grant you the opportunity to experience the spice levels enjoyed by many Lao people. This dish holds a special place in the hearts of most Lao people, evident from the street food stalls that specialize in thum mak hoong. Smashed unripe papayas are at the heart of the dish; Lao people love to *thum*, or smash, ingredients, especially papayas. The salad is typically prepared at home at least once a week and enjoyed with sticky rice. When thumps and pounding emanate from the kitchen, more times than not, Mae is making thum mak hoong. The beauty of the dish lies in the ease with which its levels of sweetness, sourness, and spiciness can be customized, making it an excellent starting point for mastering the art of balancing flavors. A touch more sugar can correct if it leans salty, while an extra splash of padaek can counter excessive sourness.

1 garlic clove

3 fresh bird's eye chiles, stemmed

2 dried bird's eye chiles, stemmed

1 tablespoon palm sugar, plus more as needed

½ teaspoon MSG

½ teaspoon black crab paste

½ teaspoon shrimp paste

3 tablespoons padaek, or more as needed (see page 97)

1 tablespoon tamarind paste

2 cups green (unripe) papaya, peeled and shredded (see page 22)

1 Lao plum (see Note)

1 lime, halved

12 cherry tomatoes, halved

1 frozen salted whole black crab, defrosted, liquid reserved

To Serve

1 cup sliced morning glory (2-inch pieces); see page 23

1 cup sliced purple cabbage (2-inch pieces)

1 cup cooked vermicelli rice noodles

2 round green Thai eggplants, quartered

½ cup sliced green beans (2-inch pieces)

Make the base paste: In a deep mortar, combine the garlic, fresh and dried chiles, palm sugar, and MSG and pound into a paste. Add the black crab paste and shrimp paste and pound until fully incorporated.

Prepare the sauce: Add the padaek and tamarind paste to the mortar. Continue pounding to create a fairly smooth sauce.

Incorporate the papaya and plum: Add the shredded papaya to the mortar. Prepare the Lao plum by separating the skin from the seed. Scrape the thin layer of plum flesh from the seed into the mortar, then add both the skin and the seed to the mortar. Squeeze half a lime into the mortar and add the spent lime half.

Continued

Thum Mak Hoong ◆ Lao Papaya Salad
continued

Add the tomatoes and crab: Add the halved cherry tomatoes and the salted black crab to the mortar, along with 2 tablespoons of its liquid. (If your mortar is too small, transfer the mixture to a large bowl at this stage for easier mixing.)

Mix and blend: Use a large spoon along with the pestle to gently smash and mix the ingredients, turning the mixture from top to bottom to ensure the papaya and sauce are thoroughly blended.

Taste, adjust, and serve: Taste the salad and add more palm sugar, lime juice, or padaek as needed to balance the flavors. Serve immediately accompanied by the morning glory, purple cabbage, vermicelli noodles, round eggplant, and green beans.

Note

You can substitute 1 tablespoon of peeled, shredded Granny Smith apple for the Lao plum if needed.

Thum Luang Prabang ◆ Luang Prabang-Style Papaya Salad

ຕຳຫຼວງພະບາງ

Serves 3 or 4

Having grown up with hand-shredded papaya salad, I was delighted to discover this fettuccine-style version, where the papaya is cut into long, flat strands that create a different texture with each bite. As its name suggests, this dish originated in Luang Prabang, and it has become so popular that even celebrities from neighboring Southeast Asian countries visit to try it. Unlike the traditional Lao version (thum mak hoong; see page 99), this papaya salad is vibrant green and has a tangy flavor, thanks to the inclusion of unripe green tomatoes, bird's eye chiles, and eggplant. If green tomatoes aren't available, tomatillos make an excellent substitute, adding a similar tanginess to the dish while introducing a slightly earthy undertone to the sauce. This variation showcases how regional Lao dishes can adapt to local ingredients, blending traditional flavors with North American produce. It's a refreshing example of how Lao cuisine continues to evolve and innovate.

1 ounce palm sugar (about 2 crushed tablespoons)

6 fresh green bird's eye chiles, stemmed

½ teaspoon shrimp paste

1 tablespoon tamarind paste

1 tablespoon padaek (see page 97)

2 tablespoons fish sauce (see page 18)

½ teaspoon MSG

2½ cups unripe papaya (see page 22), shredded into long strips (see Note)

½ cup thinly sliced round purple Thai eggplant

½ cup sliced tomatillo or green tomato

½ cup halved small yellow tomatoes

About 1 tablespoon lime juice, from ½ lime

To Serve

1 cup chopped green cabbage (2-inch pieces)

1 cup cooked sticky rice (see page 73)

Make the dressing: Place the palm sugar in a deep mortar and crush it into a fine powder. Palm sugar is dense, so this may take some effort. Add the chiles to the mortar and smash them into a paste with the palm sugar. Add the shrimp paste to the mortar and mix until fully combined with the chile-sugar paste. Add the tamarind paste, padaek, fish sauce, and MSG to the mortar. Use the pestle in a circular motion to mix everything together, scraping down the sides with a spoon as needed.

Add the fruits and combine: Add the shredded papaya, sliced eggplant, tomatillo, and yellow tomatoes to the mortar. Squeeze the lime half over the mixture, then toss the squeezed lime into the mortar for extra flavor.

Use a large spoon and the pestle to gently smash and toss the ingredients together. Turn the mixture from top to bottom to ensure the papaya and liquids are evenly combined. Serve immediately with green cabbage and sticky rice on the side.

Note

This style of papaya salad is known for its shredded texture. You can achieve this by using a peeler, or by cutting the papaya in half lengthwise, removing the seeds, and then slicing it into thin, wide strips. The slices should resemble fettuccine noodles.

Serves 4 to 6

Soop Nor Mai ◆ Shredded Bamboo Salad

ຊຸບໜໍ່ໄມ້

Sticky Rice Paste

¼ cup shallot quarters

3 tablespoons peeled, thinly sliced galangal

2 tablespoons minced lemongrass (from the soft parts of 1 stalks)

2 fresh bird's eye chiles, stemmed

2⅓ cups water, divided

¼ cup uncooked sticky rice

1 (14-ounce) can yanang leaf extract

Salad

28 ounces canned whole bamboo shoots

2 tablespoons padaek (see page 97)

2 tablespoons fish sauce (see page 18)

1 teaspoon MSG

1 cup chopped rice paddy herb (see page 25)

½ cup chopped scallions, white and green parts

¼ cup minced cilantro leaves and soft stems

To Serve

2 tablespoons white sesame seeds, for garnish

Fresh bird's eye chiles, for garnish (optional)

Cooked sticky rice (see page 73)

Fresh bamboo shoots are like a treasure to Mae. When she visits me in Los Angeles you can often find her near the bushes around LACMA, searching for wild bamboo. A true forager at heart, Mae finds joy in gathering her meals from the forest, the jungle, and even the bustling city. For Mae, these moments in nature aren't just about foraging; they are about finding little pieces of home. It is her way of staying connected to Laos, using the skills she honed there to thrive anywhere in the world. She has an amazing ability to identify plants, insects, and even algae, almost instinctively knowing what is safe to eat and what isn't. When I asked how she knew, she explained that her knowledge came from years of conversations with other Lao foragers, wisdom passed down within the community. One of the prized foraged ingredients is bamboo, and a classic dish where it takes center stage is soop nor mai, a bamboo salad thickened with a fragrant sticky rice paste. In Lao cuisine, bamboo is almost always paired with yanang leaf extract (see Note, page 189), as they are a well-known duo. The bamboo is prepared by using a thin needle to shred it into delicate, fibrous strands, allowing it to absorb the thickened paste and resemble noodles in texture.

Make the sticky rice paste: In a 10-inch skillet, arrange the shallots, galangal, lemongrass, and chiles evenly and cook on high heat for 5 minutes without stirring. Turn down the heat to low, add ⅓ cup of the water, cover, and let simmer for 5 minutes. Transfer the softened aromatics to a deep mortar and pound them into a paste. Rinse the sticky rice three times and drain it, then place it in a bowl. Bring the remaining 2 cups of the water to a boil, and pour it over the rice to fully cover it; let soak for 10 minutes. Drain the rice, add it to the mortar, and mash it with the aromatics until everything is well combined. Mix the yanang extract into the paste until it is fully incorporated.

Prepare the bamboo shoots: Using a needle, toothpick, or fork, shred the bamboo shoots into thin strands about the same thickness as angel hair pasta, then cut the strands into 3-inch pieces. Place the shredded bamboo in a medium pot, cover with water, and bring to a simmer over medium heat. Cook for 10 minutes, then drain and set aside.

Cook the bamboo mixture: In a clean medium pot, combine the cooked bamboo shoots, sticky rice paste mixture, and 1 cup of water. Cook over medium-low heat for 10 minutes, stirring occasionally, until the mixture thickens. Add the padaek, fish sauce, and MSG and stir well. Remove from the heat and add the rice paddy herb, scallions, and cilantro. Stir to incorporate.

In a small pan, dry-toast the sesame seeds over medium heat for about 3 minutes, until golden and fragrant.

To serve, scoop the bamboo mixture into a serving bowl. Garnish with toasted sesame seeds and whole bird's eye chiles (if using). Serve alongside sticky rice and enjoy!

Thum Mak Tua ◆ Smashed Long Bean Salad

ຕຳໝາກຖົ່ວ

Serves 2 to 4

The star ingredient in this salad is the long beans, which stand out for their earthy, nutty, and mildly sweet flavor. They are served alongside many Lao dishes as a crispy, refreshing vegetable. Long beans hold their structure and vibrant color well during cooking; lightly smashing some of them here releases their distinctive flavor into the sauce, enhancing the overall taste of this dish.

4 fresh bird's eye chiles, stemmed

1 teaspoon MSG

1½ teaspoons granulated sugar

1½ teaspoons brown sugar

1½ teaspoons shrimp paste

2¼ cups chopped long beans, 2-inch pieces, divided

1 tablespoon fish sauce (see page 18)

1 tablespoon padaek (see page 97)

2 cups halved cherry tomatoes

1 lime, halved, for juice

Make the paste: In a deep mortar, combine the chiles, MSG, granulated sugar, brown sugar, and shrimp paste. Smash into a rough paste. Add ¼ cup of the long beans to the mortar and lightly smash them into the paste.

Finish making the salad: Add the remaining 2 cups long beans and the fish sauce, padaek, and cherry tomatoes to the mortar. Squeeze the lime halves over the mixture, then drop the squeezed lime rinds into the mortar to add flavor.

Use a large spoon and the pestle to gently smash and toss the ingredients together. Turn the mixture over in the mortar to ensure everything is evenly combined and coated in the paste.

Serves 4 to 6

Soop Pak ◆ Blanched Vegetable Salad

ຊຸບຜັກ

¾ cup halved shallots

4 fresh bird's eye chiles, stemmed

¼ cup ¼-inch slices peeled ginger

2 tablespoons minced lemongrass (soft part of 1 stalk)

5 garlic cloves, lightly smashed

¾ cup water

1 tablespoon padaek (see page 97)

2 tablespoons fish sauce (see page 18)

1 teaspoon MSG

3½ cups chopped bok choy

4 cups chopped mustard greens

2 cups chopped oyster mushrooms

1 cup thinly sliced wood ear mushrooms

Toppings

2 tablespoons white sesame seeds

⅓ cup chopped cilantro leaves and soft stems

⅓ cup finely chopped scallions, white and green parts

Recipes in Laos have traditionally been passed along in the community through word of mouth, and this dish is a perfect example of that. I didn't grow up eating this particular salad, but it quickly became a favorite after my friend Ava, the creator behind CookingOutLao, introduced me to it. Ava is one of the most talented Lao cooks I know, with a deep well of culinary knowledge passed down from her parents. Our friendship mirrors my parents' connections with other Lao families in our community, a relationship built over food served at gatherings. This dish, passed from friend to friend, carries signature funky Lao flavors from the paste that seasons the vegetables. While sesame seeds aren't common in Lao cooking, they add a rich, nutty depth to this salad. It's also highly adaptable; simply swap in any seasonal vegetables you have on hand.

Pan-roast the aromatics and prepare the paste: Heat a 10-inch cast-iron skillet on high heat for 5 minutes. Arrange the shallots, bird's eye chiles, ginger, lemongrass, and garlic evenly in the skillet. Cook for 2 minutes without stirring, then flip. Reduce the heat to low, pour the water into the skillet, and cover the pan. Let the aromatics simmer for 10 minutes. Remove the lid, and if water remains in the pan, increase the heat to high and cook until it evaporates.

Transfer the simmered ginger to a deep mortar and smash it into a paste. Add the chiles, lemongrass, and garlic and smash them into a rough paste with the ginger. Mix in the padaek, fish sauce, and MSG, combining thoroughly.

Blanch the vegetables and mushrooms: Bring a large pot of water to a rolling boil. In separate batches, blanch the bok choy, mustard greens, oyster mushrooms, and wood ear mushrooms by boiling them for 2 minutes each, then immediately transferring them to an ice bath to cool. Drain and set aside.

Assemble the dish: In a small pan, dry-toast the sesame seeds over high heat for 2 minutes. Set aside.

In a large bowl, combine the blanched vegetables and mushrooms. Add the aromatic paste and mix thoroughly to coat the vegetables. Top with the cilantro, scallions, and toasted sesame seeds, and toss lightly to combine.

Thum Khao Poon ◆ Cold Vermicelli Noodle Salad

ຕໍາເຂົ້າປຸ້ນ

Serves 4 to 6

Unripe papaya was a staple in our fridge when I was growing up, and we made papaya salad at least once a week. But when we ran out of papaya, I'd turn to the pantry, where vermicelli rice noodles were always on hand. Thum khao poon was my childhood version of spaghetti, but instead of being mild and tomato sauce–based, it's spicy, sour, funky, aromatic, and padaek-based: a dish that truly felt like my own. On hot summer days, these cold noodles were refreshing, even while the spicy peppers left me breathless and reaching for ice-cold water. I couldn't stop slurping. The thum sauce is extra saucy so the noodles can soak up all its flavors. Once you make it, be sure to enjoy it within the hour, as the sauce-soaked noodles will begin to change texture. You can make the sauce ahead of time, drizzling it over right before serving the salad.

Vegetable oil, for frying

8 Asian pork meatballs (see Note)

3½ tablespoons sugar

3 tablespoons water

1 garlic clove

6 fresh bird's eye chiles, stemmed

2 tablespoons lime juice

½ teaspoon shrimp paste

⅓ cup padaek (see page 97)

¼ cup tamarind paste

¼ cup chili garlic sauce (sambal)

1 teaspoon MSG

1 cup halved cherry tomatoes

14 ounces thick-style dried vermicelli rice noodles

To Serve

Cilantro leaves

Fried shallots (see page 21)

Prepare the meatballs: In a small pot, heat ¼ inch of oil over medium-high heat until it reaches 350°F, about 4 minutes. Fry the pork balls in two batches of four, cooking, stirring occasionally, until they turn golden, about 2 minutes per batch. Transfer the fried meatballs to a bowl and set aside to cool.

Make the sauce: In a small pan, heat the sugar over medium-high heat, stirring occasionally, until it caramelizes and turns golden, about 2 to 3 minutes. Once it's melted and caramelized, add the water to the pan and mix well, then transfer to a bowl and set aside to cool.

In a deep mortar, pound the garlic and chiles into a paste. Add the lime juice and shrimp paste, mixing until smooth. Stir in the padaek, tamarind paste, chili garlic sauce, MSG, and cherry tomatoes. Lightly crush the tomatoes into the sauce to release their juices. Add the cooled caramelized liquid to the sauce and stir to combine.

Cook the noodles: In a large pot, bring enough water to fully submerge the noodles to a boil. Add the noodles and cook for 10 minutes, then drain the noodles and rinse them under cold water. Transfer the cooked noodles and meatballs to the mortar with the sauce and stir to coat the noodles and meatballs with the sauce. Garnish with the cilantro and fried shallots and serve.

Note

Asian pork meatballs are found at Southeast Asian markets vacuum sealed in plastic in the fridge section. These meatballs are the bouncy kind and often used in pho as well.

Makes about 6 cups | Serves 4 to 6

Som Pak Galum Sai Hoo Moo ◆ Pickled Cabbage with Pork Ears

ສົ້ມຜັກກະລ່ຳໃສ່ຫູໝູ

½ pound uncooked pork ears

4 tablespoons plus 1 teaspoon coarse kosher salt, divided

1 (2½-pound) green cabbage, cored and chopped into 2-inch pieces

5 cups chopped Chinese chives or scallions (3-inch pieces)

2 tablespoons uncooked sticky rice

1 cup water

To Serve

Ginger slices

Whole fresh bird's eye chile

If you love kimchi, this pickled cabbage will quickly become another favorite. Like kimchi, it undergoes a lactic acid fermentation process, with sticky rice serving as the sugar source that breaks down to produce the signature tangy flavor. This fermentation method infuses the cabbage with rich, complex flavors; it typically takes about three days. In Lao cuisine, fermented cabbage is often served as a side dish alongside other foods. Each bite pairs the tangy cabbage with the heat of fresh bird's eye chiles and the zing of ginger. The pork ears bring a satisfying crunch, making every bite a deliciously textured experience.

Prepare the pork ears: Wash the pork ears thoroughly in a large bowl, scrubbing them with 1 tablespoon of the salt. Rinse well in water and transfer to a medium pot. Cover the pork ears with water, add the 1 teaspoon of salt, cover the pot and set it over medium heat, and simmer for 1 hour. Once they're cooked, take them out of the pot to cool, then thinly slice them and set aside.

Prepare the vegetables: Submerge the sliced cabbage in water and gently separate the pieces to clean them; drain thoroughly. In a large nonreactive tub, combine the drained cabbage and chives. Sprinkle 1½ tablespoons of the coarse salt over the vegetables. With your hands, mix and press the vegetables gently for 5 minutes, until they soften and release liquid and have reduced to about half their original volume. Pack them down evenly on the bottom of the tub, cover, and let sit for 30 minutes. Rinse the vegetables in three changes of fresh water to remove excess salt, then drain and set them aside.

Prepare the sticky rice mixture: Rinse the sticky rice three times and drain it. In a small nonstick pot, combine the rice and ½ cup of water. Bring to a simmer, cover, and cook on low heat for 10 minutes, until a thick rice-water mixture forms. Let it cool, then add the remaining ½ cup of water to thin it out.

Assemble the pickled greens: In a large bowl, combine the drained cabbage and chives with the sliced pork ears. Pour the cooled sticky rice mixture over the vegetables and add the remaining 1½ tablespoons of salt. Gently mix and massage everything to coat the vegetables evenly with the rice mixture.

Pack and ferment: Transfer the mixture to a clean, sterilized 2-quart glass jar, packing it tightly to remove air pockets. Place plastic wrap on top of the mixture to ensure the vegetables remain fully submerged in the liquid and are not exposed to air. Place the lid on the jar and fasten it loosely, leaving room for gases to escape during fermentation. Place the jar in a basin to catch any overflow. Ferment in a cool, dark place for 2 to 3 days, or until the greens reach your desired level of sourness. Serve them with ginger slices and fresh bird's eye chiles. Any leftovers can be stored in the refrigerator for up to 4 months.

Som Moo ◆ Fermented Pork Sausage

ສົ້ມໝູ

Serves 4 to 6

Containers in our house always held surprises. Mae found creative uses for everything she had. The tin canisters from Christmas cookies were filled with her sewing supplies. Five-gallon buckets outside were for fermenting fish to make padaek, and small jars were for vegan padaek (made of mushrooms). My favorite containers held fermenting ground pork sausage, or som moo. This sour Lao sausage is made from pork loin wrapped up in plastic with cooked sticky rice, chewy pork skin, a whole garlic bulb, and a fresh bird's eye chile. After a few days of fermenting, it transforms into a tangy, firm, bouncy treat, ready to eat uncooked. It is the perfect Lao protein bar.

- 1 pound pork loin, trimmed of fat and cubed (see Note)
- 2 teaspoons coarse kosher salt
- ½ teaspoon MSG
- 1⅛ ounces finely minced garlic (about 11 cloves)
- 2¼ ounces cooked room-temperature sticky rice (about ⅓ cup)
- 2 ounces pork skin, cut into 2-inch strips (optional)
- 7 green bird's eye chiles, stemmed
- 14 (8-inch) round banana leaves (or substitute pieces of aluminum foil)

Grind the pork: Grind the cubed pork in a food processor for 1 to 2 minutes, until it reaches a sticky, paste-like consistency. Transfer the ground pork to a large bowl and add the salt, MSG, minced garlic, sticky rice, and pork skin (if using). Mix thoroughly with gloved hands until everything is evenly incorporated. Divide the mixture into seven portions, rolling each into a 3-ounce ball.

Wrap the sausages: Lay two banana leaves on a flat surface with the veins horizontal, overlapping them slightly (one closer to you and the other farther away). Place a 9-inch-long piece of plastic wrap over the banana leaves. Place a pork ball near the edge of the banana leaf closest to you. Press one green chile into the top of the pork ball. Roll the banana leaves tightly around the pork ball to form a cylinder, ensuring that the chile stays embedded in the pork. Pinch and fold the ends of the banana leaves downward to secure the wrap. Repeat six times, to wrap seven sausages.

Ferment the sausages: Place the wrapped sausages in a zip-top bag, removing as much air as possible. Seal the bag and place it inside a large pot with a lid. Let the sausages ferment at room temperature (about 75°F) in a dark place for 3 to 4 days. Partially unwrap one of the sausages to test for doneness: They are ready when the texture has firmed up and is slightly bouncy when squeezed. Transfer the sausages to the refrigerator. Keep the sausages wrapped in plastic and banana leaves until you're ready to eat them.

The sausages can be enjoyed raw (traditional style) or cooked. To cook, cut the sausages into 1-inch pieces and sear in a hot pan with ½ tablespoon of vegetable oil until lightly browned. The fermented sausages will keep in the refrigerator for up to one week.

Note

For these sausages (especially if you do not plan to cook them), it's important to source high-quality meat from a butcher to ensure both safety and flavor. Handle the raw meat with gloved hands.

Serves 3 or 4

Som Moo Ton ◆ Stir-Fried Fermented Pork

- 2 tablespoons uncooked sticky rice
- ¾ cup water
- 1 pound pork belly, chopped into 1-inch pieces, ¼ inch thick
- 3 tablespoons minced garlic
- 1 tablespoon coarse kosher salt
- 1 teaspoon freshly ground black pepper
- Vegetable oil, for frying
- ¼ cup thinly sliced ginger
- 1 green bell pepper, diced into 1-inch pieces
- ½ yellow onion, diced into 1-inch pieces
- 1½ cups enoki mushrooms
- 1 tablespoon oyster sauce
- 1 teaspoon sugar
- Fried shallots, for garnish (see page 21)
- Cooked jasmine rice, for serving

On a corner street in Luang Prabang, you'll find some of the best fermented pork skewers in the region. As the skewers cook over a charcoal grill, the pork caramelizes, and the dripping fat intensifies the flames, adding a smoky richness. Though it may seem simple at first glance, this dish is anything but ordinary. The preparation requires days of fermentation, creating a deep, tangy flavor bursting with umami. The fermented pork's already complex flavors are elevated to another level when it's pan-fried, then tossed into a stir-fry.

Prepare the sticky rice: Rinse the rice in a small bowl three times to remove excess starch. In a small nonstick pan, combine the rice with the ¾ cup of water. Cook over medium heat for 5 minutes, stirring constantly. Reduce the heat to low, cover, and simmer for 5 minutes, until the rice is thick and slightly wet. Transfer the rice to a small bowl and let it cool to room temperature, about 15 minutes.

Marinate and ferment the pork belly: In a large bowl, combine the pork belly, cooled sticky rice, garlic, salt, and black pepper. Mix thoroughly, ensuring the seasoning coats all pieces evenly. Transfer the pork mixture to a lidded glass container, pressing it down to remove any air pockets at the bottom and sides. Cover with plastic wrap, pressing it gently over the pork's surface, and place the lid on top without fully sealing it. Store the container in a dark space at room temperature (about 75°F) for 3 to 4 days to allow the pork to ferment. The texture will be firm when it's ready.

Cook the pork belly: Remove any excess rice from the fermented pork belly pieces. In a large sauté pan, heat a ½-inch depth of vegetable oil over medium-high heat. Add half of the pork belly in a single layer and fry for about 5 minutes, stirring constantly, until golden brown. Remove the pork from the pan and place it in a paper towel–lined bowl to drain. Remove any rice or garlic from the oil to prevent burning, and fry the remaining pork, adding more oil as needed.

Stir-fry the vegetables: In a wok, heat 1½ teaspoons of vegetable oil over medium-high heat. Add the ginger and sauté for 1 minute. Add the bell pepper, onion, and mushrooms. Stir-fry for 3 minutes, until the vegetables are slightly softened. Add the cooked pork belly to the wok and season with the oyster sauce and sugar. Increase the heat to high and stir-fry for 2 minutes, or until the onions are tender. Remove the stir-fry from the heat, garnish with fried shallots, and serve with jasmine rice.

5

LAAB & ACCOMPANIMENTS

Laab Means Luck

In Laos, food is more than sustenance; it's an expression of community, heritage, and celebration. At the heart of many gatherings, one dish perfectly represents the flavors of Laos: laab. A flavorful and aromatic meat salad, laab is much more than a dish in Lao cuisine; it's a symbol of prosperity and community and the perfect introduction to the country's culinary traditions.

In Lao households, meals are eaten at a low table made of rattan or bamboo, called a phakhao, which is placed on top of a woven rattan mat. People sit on the mat, gathering around the table with a Beerlao or pandan-scented water in hand. The meal isn't complete without the quintessential dishes spread across the phakhao: laab, mild bone broth soup, spicy smashed salad, charred BBQ, and a bowl of warm sticky rice nestled in the center. Fresh herbs that are layered in bundles are always within reach, while the ever-present bird's eye chiles add a spicy jolt. This experience reflects the Lao people's love for community, their sustainable practices whereby nothing goes to waste, and the sheer joy of eating with one's hands.

Laab, a star of the Lao table, is a colorful meat salad. Mixed with fresh herbs like scallions and cilantro, it often packs a punch from bird's eye chiles. Roasted sticky rice powder adds nuttiness and texture, and galangal adds a citrusy, earthy note. But laab is not just a dish; it's an umbrella term in Lao cuisine, encompassing various types of salads. Whether it's minced chicken salad (laab gai), chopped fish salad (goi pa), or even cold seaweed salad (laab tao), each version offers a unique exploration of Lao flavors.

Eating laab comes with its own traditions. To fully enjoy it, grab some sticky rice with your fingers, gently form it into a bite-sized ball, and dip it into the dry laab, pressing the rice against the meat. Scoop the laab onto the rice (like placing salami on bread) and top it with fresh leafy herbs like cilantro, lettuce, or cucumber slices; if you like your food extra spicy, bird's eye chile gives a kick. After each bite, a spoonful of bone broth washes everything down. This method of eating laab mirrors the way many other Lao dishes are enjoyed, with sticky rice always at the heart of the meal.

My parents brought their village traditions from Laos to our home in Wisconsin, and they became part of my own growing up. In Laos, they sourced the freshest meats by slaughtering their own animals, and they continued this practice in America. Although they recognized that slaughtering your own meat wasn't typical in American households where farmers and butchers handled such tasks, they still befriended, and negotiated with, local farmers to buy chickens, ducks, and cows, which were then shared among several Lao families. The more tender cuts of meat became raw laab, while the bones and tendons were simmered into rich pots of Lao pho. For me, those weekends of butchering and preparing felt endless and boring. The process took hours at the farm, and once everyone returned home, a marathon of preparing the meat stretched late into Sunday. I was never allowed to watch the adults work in the closed garage, where they carefully processed the meat. Perhaps they kept me away from the butchering so I could hold on to a childish picture of these foods coming from the shelves of an American market instead of a weekend's hard work in the garage. As a child, I found the process intimidating, but I've come to understand that it instilled in me

a deep respect for where our food comes from. I can definitely confirm how much more flavorful a dish can be when the ingredients are sourced directly from farms and gardens. This connection to the land, and to the animals and plants it nurtures, is essential to Lao cooking, and dishes like laab, where freshness makes all the difference, is a perfect example.

Beyond providing nourishment, laab holds deep cultural significance. It symbolizes luck and prosperity, which makes it a staple at weddings, funerals, and holidays. During boun (festivals or ceremonies where merit-making takes place), laab is always present. Its importance is echoed in Lao blessing rituals with chants like "Kor haii sok haii laab; haii lum haii louai der," a wish for opportunity, luck, and abundance.

Despite its deep roots in Lao culture, laab's identity is often obscured in mainstream recognition. Its Westernized name, *larb,* incorporates a pronunciation change, as the hard *r* sound is not part of its original pronunciation. (The added *r* sound stems from a British transliteration, intended as a signal to a speaker to draw out the vowel sound.) Over time, this mispronunciation has taken on its own identity, even finding its way to Hollywood, including the movie *Spiderman: No Way Home.* While seemingly minor, this shift reflects how Lao cuisine is frequently misrepresented or folded into broader categories without proper attribution.

Most laab dishes share common elements: a protein is seasoned with padaek, coated in roasted sticky rice powder, and mixed with fresh herbs and aromatics. There are some variations that follow specific rules. For example, lime juice is typically used for acidity, but beef laab often uses beef bile instead, which has a bitter flavor profile. And fish and shrimp laab come in the form of pastes instead of salads. At restaurants, the most common laab dishes are made with cooked beef, chicken, or pork, and are sometimes referred to by different names like nam tok, goi, or sua. To preserve the freshness of the herbs, the meat is always cooled before being mixed with them. A soup made from the bones of the protein is always served alongside the laab; one takes a bite of laab, with sticky rice to help mellow the flavors, then sips the soup. The soup's light seasoning creates a perfect balance with the laab's boldness, bringing harmony to the meal.

Enjoyed with fresh herbs, warm sticky rice, and a simple broth, laab is the essence of a traditional Lao meal, from rural family suppers to grand celebrations. Laab is a key to understanding the connections among Lao food, culture, and community. This chapter is an opportunity to explore laab and the dishes that often accompany it.

Laab Dip ◆ Raw Beef Salad

ລາບດິບ

Serves 3 or 4

This dish is a coming-of-age milestone for me, my embrace of something I once viewed (through the eyes of a ten-year-old) with shame and embarrassment. The kids around me in Wisconsin never experienced their parents butchering a cow and turning it into a raw dish seasoned with funky padaek. No one I knew outside of our home ate laab, and I desperately wanted the foods my friends had: pizza and hamburgers. Being on the low-income free lunch program was, in a way, a relief. It spared me from bringing my parents' homemade meals to school, giving me a chance to fit in, even if just for the brief window of lunchtime. Years later, I ate laab dip for the first time and enjoyed it. I felt a wave of regret for having been so ashamed of my culture's food, and I called Mae. I could hear the surprise and pride in her voice, as she realized her son finally understood the richness and significance of our food. I wasn't just eating laab dip; I was reconnecting with part of myself I had sought to leave behind, and it felt like finding home again.

8 ounces beef flank steak or filet mignon

1 ounce beef tripe

2 tablespoons fish sauce (see page 18)

1 tablespoon padaek (see page 97)

½ teaspoon beef bile (see page 32), or 1 tablespoon lime juice (see Notes)

½ teaspoon MSG

2 tablespoons roasted sticky rice powder (see page 17)

1 teaspoon dried ground bird's eye chile (see page 18)

1 tablespoon minced fresh makrut lime leaves (about 5 leaves)

1 tablespoon minced peeled galangal

¼ cup thinly sliced shallot

½ cup chopped scallions, white and light-green parts

½ packed cup chopped cilantro leaves and tender stems

½ packed cup chopped mint leaves

To Serve

Mint leaves

1 cup peeled, chopped cucumber

1 cup 2-inch-cut long beans

1 cup chopped purple cabbage

Roasted sticky rice powder

Whole fresh bird's eye chiles

Cooked sticky rice (see page 73)

Prepare the beef: Use a paper towel to pat the beef dry and remove excess blood. Wrap the meat in fresh paper towels, place it in a small bowl, and put in the freezer for 15 minutes to firm up. Remove the beef from the freezer, discard the paper towels, and mince it into ¼-inch cubes, discarding any large chunks of fat. Refrigerate the cubed beef until needed.

Prepare the tripe: Cut the tripe into 2-inch chunks, then slice each piece into thin strips. You'll have about ⅓ cup of strips. Half-fill a small pot with water and bring to a boil over high heat. Add the tripe and cook for 3 minutes. Drain the water and let cool in the pot.

Make the sauce and assemble the salad: In a small bowl, combine the fish sauce, padaek, and beef bile (or lime juice); mix well. In a large bowl, combine the cubed beef and cooked tripe strips. Drizzle the fish sauce mixture over the top and mix thoroughly with gloved hands. Add the MSG, roasted sticky rice powder, ground chile, lime leaves, galangal, and shallots, mixing well to evenly coat the beef and tripe with the other ingredients. Add the scallions, cilantro, and mint leaves and toss gently, being careful not to crush the herbs.

Transfer the laab to a serving platter and garnish with extra mint, roasted sticky rice powder, and fresh bird's eye chiles. Serve with cucumbers, long beans, cabbage, more fresh whole chiles, and sticky rice.

Notes

One crucial aspect of making this laab is the need to choose between two distinct flavor profiles: bitter or sour. The dish can be made with beef bile (the traditional preference) or lime juice, but never both at once. Combining them would create clashing flavors that detract from the dish.

Beef bile can be found in the frozen section of most Asian grocery stores, making it accessible for those wishing to explore traditional Lao ingredients.

Use the freshest cuts of beef for this dish, ideally sourcing from a trusted local butcher.

Serves 6 to 8

Tom Kuang Nai ◆ Rustic Beef Innards Soup

ຕົ້ມເຄື່ອງໃນ

Organ Meats

1 pound beef intestine

½ pound beef tripe

½ pound beef tendon

½ pound beef liver

½ cup tapioca flour

1 tablespoon salt

Soup Base

1 pound beef shank, cut into ½-inch chunks

1 lemongrass bundle (see page 21)

⅓ cup ¼-inch-sliced peeled galangal

4 fresh makrut lime leaves

1 tablespoon uncooked sticky rice

1½ teaspoons coarse kosher salt

1 teaspoon MSG

2½ quarts water

Finishing Touches

4 betel leaves (optional)

1 bunch scallions, green and white parts, trimmed and sliced into 2-inch pieces

1 bunch cilantro, stems only

1 teaspoon beef bile (see page 32) or 1 tablespoon tamarind paste

Thinly sliced scallions, green parts only, for garnish

In villages in Laos, cows play a vital role in the economy, serving as more than just a food source. They provide income, wealth, a means of transportation, and even fertilizer. For my family in the United States, cows also symbolized a sense of community. Families would collectively buy a whole cow from a farmer, distributing the meat and other materials (including bile) among the group. This ensured that nothing from the cow was wasted. This soup is a good example of the practice of using many parts of the cow, including organ meats and tendon and muscle meat. This recipe reflects a style of cooking that values sustainability and minimizes waste, honoring both tradition and our resources. Serve this soup hot with Jeow Bee (page 32), Laab Dip (page 125), and sticky rice (page 73).

Prepare the organ meats: Place the beef intestine, tripe, tendon, and liver in a large bowl. Sprinkle the tapioca flour and salt over the organ meats, then mix to coat evenly. Add enough water to fully submerge the meats and mix well to ensure the flour and salt dissolve evenly throughout the water. Let soak for 15 to 30 minutes. Drain away the water and rinse the organ meats in several changes of fresh water, until the water runs clear. Cut the intestine into 2-inch pieces, slice the tripe into 1-inch pieces and leave the tendon whole. Cut the liver into ¼-inch-thick pieces and place it in a bowl (it will be cooked separately).

Prepare the soup base: In a large stockpot, combine the beef shank, tripe, intestine, tendon, lemongrass, galangal, lime leaves, sticky rice, salt, MSG, and water. Bring the pot to a boil over high heat and boil for 5 minutes, skimming off foam or impurities. Cover, reduce the heat to low, and let simmer for 40 minutes.

Cook the liver: Meanwhile, place the sliced liver in a medium pot, and cover with water. Cover the pot, place it over high heat, and simmer until the color changes to brown with no trace of pink, about 15 minutes. Drain the liver and set it aside.

Finish the soup: Remove the tendon from the stockpot, slice it into ½-inch pieces, and return it to the pot. Add the betel leaves (if using), scallions, and cilantro stems. Let the soup simmer for an additional 10 minutes over low heat. Season the soup with beef bile for a slightly bitter flavor, or tamarind paste for a tangy alternative.

Garnish with the green scallions.

Laab Gai ◆ Minced Chicken Salad

ລາບໄກ່

Serves 4 to 6

Laab is the national dish of Laos, beloved for its robust and pungent flavors and associated with luck and prosperity during Lao New Year in April. It also exemplifies how culinary traditions transcend borders. Laab is a dish that originated in Laos, and that has been borrowed and adopted by Thailand throughout its history. The Isaan region, now part of northeastern Thailand, was once part of various Lao kingdoms. After Siam asserted dominance over Lao territories in 1828, tens of thousands of Lao people in Vientiane were forced to relocate to Isaan, bringing their foodways with them. When French colonial power rose in 1893, the Mekong River was established as the formal border, placing Isaan under Siamese control. This history is key to understanding how Lao food traditions, including laab, survived in the Isaan region even as the area underwent a long process of Thaification. Decades later, while Thai cooks were popularizing laab in the West, Lao refugees were also bringing the dish to the United States often without the same visibility or recognition. Notably, laab made in Thailand typically omits padaek; this is similar to the country's take on Lao papaya salad (page 99).

In Laos, laab gai is one of the most common variations of laab, since chickens are easier than cows to raise and slaughter. If you have access to a freshly slaughtered chicken, the dish has a richer, more authentic flavor when it's made with all the organ meats, including the heart, gizzard, and liver.

1 pound bone-in, skin-on chicken thighs

1 tablespoon minced garlic

2 tablespoons padaek (see page 97)

2 tablespoons lime juice

1 tablespoon roasted sticky rice powder (see page 17)

1 tablespoon minced fresh bird's eye chile, with seeds

1 tablespoon peeled, minced galangal

1 tablespoon minced fresh makrut lime leaves (about 5 leaves)

2 tablespoons minced lemongrass (from the soft parts of 1 stalk)

½ packed cup chopped cilantro leaves and tender stems

¼ cup thinly crosswise-sliced shallot

3 scallions, white and light-green parts, thinly sliced crosswise

To Serve

½ cup packed cup mint leaves

Whole fresh chiles, for garnish (optional)

1 cup peeled and chopped cucumber

1 cup thinly sliced round Thai eggplant

Leaves from 1 bunch lettuce

Cooked sticky rice (see page 73)

Prepare the chicken: Remove the skin from the chicken thighs and cut it into 1-inch pieces. Use a cleaver or sharp knife to separate the meat from the bones. Reserve the bones for your next batch of Tom Gai (see page 134). Chop the meat into small pieces, then continue chopping until it looks like it's been coarsely ground.

Cook the chicken skins: Heat a sauté pan over medium heat. Add the chicken skin pieces and cook for 6 to 8 minutes, turning with tongs as needed as the chicken skin renders fat and becomes golden and crispy. Be cautious, as the skins may spit hot fat while they're cooking. Transfer the crispy skins to a paper towel–lined plate and set aside.

Cook the chicken: In the same pan with the rendered fat, sauté the minced garlic for 30 seconds, until fragrant. Add the ground

Continued

Laab Gai ◆ Minced Chicken Salad
continued

chicken and cook for 8 to 12 minutes, stirring frequently to break up any clumps. Cook until the chicken is no longer pink, most of the moisture has evaporated, and the meat is slightly darker in color. Transfer the cooked chicken to a large bowl and let cool to room temperature.

Assemble the laab and serve: Add the padaek and lime juice to the cooled chicken, tossing to coat evenly. Fold in the roasted sticky rice powder, chile, galangal, lime leaves, lemongrass, cilantro, shallots, and scallions, mixing until well combined.

Transfer the laab to a serving platter. Garnish with mint leaves, crispy chicken skin, and extra chile if desired. Serve alongside the cucumber, eggplant slices, lettuce leaves, and sticky rice, using the lettuce leaves to make wraps to your liking.

Sua Gai ◆ Roasted Rice Chicken Soup

ຊົ້ວໄກ່

Serves 4 to 6

This flavorful soup, one of Paw's specialties, miraculously transforms leftover chicken. When I was growing up, I would sometimes discover it in a pot on the stove, and based on its intense spiciness, I'd instantly know he made it (Paw's spice tolerance seems limitless). This soup is dark and rich, its color deepened by roasted sticky rice powder, while bright specks of scallion and cilantro float on top, adding a vibrant contrast. Paw's way of eating the soup is all about maximizing flavor: He presses a ball of sticky rice into the soup with his metal spoon, letting it soak until the rice starts to break apart and absorb the broth's bold flavors. Whenever I crave something that's both warm and comforting and also packed with laab-inspired flavors, I turn to this soup. It never fails to remind me of Paw's kitchen skill and his love for bold, hearty dishes.

4 scallions

2 tablespoons vegetable oil

1½ pounds bone-in, skin-on chicken thighs (about 4 thighs)

2 quarts water

½ cup thinly sliced ginger

1 lemongrass bundle (see page 21)

4 fresh makrut lime leaves

1 teaspoon coarse kosher salt

1 teaspoon MSG

1 tablespoon fish sauce (see page 18)

2 tablespoons roasted sticky rice powder (see page 17)

1 teaspoon ground dried bird's eye chile (see page 18)

2 tablespoons lime juice

½ cup chopped cilantro leaves

Cooked sticky rice (see page 73), for serving

Make the broth: Trim the scallion roots and, leaving the white parts whole; chop the green parts and set them aside. In a large pot over high heat, heat the vegetable oil for 2 minutes or until very hot. Place the chicken thighs skin-side down in the pot and cook until the skin side is lightly browned, about 3 minutes. Add the water, ginger, lemongrass bundle, lime leaves, scallion whites, salt, and MSG. Bring the pot to a boil over high heat and cook for 5 minutes. Skim any foam from the surface with a large spoon. Lower the heat, cover the pot, and let it simmer for 45 minutes.

Prepare the chicken: Remove the chicken thighs from the pot and allow them to cool. Separate the meat from the bones, tearing the meat and skin into bite-size pieces. Return the meat, skin, and bones to the broth. Bring the pot back to a boil for 1 minute, then turn off the heat.

Season the soup: Add the fish sauce, roasted sticky rice powder, ground chile, lime juice, scallion greens, and cilantro. Stir well to combine all the flavors. Enjoy with sticky rice, à la Paw.

Serves 6 to 8

Tom Gai ◆ Comforting Chicken Soup

ຕົ້ມໄກ່

- 1 tablespoon vegetable oil
- 1 medium yellow onion, peeled and halved
- ⅓ cup ¼-inch-sliced peeled galangal
- 1 lemongrass bundle (see page 21)
- 2 quarts water
- 2 pounds bone-in, skin-on chicken thighs (or 1 whole small chicken; see Note)
- 2½ teaspoons coarse kosher salt
- 1 teaspoon MSG
- 2 tablespoons uncooked sticky rice
- 2 Roma tomatoes, quartered
- 1 tablespoon tamarind paste
- Thinly chopped scallions, for garnish
- Cilantro, for garnish
- Cooked sticky rice (see page 73), for serving

When my nieces and nephews were growing up, this soup was always the one Mae made for them. Each bite was a ritual: a small clump of sticky rice dipped into the broth, soaking up the flavorful soup, with a tender piece of chicken carefully placed on top. The kids would blow on it to cool it down before taking the bite, and their delighted "yum" after each mouthful was unmistakable. This wasn't just any chicken soup; it was infused with the fresh aromatics from Mae's garden. When I tried re-creating it myself, something always seemed to be missing. I eventually realized it wasn't just the ingredients, it was the care and love Mae poured into her garden. The lemongrass and juicy tomatoes she grew gave the soup its special flavor. I've since started growing my own garden, hoping to capture even a fraction of that essence. My goal is not only to replicate this dish but also to pass it down to the next generation, preserving its story on paper and its flavor in a bowl.

Prepare the broth: Heat a large stockpot over medium-high heat. Add the vegetable oil and let it heat for 2 minutes. Add the onion (cut-side down), galangal, and lemongrass and let cook undisturbed for 1 minute, until aromatic. Add the water, and carefully place the chicken in the pot. Bring to a boil over high heat and then let it boil for an additional 5 minutes, skimming off any impurities from the surface using a small sieve or spoon.

Simmer and season: Reduce the heat to low and add the salt, MSG, sticky rice, and tomatoes. Cover the pot and let it simmer gently for 30 minutes. Stir in the tamarind paste and mix well to balance the flavors.

To serve, ladle the soup into bowls and garnish with scallions and fresh cilantro plucked from the bunch. Serve hot, accompanied by sticky rice on its own.

Note

For a richer broth, use a whole chicken—ideally one with its feet still attached. The bones and parts like the feet add depth and body to the soup. Break down the chicken into smaller pieces. Remove the thighs and separate the feet from the drumsticks by cutting through the cartilage. Detach the wings, then separate the breastbone from the back. Use a cleaver to cut the breast in half. Remove the nails from the chicken feet with kitchen shears before adding the feet to the soup.

Laab Tohu ◆ Crispy Tofu Herb Salad

Serves 3 or 4

Lao cuisine naturally has a strong plant-based foundation, with a wealth of fresh herbs and other plants often sourced through foraging. While I'm not vegetarian, I do try to eat less meat and incorporate more plant-based dishes into my meals. This vegan tofu laab recipe is my plant-based take on the traditional dish. The tofu is coated in a layer of sticky rice flour, giving it a crispy exterior that soaks up the vibrant flavors of a sauce made with vegan fish sauce. The result is a delicious and satisfying dish with a texture and taste that highlights the possibilities of plant-based cooking in Lao cuisine.

Tofu and Batter

1 pound firm tofu

½ cup sticky rice flour (see page 18)

½ cup cornstarch

1 teaspoon baking powder

Vegetable oil, for frying

Laab Sauce

1 garlic clove, minced

2 tablespoons lime juice

2 tablespoons vegan fish sauce

¼ teaspoon MSG

¼ teaspoon minced fresh makrut lime leaf (about 2 leaves)

1 teaspoon sugar

1 teaspoon soybean paste

Herb Bed

½ cup chopped cilantro tender stems and leaves

½ cup chopped scallions, green parts only

½ cup whole mint leaves

Whole butter lettuce leaves, from 1 bunch

1½ tablespoons roasted sticky rice powder (see page 17)

2 fresh bird's eye chiles, stemmed and minced

Prepare and fry the tofu: Pat the tofu dry and cut it into ½-inch cubes. In a large bowl, whisk together the sticky rice flour, cornstarch, and baking powder. Toss half of the tofu cubes in the flour mixture, ensuring they are evenly coated. (You will be coating and frying the tofu in two batches.)

In a wok or frying pan, heat about ½ inch of oil to 350°F. Use a thermometer to monitor the temperature while you are frying. Gently place the coated tofu into the hot oil and fry for 5 to 6 minutes, stirring occasionally to prevent sticking, until golden brown. Transfer the tofu to a paper towel–lined bowl to drain excess oil. Repeat with the remaining tofu cubes, coating, frying, and draining the second batch.

Increase the oil temperature to 375°F, adding more oil if necessary. Fry half of the tofu again for 2 minutes, until extra crispy. Remove to the paper towel–lined bowl, then re-fry the remaining tofu, and drain.

Make the sauce: In a small bowl, mix together the garlic, lime juice, vegan fish sauce, MSG, lime leaves, sugar, and soybean paste until well combined.

Assemble the salad and serve: Prepare the herb bed by mixing the cilantro, scallions, and mint leaves in a bowl. Arrange this mixture on a serving plate, and place whole lettuce leaves on the side. Drizzle the sauce over the crispy tofu and gently toss to coat. Sprinkle the roasted sticky rice powder over the tofu and mix again. Place the tofu on top of the herb bed, and sprinkle with minced bird's eye chiles. Serve immediately to maintain the crispiness of the tofu: place tofu and herbs into a lettuce leaf, wrap, and eat.

Laab Luat Beet ◆ Jelled Beet Salad

ລາບເລືອດບີດຣູດ

Serves 3 or 4

One of the rarer and more distinctive laabs, laab luat (also known as luat bang) features fresh duck blood, creating a striking red, almost bloody-looking dish. The blood is collected immediately after slaughter, then coagulated and mixed with the familiar laab ingredients. I've had laab luat a few times during visits to Laos, on occasions when the animals had been freshly slaughtered right in front of us. One of my friend's uncles, thrilled by my curiosity, eagerly shared his recipe with me. However, growing up in America meant that I wasn't exposed to slaughtering animals as often as people in Laos, and this made me a bit hesitant about fully embracing the dish.

With full respect for the original recipe, I developed a vegan version that uses beet juice to replicate the iconic red color. While this version doesn't deliver the iron-rich taste of traditional blood laab, it offers a refreshing and vibrant alternative. Perfect for a first course at a summer dinner, this dish pairs wonderfully with your favorite beer or fruity cocktail. Beet-based laab is an approachable alternative with a modern, plant-based twist, perfect for those who might hesitate to try the original.

1 cup chopped peeled beet

2 cups water, divided

2 tablespoons tua nao (Lao fermented soybean paste) or other Asian soybean paste

½ teaspoon coarse kosher salt

¼ teaspoon agar-agar powder

1 teaspoon roasted sticky rice powder (see page 17)

½ cup silken tofu

Garnishes

¼ cup cilantro leaves

¼ cup whole mint leaves

¼ cup thinly sliced scallions

1 fresh bird's eye chile, stemmed and thinly sliced, with seeds

1 tablespoon fried shallots (see page 21)

1 tablespoon roasted peanuts, crushed

1 tablespoon peeled shallot, thinly sliced

1 tablespoon thinly sliced lemongrass (from the soft part of ½ stalk)

1 lime, quartered

Extract the beet juice: Combine the chopped beet and 1 cup of the water in a blender. Blend until smooth. Strain the mixture through a fine-mesh sieve into a bowl, squeezing out all the juice from the pulp. Discard the solids.

Prepare the soybean mixture: In a small pot over medium heat, combine the remaining 1 cup of water with the tua nao, salt, and agar-agar powder. Whisk until well mixed. Bring the mixture to a simmer and cook for 30 seconds. Strain the liquid into the bowl with the beet juice. Add the roasted sticky rice powder and whisk until smooth.

Assemble the salad base: Pour the beet-soybean mixture into a wide 8-inch serving bowl and, using a small spoon, scoop up slices of silken tofu and distribute them artfully around the beet mixture. Let the mixture rest at room temperature for 15 minutes to solidify.

Garnish and serve: Garnish the dish with cilantro, mint, scallions, bird's eye chile, fried shallots, roasted peanuts, sliced raw shallot, and lemongrass. Squeeze lime juice over the top to taste. Serve at room temperature, or refrigerate to enjoy it cold.

Serves 4 to 6

Laab Tao ◆ Spinach Snail Salad

ລາບເທົາ

Spinach Broth

8 ounces spinach, well washed

½ cup water

Two (8 by 8-inch) nori sheets (dried seaweed paper), torn into 1-inch pieces

Fish Broth

12 ounces frozen snail meat, thawed

8 ounces skinless tilapia fillet

2 cups water

1 lemongrass bundle (see page 21)

⅓ cup ¼-inch-sliced peeled galangal, plus 1 tablespoon minced galangal, divided

3 fresh makrut lime leaves

½ teaspoon MSG

1 tablespoon padaek (see page 97)

1 (4-ounce) round green Thai eggplant, thinly sliced

⅓ cup minced scallions, green parts only

⅓ cup chopped cilantro leaves and soft stems

⅓ cup thinly sliced mint leaves

⅓ cup chopped long beans (¼-inch pieces)

1½ teaspoons crushed dried bird's eye chile (see page 18)

2 tablespoons roasted sticky rice powder (see page 17)

2 tablespoons fish sauce (see page 18)

Fresh bird's eye chiles, for garnish

Cooked sticky rice (see page 73), for serving

Laab is often associated with ground meat mixed with herbs, but laab tao takes the concept in a completely different direction, demonstrating the versatility of Lao cuisine. This dish has a thick, stew-like consistency, with spinach substituting for the traditional soft riverweed (see Note). Laab tao's use of snail meat and tilapia paste for protein gives it a unique flavor profile. The thick consistency of the broth paired with slices of eggplant and long beans gives texture to every bite. As a kid, I loved fishing out the pieces of snail (which I would enjoy with sticky rice), leaving the vegetables for my parents. Sometimes, Mae would even harvest and process her own riverweed from rivers in Wisconsin, using techniques she learned in Laos. She would return home with bags full of riverweed, then carefully wash and freeze it for special occasions when she wanted to serve this dish. It was one more way she brought a piece of Laos into our home and maintained a connection to her roots through food.

Make the spinach broth: Fill a large pot halfway with water and bring to a boil over high heat. Blanch the spinach for 20 seconds, then transfer it to an ice bath to stop the cooking process. Drain well. In a blender, combine the blanched spinach, ½ cup water, and the torn seaweed paper. Blend until smooth, and set aside.

Make the fish broth: Wash the thawed snail meat thoroughly and cut each piece in half. Mince the tilapia fillet into a fine paste, or pound it into a paste using a mortar and pestle. In a medium soup pot, combine the 2 cups of water and the minced fish, breaking the fish paste apart in the water. Add the snail meat, lemongrass bundle, ⅓ cup galangal slices, lime leaves, MSG, and padaek. Stir to combine. Bring to a boil over medium-high heat, then reduce the heat to low and simmer for 10 minutes. Remove the pot from the heat and let the broth cool to room temperature, about 30 minutes.

Assemble and serve: In a large bowl, combine the spinach broth, fish broth, 1 tablespoon minced galangal, eggplant, scallions, cilantro, mint, and long beans. Season with the crushed bird's eye chile, roasted sticky rice powder, and fish sauce. Mix thoroughly to combine. Garnish with whole bird's eye chiles. Serve the laab tao at room temperature alongside sticky rice.

Note

The traditional version of laab tao uses soft riverweed instead of spinach. Riverweed is harvested before it becomes firm and is often used to make kaipen, a crispy, chip-like snack. If you live in an area with a large Lao community, you may be able to source fresh riverweed from a local Lao vendor familiar with this rare ingredient.

Goi Pa ◆ Zesty Marinated Fish Salad

ກ້ອຍປາ

Serves 2 to 4

Goi is a type of dish closely related to laab. Often made with fish or seafood, and occasionally with beef, it shares some similar ingredients with laab. The main difference lies in the preparation method. Goi is made with thinly sliced meats, while laab uses ground or paste-like meat. For example, in laab pa (fish laab), the fish is processed into a raw paste-like consistency, whereas in goi pa, the fish is thinly sliced and marinated in lime juice, giving it a texture similar to ceviche. The lime juice not only slightly changes the fish's texture but its acidity also helps kill off some bacteria. It's the subtle differences in preparation, even when dishes share similar ingredients, that root these recipes in a culinary tradition.

1 pound skinless sushi-grade tilapia fillet, fresh or thawed from frozen, sliced into ¼-inch-thick pieces

2 tablespoons lime juice

½ cup chopped long beans (¼-inch pieces)

1 tablespoon minced galangal

1 tablespoon thinly sliced lemongrass (from the soft part of ½ stalk)

½ teaspoon coarse kosher salt

½ teaspoon MSG

1½ teaspoons ground dried bird's eye chile (see page 18)

2 tablespoon padaek (see page 97)

2 tablespoons roasted sticky rice powder (see page 17)

¼ cup chopped cilantro, tender stems and leaves

½ cup chopped scallions, green and white parts

½ cup chopped mint leaves

½ cup chopped Vietnamese coriander (rau ram) leaves

To Serve

Additional Vietnamese coriander (rau ram), for garnish

Whole fresh bird's eye chiles, for garnish

Cooked sticky rice (see page 73)

Prepare the fish: Place the sliced tilapia in a large bowl. Add the lime juice and gently mix to coat evenly. Let the fish marinate for 10 minutes.

After marinating, take a handful of fish at a time, gently clump it into a ball, squeezing out the lime juice into the bowl. The fish should be slightly dry but remain intact. Reserve the squeezed lime juice and transfer the fish to another large bowl.

Heat the fish (optional): In a small saucepan over medium heat, bring the squeezed lime juice to a simmer. Add the fish pieces and gently stir to coat them in the hot liquid. The fish will turn slightly opaque, but it does not need to be fully cooked. Transfer the fish and any liquid back to the bowl. If you prefer to eat the fish raw, skip this step and proceed with the squeezed fish, omitting the reserved liquid.

Assemble the salad: Add the long beans, galangal, lemongrass, salt, MSG, ground dried chile, and padaek to the fish. Mix gently but thoroughly. Sprinkle in the roasted sticky rice powder and mix well to coat evenly. Add the cilantro, scallions, mint, and Vietnamese coriander, gently folding the herbs into the mixture to maintain their freshness and texture.

To serve, transfer the fish salad to a serving plate. Garnish with additional Vietnamese coriander and fresh bird's eye chiles. Serve with sticky rice and enjoy!

Serves 3 to 5

Pon Pa ◆ Poached Fish Soup

ປົ່ນປາ

Catfish holds a special place in Lao culture, particularly the Mekong giant catfish (*Pangasianodon gigas*). These freshwater giants grow quickly and can reach over 400 pounds within a few years. Once a common catch, the catfish has drastically declined due to overfishing and to dams that block its migration routes. Conservation efforts are in effect to protect this species, in recognition of its significance as both a cultural symbol and a part of the Mekong's ecosystem. This recipe transforms catfish and smashed eggplants into a thick, spicy, herbaceous soup. It pairs perfectly with sticky rice and fresh vegetables.

Broth

1 pound bone-in catfish (yielding about 11 ounces of flesh)

1 lemongrass bundle (see page 21)

3 tablespoons ¼-inch-sliced galangal

2 fresh makrut lime leaves

4 round Thai eggplants (skin peeled off after boiling; see Notes)

4 cups water

3 tablespoons padaek (see page 97)

Aromatic Paste

2 shallots, chopped

4 garlic cloves, lightly smashed

8 fresh bird's eye chiles, stemmed

¼ cup water

Salt

Seasonings

1½ teaspoons dried bird's eye chile powder (see page 18)

½ teaspoon MSG

2 fresh makrut lime leaves, minced

¼ cup chopped scallions

¼ cup chopped cilantro leaves

¼ cup chopped culantro (optional; see Notes)

To Serve

Whole fresh bird's eye chiles

Whole cilantro leaves and tender stems

Cooked sticky rice (see page 73)

Cucumber slices

Whole romaine lettuce

Thinly sliced round Thai eggplant

Make the broth: In a large soup pot, combine the catfish, lemongrass bundle, galangal, lime leaves, eggplants, water, and padaek. Bring to a simmer over medium heat, cover, and cook for 20 minutes. Remove the cooked eggplant and the catfish and place them in separate bowls. Strain the broth and set it aside. Discard the lemongrass, galangal, and lime leaves.

Prepare the aromatic paste: Heat a small sauté pan over medium-high heat for 2 minutes. Add the shallots, garlic, and whole bird's eye chiles. Dry-sauté for about 4 minutes, stirring often, until the aromatics are charred. Reduce the heat to low, add the ¼ cup of water, cover, and simmer for 3 minutes until the aromatics have softened and most of the liquid has evaporated.

Transfer the shallots, garlic, and chiles to a mortar, add a pinch of salt, and smash them into a rough paste. Add the softened eggplant to the mortar and continue crushing until well combined. Scoop this mixture into a separate bowl.

Assemble the soup: Remove and discard the bones and skin from the cooked catfish. Place the fish in a clean mortar and smash it into a rough paste; add the aromatic paste. Add the reserved broth, ¼ cup at a time, mixing well after each addition. Aim for a thick, slightly wet, porridge-like texture (it will take about 1 cup of broth), or vary the consistency of the soup to your preference.

Season the soup: Once the desired consistency is reached, season the soup with the dried chile powder, MSG, minced lime leaves, scallions, cilantro, and culantro (if using). Gently mix everything together, then transfer to a serving bowl.

Garnish with fresh bird's eye chiles and cilantro. Serve with sticky rice, cucumber, lettuce, and thin slices of round eggplant.

Notes

To peel the round eggplants, boil them until softened; the flesh will be tender and slightly mushy. Let the eggplants cool, then gently use your fingers to peel off the skin, leaving the soft inner flesh intact.

Culantro can be found in produce sections of Southeast Asian and Latin American markets placed on a foam tray and wrapped in plastic. This herb is long and narrow with saw-toothed edges and it is more tough and fibrous than cilantro.

Tom Hua Pa ◆ Zesty Fish Head Soup

ຕົ້ມຫົວປາ

Serves 4 to 6

Lao people have a deep love for fish dishes, a passion rooted in the Mekong River's role as a vital source of their food security. For many generations, fish has been a staple protein, subject to every preparation method imaginable. Lao culinary resourcefulness extends to making the most of every part of the fish, including the sometimes-overlooked heads. With a pantry often filled with leftover ingredients, Mae frequently prepared tom hua pa, a quick and easy soup that pairs perfectly with laab pa and sticky rice. Fish heads, while often discarded at markets, contribute a rich umami flavor to the broth and also naturally thicken it with their collagen.

4 cups water

1 yellow onion quartered

⅓ cup ¼-inch-sliced galangal

4 fresh makrut lime leaves

1 lemongrass bundle (see page 21)

3 garlic cloves, roughly smashed

3 fresh bird's eye chiles, stemmed

1½ cups sliced white mushrooms

1 Roma tomato, thinly sliced

1 cup chopped zucchini

4 striped bass heads, rinsed

2 tablespoons tamarind paste

2 tablespoons fish sauce (see page 18)

2 teaspoons coarse kosher salt

1 teaspoon MSG

1 cup thin crosswise-sliced scallion, white and green parts, plus more for garnish

1 cup chopped cilantro leaves and tender stems, plus more for garnish

1 cup chopped watercress

Cooked sticky rice, (see page 73), for serving

Lime wedges, for serving

Prepare the broth: In a large pot over high heat, bring the water to a boil. Add the yellow onion, galangal, lime leaves, lemongrass, garlic, and chiles. Reduce the heat and simmer for 5 minutes to infuse the flavors.

Add the mushrooms, tomato, and zucchini to the pot. Bring the broth back to a simmer and cook for 10 minutes, until the vegetables are tender.

Gently add the fish heads to the pot. Simmer for 5 minutes; be careful not to overcook the heads, as they may fall apart.

Season the soup and serve: Remove the pot from the heat. Stir in the tamarind paste, fish sauce, salt, and MSG, mixing well to combine. Add the scallions, cilantro, and watercress to the pot. Stir gently to incorporate. Serve hot with sticky rice and a squeeze of lime. Top with additional cilantro and scallions.

6

NOODLE DISHES

Threads of Connection

The Lao people's love affair with noodles is evident in the myriad noodle preparations found throughout the country, from hearty soups to stir-fried dishes. This love for noodles is perhaps the best example of the international influences that have shaped the country's cuisine over the centuries. Laos has both influenced and been influenced by the culinary traditions of Myanmar, Vietnam, China, Cambodia, and Thailand, resulting in a national cuisine that is both unique and deeply interconnected with those of its neighbors. Regional differences also characterize Lao food and recipes, resulting in a tapestry of flavors and traditions from the northern mountains to the southern plains. Regional differences are reflected in ingredients, preparation techniques, and flavor profiles, with a common thread that ties all Lao dishes together: bold, spicy, and deeply aromatic flavors.

In northern Laos, the cuisine's character is shaped by the rugged landscape and by the influence of neighboring China. Ingredients not native to the area, including spices, were introduced to Laos through trade routes and migration from China. One such standout ingredient is mak khen, or prickly ash pepper. This relative of Sichuan pepper has a numbing spiciness that's also slightly lemony and aromatic, creating a flavor sensation that's both intriguing and addictive. (In this book, recipes that might be made with mak khen use Sichuan pepper, which is much more widely accessible.) A signature dish from the north is Lao khao soi. It features thick rice noodles in a rich tomato and pork broth, enhanced with fermented soybean paste, which is a specialty of the Tai Lue ethnic group. The paste is a common ingredient in the north, and it defines a number of northern dishes.

Traveling southward, the cuisine features thicker stews and is characterized by a heavier use of padaek, which gives the dishes a distinctive complexity and depth. Dishes like gaeng nor mai, a bamboo shoot stew, are often thickened with sticky rice paste, creating a comforting, hearty texture. One of the most unforgettable dishes from the south is thum mua, a type of noodle-papaya salad whose array of ingredients creates a complex medley of flavors and textures. The way the vermicelli noodles absorb all the bold, funky flavors of the sauce reminds me of the thum khao poon recipe in this book (see page 111).

Perhaps the most internationally recognized noodle soup, pho, has a Lao version that, like other countries' pho, is a legacy of French colonization in Southeast Asia. During the early twentieth century, when Laos and Vietnam were both part of French Indochina, the French encouraged migration from Vietnam to Laos, and this brought Vietnamese cuisine into Lao cities and towns. Over time, Lao cooks adapted the Vietnamese pho to suit local palates. While Vietnamese pho is characterized by a clear and delicate beef broth, Lao pho is a bolder and more complex affair. The broth often takes on a rich, opaque quality, and its layers of intense flavors build in sweetness, umami, saltiness, and spice. Unique features of Lao pho also include the addition of sugar to balance the heat and, in the diaspora, sliced celery for a satisfying crunch.

Despite regional differences in noodle thickness or clarity of broth, one tradition connects the country: Lao people have a penchant for personalizing their bowls of soup, creating a boong (seasoning) experience. It's common to sprinkle on chili powder, drizzle chile oil, or add fresh bird's eye chiles dipped

in kapi (a pungent shrimp paste). As the saying goes in Lao households, "baw phet baw saap" ("if it's not spicy, it's not good"). Alongside these standard condiments, fresh herbs like cilantro, scallions, and mint, and vegetables like morning glory and bean sprouts provide balance and crunch. Some noodle dishes are served with a poached egg or with a side of khanom khuu (mini Chinese doughnuts) to dip into the hot broth, either of which add satisfying richness to the meal.

Lao cuisine tells the story of a nation that is as diverse in its culinary creativity as it is united by its love of bold flavors and shared traditions. From the zesty broths of the north to the fiery noodle soups of the central plains to the rich stews of the south, each dish offers a glimpse into the lives and the nuanced culture of the people who created it. Even as the Lao diaspora has spread across the world, bringing new ingredients and influences into the fold, the essence of Lao cooking remains unchanged: a perfectly balanced pungency and spiciness and an abundance of fresh, vibrant ingredients.

In this chapter, we'll dive into regional and global variations of noodle dishes that exemplify the diversity of Lao cuisine. From the chewiness of rice and tapioca noodles to the silky smoothness of rice cubes, Lao noodle dishes are as much about texture as they are about flavor. This is your chance to embrace the Lao tradition of boong, seasoning and personalizing your bowl to suit your tastes.

Khao Piek Sen ◆ Chicken Tapioca Noodle Soup

ເຂົ້າປຽກເສັ້ນ

Serves 4

Commonly enjoyed for breakfast, this is one of Laos's most cherished noodle dishes. The heart of this delightful soup lies in the handcrafted rice-tapioca noodles. These noodles have a chewy, bouncy texture reminiscent of boba pearls, and they perfectly complement the flavors of the broth. Across every city in Laos, countless stalls tucked into corners offer variations of the broth and the noodles. This soup's adaptability extends to home kitchens, with families bringing their own touches to the dish. Growing up, I had the privilege of helping Mae make this dish. Using a pestle as a rolling pin, she crafted large batches of noodles that went straight into the pot, thickening the soup. Some cooks prefer to cook the noodles separately, which allows their family members to adjust the consistency and thickness of the soup to their liking. When you serve this soup, make enough of each condiment and topping available for everyone: the amounts listed in the ingredients list are for one serving, so scale up as needed.

Soup

1 tablespoon vegetable oil

6 garlic cloves, lightly crushed

4 quarts water

3 whole cilantro roots (see page 22), or use stems from 1 bunch cilantro

1 yellow onion, halved

½ cup sliced ginger (¼-inch-thick pieces)

1 (3-pound) whole chicken, or 2 pounds bone-in, skin-on chicken thighs

1 tablespoon MSG

1 tablespoon coarse kosher salt

1½ teaspoons fish sauce (see page 18)

Noodles

1⅓ cups water

2 cups jasmine rice flour, plus extra for dusting

2 cups tapioca flour

Condiments and Toppings (per serving)

Splash of seasoning sauce (see page 22) or soy sauce

1 teaspoon chile oil

1 tablespoon fried garlic (see page 21)

1 tablespoon fried shallots (see page 21)

2 tablespoons diced scallions, white and light-green parts

2 tablespoons chopped cilantro leaves and tender stems

1 lime, quartered

8 ounces cooked coagulated pork blood, cut into ½-inch cubes (see page 25)

Prepare the soup: Heat a large soup pot over medium heat. Add the vegetable oil and crushed garlic. Stir gently until the garlic is fragrant and lightly browned, about 3 minutes. Pour in the water, then add the cilantro root, onion, and ginger. Add the chicken, MSG, and salt. Cover the pot and simmer for 1 hour. At the end of the cooking time, skim off the fat floating on the surface of the broth. Remove the chicken from the pot and remove and discard the aromatics. Shred the chicken into bite-size pieces and set aside. Stir the fish sauce into the broth.

Make the noodles: While the soup is cooking, prepare the noodles. In a small pot over medium heat, bring the water to a boil. In a large bowl, whisk together the rice flour and tapioca flour. Gradually pour the boiling water into the flour mixture, stirring constantly with a wooden spoon. If the noodle dough feels too dry and doesn't come together, add more hot water, 1 tablespoon at a time. Avoid oversaturating the dough, as this will cause the noodles to fall apart during boiling. Knead the dough for a few minutes until smooth. Take a handful of the dough and, with a rolling pin, roll it out to ¼-inch thickness. Lightly dust the work surface and the

Continued

Khao Piek Sen ◆ Chicken Tapioca Noodle Soup *continued*

dough with rice flour to prevent sticking. With a sharp knife, cut the dough into noodles of your desired width. Dust the cut noodles with rice flour and wrap them loosely in plastic wrap to keep them from drying out.

Cook the noodles: When you're ready to serve the soup, bring a medium pot of water to a boil and add the noodles. Cook the noodles for about 3 minutes. Drain the noodles and divide them among four serving bowls.

Assemble and serve: Ladle hot broth over the noodles in each bowl and top with shredded chicken. Let each person garnish their bowl as they like, with a splash of seasoning sauce; a drizzle of chile oil; pinches of fried garlic, fried shallots, scallions, and cilantro; a squeeze of lime, and coagulated pork blood.

Khao Poon Nam Gai ◆ Red Curry Chicken Noodle Soup

ເຂົ້າປຸ້ນນ້ຳໄກ່

Serves 4 to 6

Mae didn't have the opportunity to go to school, but in the kitchen, she is the ultimate professor. Her techniques and recipes are ingrained in her memory, and she can effortlessly adapt them to suit her guests' preferences. When she taught me how to make khao poon nam gai, it took me several tries to grasp her method, which is rooted in her intuition and experience rather than a reliance on precise measurements. Often, I had to slow her down and ask her questions. When she said "a spoonful," it was always subjective, and it seemed like every spoon she used was a different size. She even brought out several buckets of padaek in various stages of fermentation (see page 97) to demonstrate how each one could subtly alter the flavor of the broth. Her use of aromatics like pandan was another lesson in subtlety and intuition: Sometimes it was just about letting an aromatic gently infuse the broth with its fragrance. Mae insisted everything be made from scratch, including her red curry paste. Her philosophy was as simple as it was demanding: If you're not going to give it your best, why bother cooking at all? As her student, I took meticulous notes, both for myself and my development as a cook, and because I knew I wanted these lessons to become second nature, so that one day I would have the confidence to both carry on her legacy and share it with others.

Broth

3 quarts water

1 pandan leaf, tied into a knot (see page 23)

6 fresh makrut lime leaves

1 lemongrass bundle (see page 21)

¼ cup sliced ginger (¼-inch-thick pieces)

2 pounds bone-in, skin-on chicken thighs

½ pound chicken feet, nails removed

Sauce and Noodles

2 tablespoons vegetable oil

⅓ cup minced shallots

6 garlic cloves, minced

½ cup Red Curry Paste (see page 21; or use store-bought)

1 (13½-ounce) can coconut milk

2 tablespoons fish sauce (see page 18)

2 tablespoons padaek (see page 97)

1 tablespoon sugar

2 teaspoons coarse kosher salt

2 teaspoons MSG

1½ teaspoons shrimp paste

½ pound cooked coagulated pork blood (see page 25), cut into 1-inch cubes

1 pound vermicelli noodles

Toppings

1 cup thinly sliced banana blossom (see page 23)

½ cup ground dried bird's eye chiles

1 cup thinly sliced purple cabbage

1 cup diced long beans

1 cup diced mustard greens

1 cup chopped cilantro

1 cup bean sprouts

4 to 6 lime wedges

Make the broth: In a large soup pot, bring the water to a boil. With the flat side of a knife, bruise the pandan leaf, lime leaves, lemongrass bundle, and ginger slices, then add them to the pot. Add the chicken thighs and chicken feet. Simmer for 5 minutes, skimming off impurities. Cover, reduce the heat to low, and simmer for 30 minutes. Remove the chicken and the aromatics from the broth; set the aromatics aside, then strain the broth and set it aside. Shred the chicken meat and pound it into a rough paste using a mortar and pestle; set aside along with the chicken feet.

Make the sauce: In a large, clean stockpot, heat the oil over high heat until it's hot. Add the shallots and garlic and sauté for 30 seconds. Reduce the heat to low, add the red curry paste, and cook, stirring often, for 6 to 8 minutes. Stir in the coconut milk and simmer for

Continued

Khao Poon Nam Gai ◆ Red Curry Chicken Noodle Soup *continued*

another 6 to 8 minutes, until the coconut fat separates. Add the chicken broth to the pot and stir to combine. In a small bowl, combine the fish sauce, padaek, sugar, salt, MSG, and shrimp paste and stir until the shrimp paste dissolves. Add this mixture to the pot along with the chicken paste, chicken feet, and reserved aromatics from the broth. Simmer for 15 minutes, then stir in the boiled pork blood. Keep it over low heat until ready to serve.

Cook the noodles: Bring a large pot of water to a boil. Add the noodles and cook for 5 to 6 minutes, stirring occasionally. Drain the noodles, rinse them under cool water, and then place them in a cold-water bath. Separate the noodles by swirling small bunches of them with your fingers, then transfer to a colander and allow to drain for 10 minutes.

Assemble the bowls and serve: Add a portion of noodles to each of 4 to 6 serving bowls. Ladle hot broth over the noodles and garnish with banana blossom, dried chile, cabbage, long beans, mustard greens, cilantro, scallions, bean sprouts, and a squeeze of lime.

Sukiyaki Lao ◆ Seafood Peanut Sauce Noodle Soup

ສຸກີ້ຢາກີ້ລາວ

Serves 4 to 6

With its particular medley of ingredients, this Lao noodle soup shows a Japanese influence. Japanese sukiyaki features thinly sliced beef and other proteins cooked in a savory broth made from soy, sugar, and mirin, often with a raw egg beaten in. Lao sukiyaki transforms these elements into a mung bean noodle soup dressed with peanut-tahini sauce. This fusion reflects the historical ties between Laos and Japan, including Japan's brief occupation of Laos in the 1940s. Today, the shared history is celebrated in events like the annual Laos festival in Tokyo.

Broth

2 pounds beef bones

4 whole cilantro roots (see page 22), or use stems from 1 bunch cilantro

1 yellow onion, halved

½ cup sliced ginger (¼ inch thick)

1 tablespoon coarse kosher salt

1 teaspoon MSG

3 quarts water

2 tablespoons fish sauce (see page 18)

Sauce

½ cup fried shallots (see page 21)

¼ cup fried garlic (see page 21)

2 tablespoons dried shrimp, soaked in warm water for 10 minutes

2 tablespoons toasted sesame oil

2 tablespoons sweet paprika

½ cup fermented red bean curd, smashed (see Notes)

1 cup coconut milk

½ cup creamy peanut butter

¼ cup tahini

2 tablespoons chili garlic sauce (sambal)

¼ teaspoon MSG

2 tablespoons sugar

¾ cup water

Noodles and Toppings

2 cups clear mung bean vermicelli

2 cups diced napa cabbage

2 cups halved baby bok choy

12 whole shrimp

1 pound beef eye of round, sliced thinly

6 Poached Eggs with Vinegar (see page 87)

12 fish meatballs (see Notes)

1 bunch scallions, chopped

2 limes, quartered

Make the broth: Add the beef bones to a large stockpot and add water to cover by about 1 inch. Bring to a boil and cook for 10 minutes. Discard the water, rinse the bones with room temperature water, and rinse the pot. Return the bones to the pot and add the cilantro roots, onion, ginger, salt, MSG, and 3 quarts of water. Bring to a boil over high heat, reduce the heat to low, and simmer, covered, for at least 1 hour, until the broth is aromatic and lightly cloudy. Stir in the fish sauce and keep the broth warm over very low heat.

Make the sauce: Blend the fried shallots, fried garlic, and soaked shrimp in a blender or mini food processor until smooth. Heat the sesame oil in a medium pot over medium heat for 1 minute. Add the paprika and sauté for 20 seconds. Stir in the red bean curd, mashing and mixing for 1 to 2 minutes. Reduce the heat to low, add the coconut milk, and bring to a gentle simmer. Stir in the peanut butter and tahini until smoothly incorporated, followed by the chili garlic sauce, MSG, and sugar. Add the fried shallot mixture, stirring frequently to prevent sticking, and cook for 5 minutes. Mix in the water and adjust for desired thickness. The sauce will thicken as it cools; add more water right before serving if necessary.

Prepare the noodles and toppings: Bring a medium pot of water to a boil. Add the vermicelli and cook for about 2 minutes, then remove them with a strainer and set aside. Blanch the cabbage and bok choy in the same pot, then remove and set aside. Lastly, boil the shrimp and thinly sliced beef to your preferred doneness, about 30 seconds to 1 minute.

Assemble the bowls: Place cooked noodles into each bowl. Ladle in about 2 cups of broth. Spoon 2 tablespoons of sauce (or more) over the top. Add the desired toppings and mix well.

Notes

Fermented red bean curd is a Chinese condiment made of tofu cubes with red rice yeast and spices. I prefer Pearl River Bridge brand.

Fish meatballs have a bouncy texture. I prefer Cha Ca Vian brand.

Khao Leng Feun ◆ Chilled Rice Cube Soup

ເຂົ້າແລ້ງຟືນ

Serves 4 to 6

Rice Cubes

1 tablespoon (¾ ounce/20 g) white limestone paste (see page 18 and Note)

7 cups water

2 cups jasmine rice flour

Broth

2 quarts water

2 large tomatoes, chopped

1 teaspoon coarse kosher salt

½ teaspoon MSG

1 tablespoon tamarind paste

¼ cup dried hibiscus flowers

To Serve

Jeow Tua Nao (see page 37)

Are rice cubes in broth considered a noodle soup dish? I think so, which is why I'm nestling the recipe in this chapter. Rice cubes, with a texture like silken tofu, are made from rice flour and served in a vibrant-red hibiscus broth. This dish is topped with fermented bean dip that adds a fiery kick to every bite. It's best enjoyed cold on a hot day (though I admit the spice might leave you feeling even warmer). One of the key ingredients in this dish is limestone paste, which is made from calcium carbonate, a compound found in seashells and coral. When mixed with water, the paste creates limestone water, an alkaline solution that helps smooth out the texture and add elasticity to the rice cubes. This unique dish originated with the Tai Lue, an ethnic community living in northern Laos and surrounding countries who have added their mark to Lao culinary traditions.

Prepare the limestone water: In a large bowl, dissolve the white limestone paste in a little of the water, stirring until smooth and clump-free. Add the remaining water, mix well, and let sit for at least 1 hour. Then, carefully pour the clear limestone water into another container, leaving the sediment at the bottom of the bowl.

Make the rice cubes: In a large nonstick pot, combine the jasmine rice flour and 5 cups of the limestone water and whisk until smooth. Cook over medium heat for 10 minutes, stirring occasionally with a silicone spatula or wooden spoon and scraping the bottom to prevent sticking. Reduce the heat to medium-low and stir continuously for another 10 minutes; the mixture will begin to thicken and become smooth. Reduce the heat to low and continue to stir continuously for 10 more minutes, until the mixture becomes silky smooth. Transfer the mixture to an 8 by 8-inch baking pan and let it cool at room temperature for 2 hours; it will solidify.

Make the broth: In a large soup pot, combine the water, tomatoes, salt, MSG, and tamarind paste. Bring to a boil over medium high heat. Reduce the heat to produce a simmer, cover the pot, and cook for 20 minutes. Add the hibiscus flowers and reduce the heat to low; steep for 5 minutes with the lid off. Strain the broth and let it cool to room temperature, then refrigerate it until chilled.

Assemble the dish: Cut the solidified rice mixture into 1-inch cubes and place them in small soup bowls. Pour the cold hibiscus broth over the rice cubes. Add a tablespoon of jeow tua nao to each bowl, mix well, and enjoy.

Note

The limestone water gives the dissolved rice flour a silky-smooth texture. Without it, the consistency of the rice cubes may turn out rough. Leftover limestone can be reused. To reuse, carefully pour off the leftover water, making sure not to disturb or pour out the white sediment at the bottom of the bowl. Add enough clean water to cover the sediment by about ½ inch, then store in the refrigerator. When you're ready to reuse it, simply add the same amount of water as you originally used. Eventually, the paste will weaken. It's time to replace it when the water no longer turns cloudy.

Kua Mee ◆ Stir-Fried Rice Noodles

Serves 3 or 4

In the small Lao community in Janesville, Wisconsin, where I grew up, weekend gatherings were a cornerstone of our lives. For Mae and Paw, cooking with their friends was a stress reliever. Everyone had a role in the kitchen: Some prepared the herbs, others handled the sticky rice, and someone always tackled the signature party noodles, kua mee. For me, these noodles are a reminder of those gatherings, and of seeing Mae and Paw laughing with their friends, finding joy in every shared moment.

16 ounces fresh thin flat rice noodles

Sweet-and-Sour Sauce

¼ cup sugar

¼ cup lime juice

1 tablespoon thin soy sauce

1 tablespoon sriracha

1 tablespoon cornstarch

¼ cup water

Omelets

4 eggs

½ teaspoon coarse kosher salt

½ teaspoon freshly ground black pepper

¼ teaspoon MSG

1½ teaspoons vegetable oil

Noodle Stir-Fry

1½ cups water

2 tablespoons sweet soy sauce

2 tablespoons seasoning sauce (see page 22)

2 tablespoons oyster sauce

2 tablespoons fish sauce

¼ cup vegetable oil

¼ cup sugar

6 garlic cloves, minced

⅓ cup minced shallot

1 cup chopped cilantro leaves and tender stems

1 cup thinly crosswise-sliced scallions, white and green parts

1 cup bean sprouts

10 fried bird's eye chiles (see page 18)

8 ounces cooked coagulated pork blood, cut into ½-inch cubes (see page 25)

Prepare the noodles and the sweet-and-sour sauce: Rinse the rice noodles, then submerge them in a bowl of room-temperature water and let soak for 30 minutes. Drain and set aside. In a small pot, combine the sugar, lime juice, thin soy sauce, and sriracha. Set over low heat and stir until the sugar dissolves, about 4 minutes. In a separate bowl, stir the cornstarch into the water, then add it to the sauce. Cook over low heat for a few minutes until it thickens but is still pourable. Set aside to serve with the noodles.

Cook the omelets: In a bowl, whisk the eggs with the salt, pepper, and MSG. Heat the oil in a medium nonstick pan over medium-low heat for 2 minutes. Pour a third of the egg mixture into the pan and cook until firm, about 2 minutes, flipping halfway through. Repeat with the remaining eggs, making three omelets. Let the omelets cool, then stack them, cut them into thin strips, and set them aside.

Stir-fry the noodles: In a bowl, stir together the water, sweet soy sauce, seasoning sauce, oyster sauce, and fish sauce; set this sauce mixture aside. Heat the oil in a large pan over medium-high heat. Add the sugar and cook, stirring, for 4 to 6 minutes, until it's caramelized and lightly golden. Add the garlic and shallots and sauté for 30 seconds. Pour in the sauce mixture and bring to a boil. Add the noodles and cook, stirring, over medium heat for 4 to 5 minutes, until most of the liquid is absorbed. Transfer the noodles to a large bowl and let cool for 45 minutes.

Assemble the dish and serve: Gently separate the noodles with your fingers. Add the cilantro, scallions, and bean sprouts, and mix gently. Transfer the noodles to a large serving platter. Top with the egg strips, fried bird's eye chiles, and cubes of pork blood. Serve with the sweet-and-sour sauce drizzled on top. If the sauce becomes too thick, add water to thin it.

Serves 4 to 6

Pho Lao ◆ Beef Noodle Soup

ເຝີລາວ

Broth

3 pounds oxtails or beef bones

Vegetable oil

1 yellow onion, halved

¾ cup ¼-inch-thick slices ginger

Base (bottom 3 inches) of 1 celery bunch

3 quarts water

1½ teaspoons sugar

1 tablespoon coarse kosher salt

¾ teaspoon MSG

1½ teaspoons fish sauce (see page 18)

1 pound beef eye round, thinly sliced

1 pound beef tripe, thinly sliced

1 pound beef meatballs, halved (1-inch diameter)

1 pound fresh pho noodles

Everything-in-the-Fridge

1 tablespoon sriracha

1 tablespoon hoisin sauce

1 tablespoon fish sauce (see page 18)

1 tablespoon sugar

1 tablespoon Jeow Bong (page 26)

1 tablespoon chili garlic sauce (sambal)

Toppings

1 Roma tomato, thinly sliced

2 cups thinly sliced celery

1 bunch scallions, thinly sliced crosswise, white and light-green parts

1 bunch cilantro, leaves and tender stems, chopped

1 cup bean sprouts

1 cup whole mint leaves

1 cup whole sweet basil leaves

2 limes, quartered

Whole fresh bird's eye chiles

Shrimp paste, for dipping chiles

½ cup crushed peanuts

When I was growing up, pho brought our family together, no matter how we were feeling. Mae's broth, rich and aromatic, was the foundation for hundreds of soul-satisfying bowls of soup. It was the one dish everyone in the family loved, and Mae knew how to tailor it to each person's preference. No matter the mood we brought to the kitchen, every slurp of noodles and hot broth and crunch of fresh lettuce and long beans had a way of soothing our souls. It's love in a bowl, a magical dish capable of melting away the day's stress and bringing everyone together in harmony.

Prepare the bones and aromatics: Preheat the oven to 425°F. Place the oxtails in a large bowl and lightly coat them with vegetable oil. Arrange the oxtails on a baking tray lined with foil and roast for 30 minutes, until charred. Lightly oil the onion, ginger, and celery and arrange them in a single layer on a second foil-lined tray. Place under the broiler, on the second rack from the top, and broil for 15 minutes, flipping the aromatics halfway through, until charred.

Make the broth: In a large pot over medium-high heat, combine the roasted oxtails, charred aromatics, and the 3 quarts of water. Bring to a gentle simmer, skimming off any scum during the first 5 minutes. Stir in the sugar, salt, MSG, and fish sauce. Set the lid slightly ajar on the pot, and simmer gently for 2 hours. (For deeper flavor, and if you have time, simmer for an additional hour.)

Make the everything-in-the-fridge sauce: In a small bowl, combine the sriracha, hoisin sauce, fish sauce, sugar, jeow bong, and chili garlic sauce. Mix until smooth and set aside.

Cook the meats and noodles: Bring a medium pot of water to a boil. Add the sliced beef, tripe, and meatballs and cook for 2 to 3 minutes, until the beef turns light brown, the tripe slightly curls, and the meatballs float to the surface or until your desired doneness. Remove the meats from the liquid and set them aside. Bring the water back to a boil and cook the noodles according to the package instructions.

Assemble the pho bowls: In serving bowls, layer the cooked noodles and each diner's choice of meats. Ladle the hot broth over the noodles, and top with tomato, celery, scallions, cilantro, bean sprouts, mint, sweet basil, and a tablespoon of the sauce; allow everyone to adjust quantities to their taste. Serve with lime wedges, chiles, shrimp paste for dipping, and crushed peanuts.

Khao Poon Nam Seen ◆ Beef Vermicelli Noodle Soup

ເຂົ້າປຸ້ນນໍ້າຊີ້ນ

Serves 6 to 8

Many of my favorite Lao dishes share two key themes: minimal to no use of coconut milk, and lots of vermicelli noodles. Among the many variations of khao poon noodle soups, the nam seen version highlights one of these themes: limited reliance on coconut milk. This rendition skips coconut milk entirely, making room for the curry paste and tangy broth to take center stage. The popularity of khao poon stems in part from the particular vermicelli noodles that are often used in the dish. In Laos, vermicelli noodles are often made fresh with some fermentation, which gives them a slight sourness and chewy texture. These fermented noodles are a rare find outside of Laos, so if you visit the country, they are worth seeking out.

Broth

10 ounces canned bamboo shoots, cut into ¼ inch slices

¼ cup vegetable oil

1 cup Red Curry Paste (see page 21; or use store-bought)

2 Roma tomatoes, chopped

2 tablespoons shrimp paste

3 quarts water

2 pounds beef shank, cut into ½-inch-thick pieces

1 pound beef tendon

2 cups sliced fresh pineapple

1 lemongrass bundle (see page 21)

1 yellow onion, peeled and halved

¼ cup fish sauce (see page 18)

1½ teaspoons MSG

2 tablespoons sugar

To Serve

2 pounds fresh vermicelli rice noodles

2 cups thinly sliced banana blossom (see page 23)

2 cups thinly sliced green cabbage

2 cups chopped green beans (¼-inch pieces)

1 cup chopped scallions, green parts only

6 to 8 whole dried bird's eye chiles

6 to 8 lime wedges

Make the broth: Place the sliced bamboo shoots in a small pot and cover with water. Set over high heat, bring to a boil, and boil for 10 minutes, then drain and set aside.

In a large pot over high heat, heat the vegetable oil for 2 minutes. Reduce the heat to low, add the curry paste, and sauté for 10 minutes, stirring continuously. Add the chopped tomatoes and shrimp paste and sauté for an additional 5 minutes. Pour in the water and add the beef shank, tendon, pineapple slices, bamboo shoots, lemongrass bundle, onion, fish sauce, MSG, and sugar. Stir to combine well. Bring the mixture to a boil, then reduce the heat to low, cover, and let it simmer for 1 hour.

Remove the beef tendon from the pot. Slice the tendon thinly and return it to the broth. Continue simmering for 30 more minutes.

Cook the noodles and assemble the bowls: Fill a large pot halfway with water, set it over medium-high heat, and bring it to a boil. Add the noodles and, stirring constantly, cook for 7 to 9 minutes, until tender. Drain the noodles and transfer them to a cold-water bath to stop the cooking process. Remove the noodles from the bath, drain, and separate them into serving-size bundles.

For each serving, add the cooked vermicelli noodles to a bowl. Ladle the hot soup over the noodles, ensuring each bowl has enough broth to cover the noodles. Garnish with banana blossom, green cabbage, green beans, scallions, and a dried chile. Serve with lime wedges.

Serves 4 to 6

Mee Katee ◆ Red Curry-Egg Drop Noodle Soup

ໝີ່ກະທິ

Broth

2 pounds pork bones, cut into pieces

¼ cup dried mung beans

2 tablespoons vegetable oil

1 yellow onion, halved

⅓ cup ¼-inch-sliced peeled galangal

1 cup ¼-inch-thick slices pork belly

2 tablespoons sweet paprika

¼ cup Red Curry Paste (see page 21; or use store-bought)

4 quarts water

¼ cup soybean paste

2 tablespoons tamarind paste

5 tablespoons fish sauce (see page 18)

1 tablespoon sugar

1 (13½-ounce) can coconut milk

3 eggs, whisked together

Aromatic Mixture

1 tablespoon vegetable oil

3 tablespoons minced garlic

3 tablespoons minced shallot

4 fresh makrut lime leaves, minced

Noodles

1 pound fresh thin flat rice noodles

1 tablespoon vegetable oil

To Serve

2 cups thinly sliced purple cabbage

1 cup chopped scallions

1 cup crushed peanuts

½ cup fried bird's eye chiles (see page 18)

2 cups thinly sliced banana blossom (see page 23)

4 to 6 lime wedges

1 cup mint leaves

2 cups bean sprouts

This noodle dish brings together elements from several beloved dishes: khao poon, pho, and egg drop soup. At first, it seems to resemble the red, coconut-based broth of khao poon, but it takes a turn with the addition of soybean paste and pork to fill out its flavorful base. The thin rice noodles, borrowed from pho, add a light and silky texture. Finally, the technique of slowly swirling whisked eggs into simmering broth to create delicate egg ribbons is reminiscent of egg drop soup. Think of this soup as a fusion of some of the best characteristics of these dishes, creating something that feels both familiar and innovative.

Prepare the broth: In a large pot, cover the pork bones with water and bring to a boil; boil for 10 minutes. Drain the water, rinse the bones under running water, and set them aside.

Place the mung beans in a medium bowl and rinse them three times with room-temperature water. Bring 3 cups of water to a boil, then pour it over the beans and let them soak for 15 minutes. Drain them and set aside.

In a clean stockpot, heat 2 tablespoons of vegetable oil over medium-high heat for 1 minute. Add the onion and galangal and sauté for 2 minutes, stirring constantly. Reduce the heat to low, add the pork belly, paprika, and red curry paste, and sauté for another 2 minutes. Add the 4 quarts of water, cleaned pork bones, soaked mung beans, soybean paste, tamarind paste, fish sauce, and sugar. Stir well and bring to a simmer over medium-high heat.

Prepare the aromatic mixture: In a medium sauté pan over medium-high heat, heat 1 tablespoons of vegetable oil for 1 minute. Add the minced garlic, shallots, and lime leaves, and sauté for 1 minute. Add this mixture to the broth and bring it back to a simmer. Cover, reduce the heat to low, and let simmer for 1 hour.

Prepare the noodles: While the broth is simmering, half-fill a pot with water and bring to a boil. Blanch the rice noodles in the boiling water for 10 to 20 seconds. Remove the noodles and place them in cold water to stop the cooking process, then drain. Toss the noodles with 1 tablespoon of vegetable oil and set aside.

Once the broth has simmered undisturbed for an hour, stir in the coconut milk. Slowly drizzle the whisked eggs into the simmering broth without stirring, then allow the broth to return to a gentle simmer over low heat.

Assemble and serve: In soup bowls, add noodles and ladle 2 to 3 cups of broth into each bowl. Garnish with purple cabbage, scallions, crushed peanuts, fried chiles, banana blossom, lime wedges, mint, and bean sprouts. Serve immediately.

Khao Soi Lao ◆ Tomato Pork Noodle Soup

Serves 4 to 6

ເຂົ້າຊອຍລາວ

Some Lao dishes remained a mystery to me until my first trip to Laos. Among them was khao soi. In Luang Prabang, I learned about a famous morning stall known for its khao soi. Like many places in Laos, the stall operates within strict time constraints, and by 10 a.m., they are often sold out. Locals line up early for the freshly made flat noodles served with fermented bean sauce crafted from fermented bean paste made by members of the local Mien community. When I finally had the chance to try this particular khao soi, I was immediately hooked. The dish's flavors were complex yet comforting: It reminded me of a soupy Bolognese, with its rich, hearty sauce. After returning to the United States, I was determined to re-create it, and this recipe is the result of my effort to capture the essence of what I had tasted in Laos.

Broth

3 pounds pork bones, cut into pieces

½ cup sliced ginger, (¼-inch-thick)

½ cup chopped cilantro root (see page 22), or use cilantro stems from 1 bunch

1 yellow onion, halved

2 teaspoons coarse kosher salt

1 teaspoon MSG

4 quarts water

Pork Sauce

3 tablespoons vegetable oil

3 tablespoons minced garlic

⅓ cup gochugaru (Korean chile flakes) or sweet paprika

⅓ cup Mien fermented bean paste or other Asian fermented bean paste such as doenjang

4 large tomatoes, roughly chopped

½ cup water

1 pound ground pork

1½ teaspoons sugar

1 teaspoon coarse kosher salt

½ teaspoon MSG

To Serve

2 pounds fresh wide rice noodles

1 cup fried garlic (see page 21)

1 cup fried shallots (see page 21)

1 cup watercress

1 cup chopped cilantro

1 cup chopped scallions, green parts only

1 cup mint leaves

4 to 6 lime wedges

Fish sauce (see page 18)

1 bunch lettuce leaves

1 cup raw green beans (optional; see Notes)

Shrimp paste, for dipping (optional; see Notes)

Make the broth: Place the pork bones in a large pot and cover them with water. Bring to a boil, then reduce the heat to medium-low and simmer for 10 minutes. Drain and rinse the bones under cold water, removing any coagulated blood. In a clean pot, combine the rinsed bones, ginger, cilantro root, onion, salt, and MSG. Add 4 quarts of water, bring to a simmer over high heat, then turn the heat to low and simmer for 1 hour.

Make the pork sauce: Heat the vegetable oil in a large pot over high heat for 1 minute. Add the minced garlic and sauté for 20 to 30 seconds, until fragrant. Lower the heat to low, add the gochugaru, and sauté for 5 minutes, stirring. Stir in the fermented bean paste, tomatoes, water, and ground pork. Raise the heat to high and bring the mixture to a boil, breaking up the pork as it cooks. Cover the pot, reduce the heat to low, and simmer for 15 to 20 minutes, until the tomatoes soften. Add the sugar, salt, and MSG, mix well, and simmer for 10 more minutes. Remove from the heat.

Assemble the dish and serve: In a clean medium pot, bring 4 cups of water to a boil. Blanch the noodles in the boiling water for about 20 seconds, then transfer them to serving bowls. Ladle hot broth over the noodles and add about ½ cup of the pork sauce to each bowl. Top with fried garlic, fried shallots, watercress, cilantro, scallions, and mint leaves. Squeeze a lime wedge over the top of each bowl and serve, allowing each person to adjust the flavor with fish sauce to their taste. Serve with lettuce on the side and raw green beans for dipping into shrimp paste (if using).

Notes

Shrimp paste is often served alongside khao soi lao. Diners can dip green beans into a tiny amount of shrimp paste (about ⅛ teaspoon).

Mien fermented soybean paste, a key ingredient in khao soi lao, gives the broth a savory and complex flavor. A popular brand in the United States is Grandma Yien Choy's Thopezay.

7

SOUPS & STEWS

Foraging for Flavors

Enter my parents' kitchen and you will find a dented aluminum pot in the center of the stove. Weathered and unassuming, it is often filled with the comforting flavors of home. It may hold freshly foraged mushrooms, earthy and aromatic; or a hearty stew infused with garden herbs and summer vegetables. At every meal, Lao cooks transform fresh, unprocessed ingredients into dishes that nourish bodies and soothe souls. Among these dishes, stews and soups hold a special place in that they both offer rich and complex flavors and also serve as natural remedies drawn from the wisdom of generations. The simple soup pot symbolizes a deep connection to the land and an enduring tradition of resourceful cooking.

For the Lao people, foraging is both a means to gather food and a way of life that ties communities to their environment. If an ingredient isn't grown in the family garden, it's likely collected from nearby forests, fields, or riverbanks. Foraging is a skill passed down through generations; it teaches inherent respect for nature and an understanding of natural rhythms. Children learn to recognize seasonal patterns, such as when mushrooms appear after the rains, or that bamboo shoots are best for harvesting when they emerge tender and pale from the soil. We are taught that hardy herbs thrive under the dry season's intense sun, that wild vegetables like watercress grow along streams, and that sesame blossoms can be gathered and used to enrich soups. Each ingredient reflects the landscape's diversity and the ingenuity required to thrive within it.

Foraging is far from a casual pastime: It's a deliberate pattern of actions guided by generational knowledge. Families forage together, turning the task into a communal experience. Elders teach younger generations how to identify edible plants and to differentiate between safe and toxic mushrooms, and then how to use every part of what is harvested to minimize waste. People learn to leave roots intact to encourage regrowth, and to gather rare plants sparingly to ensure they remain available in the future. These practices demonstrate a deep respect for the land and an ancient and necessary focus on sustainability.

Once gathered, foraged ingredients often make their way to bustling morning markets. Here, an incredible variety of fruits, vegetables, and other treasures are displayed. Some may be known in the wider world, while others are entirely unique to Lao cuisine, like mai sakahn, the wood chili vine found in northern Laos. This distinctive ingredient is used in or lam, a traditional stew known for its herbal depth and complexity. Mai sakahn lends a peppery, numbing spiciness to the dish along with a fibrous texture: It is chewed to add flavor but never swallowed. Outside Laos, finding mai sakahn can be a challenge, so Sichuan peppercorns are sometimes used as a substitute to mimic its tingling effect.

Morning markets demonstrate the Lao embrace of all the natural world has to offer. For example, edible insects have long been a staple of the Lao diet. Cicadas, ant eggs, dragonfly nymphs, and water beetles are protein-rich and bountiful, and as foods they exemplify a culinary approach that wastes nothing. In the Lao diaspora, this resourcefulness continues in new landscapes. I remember foraging with Mae and Paw in Wisconsin, where we searched parks and rivers for mushrooms, algae, and cicadas (which I fondly called "land shrimp"). Cicadas were a family favorite, with a sweet, nutty flavor when

sautéed in butter with salt and crispy makrut lime leaves. Their crisp exterior and soft, tasty interior evokes roasted peanuts or shrimp, making them seem like a taste of home.

Mae's story about my birth perfectly illustrates how the ethos of foraging can extend beyond food to, in this case, medicine. I was born in Nakhon Phanom at the Nong Saeng refugee camp, where Mae drew support from the camp's community as she gave birth to me. Mae and my older sister, Daeng, had already spent several years in the camp. Giving birth outside of a hospital was already a significant challenge, and my birth had complications. Mae told me that the community's resourcefulness and their knowledge of natural remedies (in this case medicinal leaves), helped ensure my safe arrival. Medicinal leaves were often also used at the camp as cooking ingredients, in dishes like gaeng nor mai, a bamboo stew. This dish used ingredients that could be easily foraged in and around the camp, making it accessible to everyone. The stew was often part of the shared meals within the community that not only provided physical nourishment but also a sense of hope and a reminder of home.

When word of my birth reached Paw, who was in the Napo camp at the time, he took an incredible risk. Determined to see his newborn son, Paw sneaked into a portable toilet truck on its way to Mae's camp. He was able to spend just one day with his family: his wife, small daughter, and tiny son. It was this kind of devotion and love that kept our family connection strong despite the hardships of separation. Eventually, we were reunited as a family at Napo camp, where we learned that we would have the opportunity to resettle in America as refugees.

Though we left everything material behind, one thing Mae carried with her was her food knowledge, including her recipe for gaeng nor mai from the camps. Understandably, this dish became a cornerstone of our family's story. It embodies the heart of Lao cuisine: its deep connection to nature, its resourcefulness, and its ability to adapt. Whether we were in a refugee camp in Southeast Asia or a kitchen in Wisconsin, Mae's bamboo stew was a constant for us, a symbol of resilience, resourcefulness, and the shared experience of the Lao community to which we belong. This dish carried the flavors of home even as we made new beginnings far away.

For me and for many others in Lao communities worldwide, gaeng nor mai tells a story of resilience, creativity, and profound connection to the land. It reflects the resourcefulness of Lao culture, which treats even the humblest ingredients with care and transforms them into something extraordinary. Our tradition of foraging, our vibrant markets, and the enduring appeal of our endlessly creative and satisfying dishes all demonstrate the Lao people's ability to thrive within our environment while respecting its limits. As you explore the recipes in this chapter, take a moment to consider your own relationship with the land around you, whether you forage in the wild, visit a farmers' market, or seek out seasonal produce. Lao stews tell stories of people connecting with nature's cycles and finding joy in creating something nourishing from the simplest ingredients.

Gaeng Nor Mai ◆ Yanang Bamboo Stew

ແກງໜໍ່ໄມ້

Serves 6 to 8

No dish captures the spirit of Lao stews more than gaeng nor mai. Featured in the 1981 cookbook of royal chef Phia Sing, this iconic dish embodies centuries of both tradition and ingenuity. It represents the Lao gift for turning simple, often foraged, ingredients into meals that are as nourishing as they are flavorful. Yanang leaves, prized for their dark green color and medicinal qualities, are blended with water to extract their juice. Rich in vitamins, the juice is believed to restore energy and ease ailments, earning it a revered place in Lao kitchens. Sticky rice powder is often added to thicken the stew, giving it a hearty, porridge-like consistency. The dish can include meat but shines just as brightly without it, relying on the natural flavors of its foraged components. Like many Lao dishes, gaeng nor mai tastes even better the next day, when the flavors deepen and meld into a harmonious blend.

Sticky Rice Paste

⅓ cup uncooked sticky rice

2 cups water

2 tablespoons minced lemongrass, soft part

2 fresh bird's eye chiles, stemmed and minced

¼ cup minced shallot

Stock

2 pounds pork spareribs, cut into 1-inch slices

1 cup thinly sliced canned bamboo shoots (¼-inch slices)

1 lemongrass bundle (see page 21)

2 cups roughly sliced wood ear mushrooms

1 (14-ounce) can yanang extract (see page 189)

5 cups water

Stew

1½ cups cubed kabocha squash (½-inch cubes)

1 cup sliced okra (½-inch slices)

¼ cup fish sauce (see page 18)

3 tablespoons padaek (see page 97)

1½ teaspoons MSG

½ cup chopped climbing wattle stems (see Notes); 3-inch pieces

2 cups chopped rice paddy herb (see page 25)

1 cup chopped scallions, white and green parts

½ cup whole Lao basil leaves (see Notes)

Cooked sticky rice (see page 73), for serving

Make the sticky rice paste: Rinse the sticky rice three times, then place it in a small bowl. Bring 2 cups of water to a boil. Cover the rice with the boiling water, and let soak for 10 minutes. Drain the rice and transfer it to a deep mortar; smash it into a paste with a pestle. Add the lemongrass, chiles, and shallot to the mortar, and pound until a smooth paste forms. Set aside.

Build the stock: In a large pot, combine the spareribs and bamboo shoots with enough water to cover. Bring to a boil, then lower the heat to a simmer; cover, and cook for 10 minutes. Remove the ribs and bamboo shoots with tongs, rinse them with room-temperature water and drain well. Discard the cooking water.

In a clean pot, combine the spareribs, bamboo shoots, lemongrass bundle, wood ear mushrooms, yanang extract, and the 5 cups of water. Bring to a simmer over low heat, cover, and cook for 15 minutes.

Finish the stew: Add the kabocha squash and okra to the pot. Add the fish sauce, padaek, and MSG and stir well. Bring the pot to a low simmer, then add the sticky rice paste and mix well, stirring until the soup starts to thicken. Simmer uncovered for another 10 minutes.

Add the climbing wattle stems, rice paddy herb, scallions, and basil. Simmer for another 5 minutes, then remove from the heat. Serve with sticky rice.

Notes

Climbing wattle can be found in frozen vacuum-sealed packages in Southeast Asian markets.

Lao basil, also known as lemon basil, can be a difficult variety to find. In summer months, it can be found at Southeast Asian markets and farmers' markets that specialize in Southeast Asian herbs. Sweet basil can be substituted.

Serves 2 or 3

Gaeng Kai ◆ Curried Egg Soup

แกงไข่

2 fresh bird's eye chiles, stemmed

1 tablespoon minced dill stems

¼ cup minced scallions, white part

3 garlic cloves, minced

¼ teaspoon coarse kosher salt

¼ teaspoon MSG

1½ teaspoons vegetable oil

2 cups water

2 tablespoons padaek (see page 97)

1½ teaspoons tamarind paste

2 fresh makrut lime leaves, torn

1 Roma tomato, thinly sliced

5 eggs

¼ cup chopped scallions, green parts only

2 tablespoons chopped dill, plus more for garnish

Cooked jasmine rice, for serving

No matter how much Mae prides herself on being the best in the kitchen, there are certain dishes that Paw excels at making. Paw doesn't cook often, but when he does, I know that something delicious is in the works. One of his standout dishes is this egg soup. Paw's preference for bold flavors means his version is always extra spicy and fragrant, a perfect complement to a bowl of rice. It's amazing how simple ingredients like eggs and dill can be transformed into such a deeply satisfying, belly-warming soup. Paw's mastery is evident in his technique and how he expertly creates the large, flavorful ribbons of egg that serve as an alternative to meat in this humble yet comforting meal.

Prepare the seasoning mixture and the broth: In a deep mortar, combine the chiles, dill stems, minced white scallions, garlic, salt, and MSG. Pound into a rough mixture.

Heat the vegetable oil in a small pot over medium heat. Add the seasoning mixture and sauté for 1 minute, until fragrant. Pour the water into the pot and stir in the padaek, tamarind paste, lime leaves, and sliced tomato. Bring the broth to a gentle simmer, stirring occasionally.

Incorporate the eggs: In a measuring cup with a spout, crack the eggs and whisk them until smooth. Very slowly, pour the whisked eggs into the simmering broth. Stir gently to break up the egg clumps that form, scraping the sides and bottom of the pot to prevent sticking. Continue stirring until the eggs have formed soft ribbons in the broth and are fully cooked.

Finish and serve: Add the chopped green scallions and dill. Simmer for 5 more minutes to combine the flavors. Ladle the soup into bowls and garnish with extra dill. Serve hot, with jasmine rice on the side.

Gaeng Phet Gai ◆ Red Curry Chicken Stew

แกงเผ็ดไก่

Serves 6 to 8

In 2023, Paw had a health scare, and the whole family came together to help. I decided to take on the responsibility of cooking for Paw. I wanted to make him dishes that were both nutritious and full of the flavors he loved, and I immediately thought of a dish that Mae Yai, an elder in our community, used to make for me when she watched me as a child. When I made this curry, it was one of the rare times I've found myself cooking with potatoes and carrots after rummaging through the fridge to find anything I could add to the broth. For Paw, I served the curry with jasmine rice instead of sticky rice, a dietary shift his diabetes had made necessary. He struggled to accept that sticky rice, once a staple of his daily meals, was now contributing to his health issues. It saddened him to limit enjoyment of something so deeply tied to our family's traditions and his own identity. As I prepared and served this meal, I couldn't help but reflect on how life had come full circle. It was a humbling experience for both of us, and one that deepened our bond and reminded me of the importance of family and tradition, especially in times of change.

1 tablespoon vegetable oil

¼ cup Red Curry Paste (see page 21; or use store-bought

6 garlic cloves, minced

1 (13½-ounce) can coconut milk

1 pound boneless, skinless chicken breast, chopped into ½-inch pieces

1½ cups sliced canned bamboo shoots

1 (8-ounce) can baby corn in brine, drained and cut into thirds

6 fresh makrut lime leaves

2 cups water

1½ teaspoons MSG

1½ teaspoons sugar

2 tablespoons fish sauce (see page 18)

1 (7-ounce) can quail eggs, drained

1 russet potato, peeled and chopped into 1-inch cubes

1 large carrot, chopped into 1-inch pieces

1 red bell pepper, seeded and chopped

Cooked jasmine rice, for serving

Sauté the curry paste and coconut milk: Heat the vegetable oil in a large stockpot over medium-high heat for 1 minute. Add the red curry paste and minced garlic, then reduce the heat to medium-low and sauté for 3 minutes, stirring occasionally. Stir in half of the coconut milk and cook over low heat for 3 minutes; the coconut oil will separate and rise to the surface.

Cook the chicken and vegetables: Add the chopped chicken and the remaining coconut milk. Bring the mixture to a boil, then reduce the heat to low. Simmer until the chicken is fully cooked, about 5 minutes. Add the bamboo shoots, baby corn, lime leaves, and water. Bring the mixture to a boil again, then reduce the heat to low. Cover and simmer for 10 minutes.

Season the curry, simmer, and serve: Stir in the MSG, sugar, and fish sauce, ensuring these ingredients are evenly combined. Add the quail eggs, potatoes, carrot, and bell pepper. Stir, then cover and simmer over low heat until the potatoes and carrots are tender, about 10 minutes. Serve the curry hot over jasmine rice.

Serves 6 to 8

Gaeng Het Sai Pa ◆ Forager's Mushroom Fish Soup

ແກງເຫັດໃສ່ປາ

Rice Paste

⅓ cup uncooked sticky rice

3 fresh bird's eye chiles, stemmed

Soup

6 cups water

1 pound chopped grass carp (see Note), cut into 1-inch steaks

1 lemongrass stalk, hard part only, lightly bruised

3 tablespoons padaek (see page 97)

1 tablespoon fish sauce (see page 18)

1 teaspoon MSG

½ cup chopped oyster mushroom (1-inch pieces)

½ cup separated seafood mushrooms

½ cup chopped wood ear mushroom (1-inch pieces)

½ cup separated brown shimeji mushrooms

½ cup halved straw mushrooms

4 cups chopped pumpkin leaves and vines (2-inch pieces); or use morning glory (water spinach)

3 cups chopped rice paddy herb (1-inch pieces); see page 25

Cooked sticky rice (see page 73), for serving

Mae loves every kind of mushroom, and her foraging trips often result in zip-top bags filled with a variety of edible mushrooms. She shares these with other Lao families who, like her, use them to make classic stews like this one. Mushrooms are one of her go-to ingredients for enhancing the umami flavors in many dishes, including this stew, where they deepen the richness of the fish broth and bring a variety of textures and flavors. Other ingredients Mae gathers on her foraging trips include tender vines, leaves, and herbs: A single morning trip to the park can supply many of the things she needs for her beloved soups and stews. For Mae, foraging is a way to feel connected to the jungles of Laos even as she surveys the parks and fields of her current home in Wisconsin.

Prepare the rice paste: Rinse the sticky rice three times in cool water and place it in a medium bowl. In a small pot, bring 2 cups of water to a boil. Cover the rinsed rice with the boiling water and let it soak for 10 minutes; drain the rice. Using a deep mortar and pestle, pound the soaked sticky rice into a paste. Add the bird's eye chiles and continue pounding until the mixture is smooth. Slowly add 1 tablespoon of water as you grind the mixture into a watery paste. Set aside.

Make the soup: In a large pot, bring the 6 cups of water to a simmer over medium heat. Add the fish steaks and lemongrass stalk and return to a simmer, then turn the heat down to low, cover the pot, and cook for 10 minutes.

Stir in the padaek, fish sauce, and MSG. Add the prepared rice paste to the pot, mixing gently to combine. Allow the soup to simmer until it begins to thicken slightly.

Add the oyster, seafood, wood ear, shimeji, and straw mushrooms to the pot. Simmer for 10 more minutes.

Add the vegetables and serve: Stir in the chopped pumpkin leaves and vines and the rice paddy herb. Cook for another 10 minutes, until all the ingredients are tender and the flavors are well combined. Ladle the warm soup into bowls and serve with sticky rice.

Note

Grass fish are a kind of carp; catfish, tilapia, or other firm, mild-flavored fish can be substituted.

Aw Hoy ◆ Snail Stew

ອໍຫອຍ

Serves 4 to 6

Rustic dishes like aw hoy hold a special place in my heart. It was one of Mae's go-to stews when I was a kid: Sometimes she switched out the protein she used, but thanks to the fragrant aromatics and padaek, everything in the stew always tasted incredible. Still, the snails were one of my favorites. Paw taught me how to pick snails out of their shells. Sometimes, he cut the ends of the shells to make it easier to blow the snail out. While aw hoy might sound fancy (like escargot), it is a humble meal and a common one in our household, bringing us together to happily slurp up the rich, umami-filled juices from each shell.

3 pounds fresh sea snails (periwinkles) in the shell or 2 pounds defrosted whole snail meat

¼ cup uncooked sticky rice

5 cups plus 1 tablespoon water, divided

⅔ cup chopped shallot

5 fresh bird's eye chiles, stemmed

¼ cup minced lemongrass (from the soft part of 2 stalks)

6 fresh makrut lime leaves

Pinch of coarse kosher salt

1 tablespoon vegetable oil

1 cup thinly sliced dill, tender stems and leaves

1 bunch scallions, chopped into 2-inch pieces, white and light green parts

½ teaspoon MSG

2 tablespoons padaek (see page 97)

Cooked sticky rice (see page 73), for serving

Prepare the snails: If you are using fresh snails in the shell, rinse them thoroughly in a large bowl of water. Drain and repeat two more times, or until the water runs clear and any sediment or debris is washed away. Drain the snails and set them aside.

Make the rice paste: Rinse the sticky rice three times with cool water, then place in a small bowl. Bring 2 cups of the water to a boil. Cover the rinsed rice with the boiling water and let it soak for 10 minutes. Drain the rice and, in a deep mortar, pound the soaked sticky rice into a paste with a pestle. Add 2 of the bird's eye chiles and continue pounding until they're smoothly incorporated, gradually adding the 1 tablespoon of water to achieve a slightly watery paste. Set aside.

Prepare the aromatic paste: In a clean mortar, combine the shallots, lemongrass, lime leaves, remaining 3 chiles, and salt and pound into a rough paste. Transfer to a small bowl and set aside.

Cook the stew: Heat a medium soup pot over medium-high heat. Add the vegetable oil and warm for 1 minute, then add the aromatic paste and sauté for 1 minute, until fragrant. Add the snails in their shells (or the thawed frozen snail meat), stirring to coat them evenly with the paste. Pour in the remaining 3 cups of water, add the dill and scallions, and bring the mixture to a simmer. Cover, lower the heat to low, and cook for 5 minutes, until the snails are slightly chewy but tender in texture. Stir in the MSG and padaek. Add the rice paste, mixing well to thicken the stew. Stir continuously as the stew simmers for another 5 minutes.

Serve the snail stew hot with sticky rice. Use a toothpick or skewer to gently hook and pull the snail out of the shell.

Serves 3 or 4

Tom Khem ◆ Caramelized Braised Pork Stew

ຕົ້ມເຂັມ

6 eggs

1½ pounds pork riblets, cut into two-bone segments

1 tablespoon vegetable oil

⅓ cup sugar

1 tablespoon minced garlic

2 tablespoons minced ginger

¼ cup thinly sliced ginger

2 cups water

3 tablespoons fish sauce (see page 18)

1 tablespoon sweet soy sauce

1 tablespoon dark soy sauce

1 teaspoon MSG

Cooked jasmine rice, for serving

Thinly sliced fresh bird's eye chiles, for garnish

Chopped scallions, green parts only, for garnish

Fried garlic (see page 21), for garnish

Like most stews, tom khem tastes even better the next day, as the flavors have time to meld and deepen. The dish relies on the process of sugar caramelization to create layers of sweetness, while the soy sauces balance the flavors and give each riblet a rich, golden brown color. When I was growing up, this dish was a staple in my household, always made in large batches; my siblings and I loved its perfect balance of sweet and savory flavors (and we often found ourselves competing to secure the last egg!).

Cook the eggs: Place the eggs in a medium pot and add enough water to cover them by 1 inch. Bring the water to a simmer over medium heat and cook for 7 minutes. Transfer the eggs to an ice bath for 5 minutes, then peel; set aside.

Parboil the pork riblets: Place the riblets in a pot and cover them with water. Bring to a boil and cook for 5 minutes. Drain the riblets and rinse them to remove the scum, then set them aside.

Caramelize the sugar and cook the aromatics and pork: In a medium pot over medium-high heat, heat the vegetable oil and sugar, stirring continuously for about 3 minutes until the sugar melts into the oil and and turns a caramel color. Add the minced garlic, minced ginger, and sliced ginger to the caramel oil. Sauté, stirring constantly, until fragrant, about 30 seconds. Add the riblets, stirring to coat them evenly in the caramel mixture.

Pour in the water, and add the fish sauce, sweet soy sauce, dark soy sauce, and MSG. Stir to combine, then bring the mixture to a simmer over medium-high heat. Reduce the heat to medium-low, cover the pot (setting the lid slightly ajar), and cook for 15 minutes, until the pork takes on a golden brown color.

Add the eggs, garnish, and serve: Gently add the peeled eggs to the pot. Simmer for another 15 minutes, allowing the flavors to meld. For a thicker stew, continue cooking for 5 more minutes, or longer, until the stew reaches your desired consistency. Serve hot with jasmine rice, garnish with fresh bird's eye chiles, scallions, and fried garlic, and enjoy!

Gaeng Keelek ◆ Cassia Leaf Stew

แกงขี้เหล็ก

Serves 4 or 5

This dish beautifully illustrates how Lao recipes have evolved within the diaspora, adapting to new environments and available ingredients while preserving their essence. This is my favorite Lao dish, and I've had the pleasure of trying countless variations both in Laos and elsewhere, each version tailored to its locale. Traditionally, this stew is made with ground cassia leaves to thicken the broth, enriched ox skin or another protein, and delicately topped with red ant eggs, which are harvested only during the late summer. The result is a dish that delivers a harmonious balance of mildly bitter, earthy, pungent, and fragrant flavors; a true representation of Lao cuisine's complex flavor palette.

1 (16-ounce) can cassia leaves pickled in brine, or 6 ounces of kale with tough stems removed (see Note)

1 (14-ounce) can yanang leaf extract (see Note)

Rice Paste

3 tablespoons uncooked sticky rice

2 cups water

3 fresh bird's eye chiles, stemmed

4 garlic cloves, minced

1 shallot, and minced

½ teaspoon coarse kosher salt

Pork

1 pound pork shoulder, cubed

1 lemongrass bundle (see page 21)

1 cup water

1 teaspoon MSG

¼ cup padaek (see page 97)

2 tablespoons fish sauce (see page 18)

To Serve

1 cup chopped scallions

Ground pork rinds, about 2 ounces

Cooked sticky rice (see page 73), for serving

Prepare the cassia leaves: Drain the cassia leaves and squeeze them to remove as much brine as possible. Place the leaves in a large pot, add enough water to cover, and bring to a boil over high heat. Reduce the heat to low and simmer, covered, for 15 minutes. Drain the leaves and rinse them under cool water, then squeeze out the excess moisture. In a food processor, combine the cassia leaves with the yanang extract and blend until finely pureed. Set aside.

Make the rice paste: Rinse the sticky rice three times, then place it in a small bowl. Bring 2 cups of water to a boil. Cover the rice with the boiling water and let soak for 10 minutes. Drain the rice and transfer it to a deep mortar. Add the chiles, garlic, shallot,and salt and pound it into a smooth paste. Add the cassia leaf puree to the mortar and mix until the ingredients are evenly combined.

Cook the pork: In a large pot, combine the pork cubes, lemongrass bundle, and water. Bring to a simmer over high heat and cook for 5 minutes, skimming off any foam or impurities from the surface.

Add the cassia leaf mixture, MSG, padaek, and fish sauce to the pork and stir to combine thoroughly. Continue cooking, uncovered, over medium heat, stirring occasionally, until the mixture thickens slightly. Cover, and simmer on low heat for 20 minutes.

Garnish with chopped scallions and ground pork rinds and serve warm with sticky rice.

Note

Canned cassia leaves and yanang extract are both commonly available at Southeast Asian markets. If you can't find these ingredients, 6 ounces of kale (tough stems removed) pureed in a blender with 2 cups of water will yield the desired texture and flavor.

Serves 6 to 8

Gaeng Mak Daeng ◆ Pork-Stuffed Cucumber Soup

ແກງໝາກແຕງ

Cucumbers and Filling

3 cups water

1 (1½-ounce) bundle mung bean thread noodles

1 pound ground pork

1 tablespoon minced garlic

½ teaspoon coarse kosher salt

½ teaspoon freshly ground black pepper

1 tablespoon oyster sauce

2 large English cucumbers, peeled, ends trimmed, and sliced into 2-inch-thick rounds (about 10 slices total)

Broth

1½ teaspoons vegetable oil

1 yellow onion, halved

¼ cup thinly sliced ginger

2½ quarts water

1 large carrot, peeled and diced into ¼-inch cubes

2 teaspoons coarse kosher salt

½ teaspoon MSG

1 tablespoon fish sauce (see page 18)

To Serve

Chopped cilantro

Chopped scallions, green parts only

A year after my first trip to Laos, I sat in my apartment reading an article about the legendary flavors of Laos. The accompanying photo of the morning market in Luang Prabang stirred vivid memories; it was instant nostalgia. That market was where I first tried gaeng mak daeng. In this dish, a light vegetable broth is infused with pork-stuffed cucumber, which adds a rich, fatty depth to the flavor. Trying gaeng mak daeng and other Lao foods in the motherland brought back memories of my childhood. Each of the preparations had some reflection of the flavors Mae had lovingly introduced me to. It was moments like this while I was exploring Laos that made me feel reconnected with my roots, bringing my soul into harmony. It made me hope that many more members of the Lao diaspora get the chance to visit Laos and experience the beautiful place our families came from.

In a small pot over medium heat, bring the 3 cups of water to a boil. Place the noodles in a large bowl and cover with the boiling water. Let sit for 1 minute, then drain and rinse under cool water. Drain again, and cut the noodles into 3-inch pieces. Set aside.

Make the filling and stuff the cucumbers: In a large bowl, combine the ground pork, minced garlic, salt, black pepper, oyster sauce, and prepared noodles. Mix thoroughly by hand until the filling ingredients are evenly combined. Scoop out the seeds in the cucumber rounds, creating hollow rings. Fill each cucumber ring with about 1 tablespoon of the pork mixture. Roll any remaining pork mixture into small meatballs to add to the soup.

Make the broth: Heat the vegetable oil in a large soup pot over medium-high heat. Add the halved onion and sliced ginger and cook for 2 minutes, flipping the ginger halfway through. Add the water and bring to a boil. Add the diced carrots and season with the salt, MSG, and fish sauce. Return the broth to a boil.

Cook the cucumbers and meatballs: Gently add the stuffed cucumbers and meatballs to the soup. Return the soup to a boil, skimming off any scum that rises to the surface. Lower the heat to low, cover, and simmer for 15 minutes. Ladle the hot soup into bowls, making sure to evenly distribute the cucumber rounds and meatballs, and garnish with cilantro and scallions. Serve hot.

Lao Cooks
Celebrate

Lao-Style Ragout

ລາກູ້ລາວ

Serves 4 to 6

Paw can speak French, since he grew up in Laos during a time of significant transitions for the country. When he was young, the country had only recently become politically independent from France, and French culture and language were still strong influences. Today, if you visit Laos, you'll notice a striking contrast in its architecture: Traditional wooden and bamboo homes with thatched roofs sit alongside both sharp-topped temples and buildings influenced by French colonial design. This blend reflects Laos's history as part of French Indochina. During the colonial period, between 1893 and 1953, French military posts were established in each province, and influences extended to food. Baguettes, crepes, coffee, and even a version of ragout became part of the culinary landscape. This ragout is infused with Lao flavors such as lime leaves, lemongrass, and padaek, and it's served with a baguette for dipping and sopping up the stew.

2 tablespoons oyster sauce

1½ teaspoons brown sugar

1 teaspoon coarse kosher salt

1 teaspoon MSG

2 pounds bone-in short ribs, cut into 2-inch pieces

2 tablespoons vegetable oil

4 cups plus ⅓ cup water, divided

1 bunch scallions, whites and greens separated, chopped

4 garlic cloves, minced

2 cups tomato sauce

2 tablespoons tomato paste

1 medium tomato, diced

3 fresh makrut lime leaves

2 cups sliced white mushrooms

1 large carrot, peeled and cut into 2-inch pieces

1 russet potato, peeled and cut into bite-sized pieces

1 lemongrass bundle (see page 21)

1½ teaspoons padaek (see page 97)

1 teaspoon freshly ground black pepper

Baguette, for serving

Marinate the ribs: In a large bowl, combine the oyster sauce, brown sugar, kosher salt, and MSG. Add the short ribs and coat them evenly in the mixture. Cover and refrigerate for at least 30 minutes, or overnight for deeper flavor.

Sear the ribs: Heat 1 tablespoon of the oil in a large pot over medium-high heat. Add the ribs to the pot (reserve the marinade in the bowl), meat-side down, and brown for 2 to 3 minutes on each side. Remove the ribs from the pot and set aside. Pour the ⅓ cup of water into the pot and scrape the bottom to loosen any browned bits. Add this liquid to the marinade bowl.

Sauté the aromatics and simmer: In the same pot, heat the remaining 1 tablespoon of vegetable oil over medium heat. Sauté the white parts of the scallions and the garlic for about 1 minute, until fragrant. Stir in the tomato sauce, tomato paste, diced tomato, and lime leaves. Pour in 4 cups of water and stir well to combine. Return the short ribs, reserved marinade, and any accumulated juices to the pot, ensuring the ribs are fully submerged in the liquid. Cover and bring to a gentle simmer over medium heat. Reduce the heat to low and cook, covered, for 2 hours, or until the ribs are tender. Add the mushrooms, carrots, potatoes, and lemongrass to the pot. Simmer for 10 minutes, stirring occasionally.

Season and finish: Stir in the padaek and black pepper. Cook for 5 minutes more to let the flavors meld. Top with the scallion greens and serve with the baguette.

Serves 6 to 8

Or Lam ◆ Luang Prabang Pepper Stew

ເອາະຫຼາມ

Aromatics

1 lemongrass bundle (see page 21)

⅓ cup thinly sliced galangal

6 fresh red bird's eye chiles, stemmed

1 cup halved shallots

Broth

2½ quarts water

1 pound beef chuck, cut into 1-inch cubes

½ pound beef tendon, in one piece or uncooked pork rinds

1 teaspoon coarse kosher salt

10 round green Thai eggplants, halved

⅓ cup uncooked sticky rice

2 cups water

2 cups wood ear mushrooms

2 cups king oyster mushrooms

¼ cup padaek (page 97)

1 teaspoon MSG

1½ teaspoons Sichuan peppercorn, crushed

2 cups chopped dill

1 cup chopped scallions, white and green parts

2 cups yam leaves and tender stems (see Note)

Cooked sticky rice (see page 73), for serving

Lao cuisine is unique among Southeast Asian countries for its heavy use of dill, known locally as *pak see*. Likely introduced by the French during the colonial period, dill adds subtle anise-like and earthy flavors to dishes such as mok pa (steamed fish in banana leaves), gaeng nor mai (bamboo shoot stew), and gaeng pa (Lao jungle curry).

Or lam, one of the most famous dishes in Luang Prabang, is a peppery stew that prominently features dill. Traditionally, it is made with mai sakahn, a wood vine that provides a numbing, spicy sensation. Since mai sakahn is not widely available outside Laos, this version substitutes Sichuan peppercorns to mimic the effect.

Sauté the aromatics and prepare the broth: Heat a medium pan over medium-high heat. Add the lemongrass, galangal, chiles, and shallots, and dry-sauté for 5 minutes until the aromatics are slightly charred. In a medium stockpot, combine the water and the sautéed aromatics. Add the beef chuck, whole tendon, and salt. Bring to a boil, skimming off any scum that rises to the surface.

Add the halved green eggplants to the pot and reduce the heat to low. Cover and simmer for 15 minutes. Remove the eggplants, shallots, and chiles from the pot and place them in a deep mortar. Mash them into a rough paste and set aside.

Prepare the sticky rice paste: Rinse the sticky rice three times, then place it in a small bowl. Bring 2 cups of water to a boil. Cover the rice with the boiling water, and let soak for 10 minutes. Drain the rice and crush it into a paste using a deep mortar and pestle. Set aside.

After the broth has been simmering for 30 minutes, remove the tendon from the pot. Slice it into thin pieces and return it to the broth. Add the mashed eggplant mixture, mushrooms, and the sticky rice paste to the broth. Stir well and let it cook for 5 minutes, allowing the broth to thicken. Season the stew with the padaek, MSG, and Sichuan peppercorns. Simmer for 5 more minutes. Add the dill, scallions, and yam leaves and stems and cook, uncovered, for 5 minutes. Serve the stew hot with sticky rice on the side.

Note

Yam leaves are spade-shaped and smooth, with a mild earthy taste. The tender stems can be used as well. They are found at Asian markets. Mature spinach or water spinach are good substitutions.

8

DESSERTS

Not Too Sweet

For a Lao child, cultural festivities often come alive through the promise of delicious sweets. While kneeling to listen to monks chant blessings may test a young one's patience, the anticipation of Lao desserts makes it worthwhile. Adolescence is a time to engage with and learn about these customs, but many parents in the diaspora find it challenging to pass them down while simultaneously adapting to life outside of Laos. Thankfully, community support and involvement mean that throughout the diaspora these celebrations both endure and evolve to fit new environments.

Lao celebrations, especially those tied to rice cultivation and spiritual milestones, play a crucial role in preserving community identity. Lao New Year, or Pi Mai, is the largest festival celebrated both in Laos and among diaspora communities. This celebration typically occurs around April 14 to 16, with each year's date varying based on the Indic calendar, which aligns months with the moon and years with the sun. Desserts like nam wan, khao lam, khanom nap, khao tom, and khanom mantone are staples of the celebration. These treats often feature ingredients such as coconut milk, mini tapioca pearls, and sticky rice, which is sometimes dyed a brilliant blue using butterfly pea flower. Many Lao desserts are less sweet than Western ones, a reflection of the cultural belief that excessive sweetness is unnecessary and even undesirable.

I recall Mae savoring simple desserts like freshly cooked sticky rice with mango or steamed kabocha squash, humble combinations that taught me to appreciate the nuanced sweetness of natural ingredients. One rare and memorable dessert is made with khao mao, which is green sticky rice that's harvested young, while it's still tender. The young rice plumps up beautifully when combined with sweetened hot coconut water. Freshly grated coconut is then mixed in, creating a delicate dish that perfectly balances sweetness with the flavor of the rice.

Lao New Year celebrations in diaspora communities retain rich traditions, even far from home. During Pi Mai, families clean their homes and say goodbye to the old so they can welcome the new year. At temples, statues of the Buddha are lovingly washed and perfumed for good luck, and the water that's blessed by this use is then taken home. Water festivals are celebrated in many Southeast Asian cultures, and Pi Mai is one of the world's largest. People often splash the blessed water on one another to cleanse away negativity and extend wishes for a long life. The wetter you are, the luckier you're considered to be.

Another significant tradition during Lao New Year is duk baht, the offering of food to monks as an act of merit and respect. Families bring an assortment of offerings, from sticky rice and traditional sweets to packaged Western treats like Twinkies, placing them in intricately designed containers called kun. These are then placed into the monks' alms bowls during the ceremony, as offerings symbolizing the importance of generosity and sharing.

The baci ceremony, which is central to the celebration of many Lao milestones, such as the birth of a child, marriage, recovery from illness, or moving away from home, unites the community in blessings and good wishes. A pa kwan, a cone-shaped centerpiece crafted from banana leaves,

flowers, and white blessing threads, takes center stage. Surrounding it are bowls filled with symbolic foods: hard-boiled eggs to represent fertility, rice whiskey for purification, a whole boiled chicken for divination, and so on. Desserts like khao tom (a sweet sticky rice–and-banana parcel wrapped in banana leaves) and rice puffs are also included as symbols of community and abundance.

As the ceremony begins, the mo pawn, a respected elder versed in Buddhist teachings, leads the gathering in chanting blessings. Participants then tie the blessed white threads around one another's wrists, offering heartfelt wishes for health and prosperity. This act symbolizes reuniting the soul with the body, a vital step for maintaining balance and well-being. Lao tradition holds that thirty-two spirits reside in the body, each tied to an organ, and this ceremony restores harmony during life's pivotal moments.

I was once a child unaware of the significance of these customs, but now I've come to realize that they are vital threads connecting us to our roots. They carry the essence of joy, health, and community, offering us a sense of belonging even when we are far from home. This chapter invites you to explore the sweets that enrich these traditions, with the hope that each bite brings not only delicious flavors but also a deeper connection to Lao culture and its enduring spirit.

Khao Lod Song ◆ Pandan Gems in Sweetened Coconut Milk

ເຂົ້າລອດຊ່ອງ

Serves 4 to 6

Whenever we ran out of our fifty-pound supply of sticky rice, my family would take an hour-long road trip to Madison, which had the closest Southeast Asian market. Mae always had a carefully planned grocery list, which typically included beef meatballs, pho noodles, blue crabs, balut eggs, Tito's burritos, unripe papaya, MSG, and fish sauce. As a ten-year-old, I had my own list of must-haves: dried squid, coconut juice, khanom ooloo, and khao lod song. We always aimed to go in the morning, because khao lod song was made fresh and it sold out quickly. It was my favorite dessert, not just because of its vibrant green color, but because it floated in a sweet, creamy coconut syrup. Grocery shopping can still bring back the joy of those childhood trips, especially when my shopping list includes the nostalgic treats of my youth.

Limestone Water

2 teaspoons (⅖ ounce/12 grams) white limestone paste

3 cups water

Pandan Puree

2 cups water

10 pandan leaves (1¾ ounces), chopped (see page 23)

Green Gems

1½ cups (7 ounces/200 grams) jasmine rice flour

½ cup (1¾ ounces/50 grams) tapioca flour

Syrup

1 cup sugar

1 cup water

Coconut Mixture

2 (13.5-ounce) cans coconut milk

2 cups water

1 pandan leaf

1 teaspoon coarse kosher salt

Make the limestone water: In a large bowl, combine the limestone paste with ½ cup of the water. Stir until the limestone paste is fully dissolved. Add the remaining 2½ cups of water and mix well. Let the mixture sit for at least 1 hour. Carefully pour the clear water into another container, leaving the sediment at the bottom of the bowl. Discard the sediment or save it to use again (see Note, page 160).

Make the pandan puree: In a blender, blend the water and the chopped pandan leaves until pureed, about 1 minute. Strain the mixture through a fine-mesh sieve or cheesecloth, squeezing out as much liquid as possible. Set the pandan extract aside.

Make the green gems: On a work surface near the stove, place a large bowl of cold water and a strainer with holes that are at least 3 millimeters in diameter (such as a potato ricer). In a large nonstick pan with a handle, combine the 3 cups of limestone water and the pandan extract with the rice flour and tapioca flour and whisk until smooth. Place over medium-high heat, bring to a simmer, and cook for 5 minutes, stirring with a silicone spatula or wooden spoon and scraping the bottom occasionally to prevent sticking. Reduce the heat to medium and cook, continuing to stir occasionally, for another 10 minutes. The mixture will start out clumpy but will become smooth as you continue cooking and stirring it.

Continued

Khao Lod Song ◆ Pandan Gems in Sweetened Coconut Milk

continued

At the end of the cooking time, hold the strainer about a foot above the cold water bath and immediately begin pouring the mixture from the pot into the water, letting the green strands fall into the water. Apply light pressure if needed to push the mixture through. Set the bowl of water and gems aside until it's time to assemble the dish.

Make the syrup: In a small pot over medium-high heat, cook the sugar, stirring and letting it melt and caramelize, about 4 to 5 minutes. Once the sugar is golden brown, carefully add the water and stir. Reduce the heat to medium-low and simmer for about 6 minutes, until the sugar is fully dissolved. Set aside to cool.

Make the coconut sauce: In a small pot, combine the coconut milk, water, pandan leaf, and salt. Place over low heat and cook for about 8 minutes, stirring occasionally until the salt has melted. Pour the mixture into a pitcher and let it cool to room temperature.

Assemble the dessert: Once all the components have cooled to room temperature, use a slotted spoon to transfer the green gems to small serving bowls. Place 4 ice cubes in each bowl and top with drizzles of syrup and coconut sauce. Serve immediately and enjoy!

HK
SAMSUNG
2024

Serves 4 to 6

Vun Mak Muang ◆ Mango Coconut Jelly

ວຸ້ນມັກໝ່ວງ

Mango Layer

1 tablespoon agar-agar powder

⅓ cup sugar

3 cups water

Orange food coloring (optional)

1 cup ¼-inch cubed ripe mango

Coconut Layer

1 tablespoon agar-agar powder

⅓ cup sugar

1 (13.5-ounce) can coconut milk

1¼ cups water

In Lao cuisine, the jellylike dessert vun uses agar-agar as its main solidifying ingredient. Agar-agar is a plant-based gelatin substitute that gives the dessert a firm texture while making it suitable for vegan diets. Vun is often made with layers of multiple flavors such as coconut, pandan, or mango.

This vun is inspired by my love of mango sticky rice: Each bite pairs pieces of sweet mango with smooth coconut milk jelly, offering a perfect balance of sweetness and creaminess. Unlike gelatin-based jellies, vun does not melt at room temperature, making it an ideal dessert to serve at gatherings.

Make the mango layer: In a small pot, combine the tablespoon of agar-agar powder, the sugar, and 3 cups of water. Mix well to dissolve. Set the mixture over medium-low heat and bring to a simmer then reduce the heat to low; cook, stirring occasionally, for about 8 minutes, until the sugar is dissolved. Stir in a drop of orange food coloring (if using), then pour the mixture through a fine-mesh sieve into a 9 by 13-inch pan. Evenly distribute the cubed mango pieces in the jelly layer. Let the layer sit at room temperature for 20 minutes to set, popping any bubbles that form on the surface using a fork or toothpick.

Make the coconut layer: In a clean pot, combine the tablespoon of agar-agar powder, sugar, coconut milk, and 1¼ cups water. Mix well to dissolve the sugar and agar-agar. Place the mixture over medium-low heat, heat to a simmer, then reduce the heat to low and cook, stirring occasionally, until the sugar is fully dissolved, about 8 minutes. Carefully pour the coconut mixture through a fine-mesh sieve over the mango jelly layer. Pop any bubbles on the surface as before, and let the jelly cool at room temperature for about 40 minutes, until fully set.

Once the jelly has set, you can chill it before serving, or serve it at room temperature, cut into squares or whatever shapes you wish.

Khao Tom Ping ◆ Grilled Yam Sticky Rice

ເຂົ້າຕົ້ມປີ້ງ

Serves 8 to 10

Khao ping is beautifully wrapped sticky rice dessert shaped like a triangle. When unwrapped, the rice triangle reveals patches of vibrant colors from orange and purple yams. I first enjoyed this dessert during a visit with a friend's family in Vientiane. They took us to a stunning restaurant in a bamboo hut floating over a pond, where dish after dish arrived in an endless show of hospitality. At the end of the meal, my friend surprised us with khao ping. I was moved by her family's generosity and their effort to help me discover Lao dishes that are less widely known. I hope you try this recipe and share it in a similar spirit of exploration.

1½ cups uncooked white sticky rice

½ cup uncooked purple sticky rice (black glutinous rice)

1 cup water

1 (13.5-ounce) can coconut milk

½ cup sugar

½ teaspoon coarse kosher salt

1 pandan leaf, tied into a knot (see page 23)

½ cup ¼-inch cubes orange yam

½ cup (¼-inch cubes) purple yam

10 (11 by 11-inch) banana leaves

Prepare the sticky rice: In a large bowl, combine the white and purple sticky rice. Rinse under cool water three times to remove excess starch. Transfer the rinsed rice to a rice cooker, add the 1 cup of water, and cook for 20 minutes; the rice should be slightly undercooked (it will finish cooking as it steams in the banana leaves).

Make the coconut mixture: In a large pot, combine the coconut milk, sugar, salt, and pandan leaf. Heat over medium heat until it reaches a low simmer, about 5 minutes, stirring occasionally. Turn off the heat and remove the pandan leaf from the pot.

Combine the rice and yams: Add the cooked sticky rice and the yams to the coconut mixture and stir, ensuring the rice absorbs all the liquid.

Assemble the parcels: Fold a banana leaf in half with the folded edge closest to you. Take the bottom left corner and fold it toward the center at a 90-degree angle to create a triangular pocket. Wrap the right side of the leaf around to form a triangular cone. Scoop ½ cup of the rice filling into the cone and use a spoon to press it down gently. To close the top of each parcel, fold the bottom flap inward over the top of the filling. Fold the left flap inward, followed by the right flap, to completely seal the opening. Secure the top of each parcel with two toothpicks, piercing through the layers of banana leaf to hold the flaps in place.

Steam and broil the parcels: Bring a large pot of water to a boil. Place the banana leaf parcels in a single layer in a steamer basket and steam over medium-high heat for 30 minutes. Carefully move the parcels to a sheet pan and place it on the top rack of the oven. Set the oven to broil, and broil the parcels for 30 to 60 seconds on one side, then flip them over and broil for 30 to 60 seconds on the other side; the leaves should darken slightly. Take the pan out of the oven and allow the parcels to cool until they are warm or room temperature before serving.

Serves 4

Mak Muang Yat Khao ◆ Sticky Rice-Stuffed Mango

ໝາກມ່ວງຍັດເຂົ້າ

- 1 cup uncooked sticky rice
- 4 Champagne mangoes (see Note)
- ¼ cup sugar
- 1 cup water
- ¼ teaspoon coarse kosher salt
- 1 tablespoon uncooked mung beans
- 1 tablespoon dried shredded coconut
- 1 tablespoon roughly crushed lightly salted peanuts

The combination of tropical fruits and sticky rice always reminds me of Mae, who loves to eat her freshly cooked sticky rice with fruit, steamed kabocha squash, or corn. She doesn't add sugar, preferring to savor the natural sweetness of the ingredients, and for a long time, I couldn't understand her enjoyment of such simplicity. Later, of course, I grew to realize how our taste preferences evolve throughout our lives. This recipe is inspired by Mae's not-too-sweet approach: a sticky rice and mango dessert that highlights the fruit's natural flavors. The sticky rice is infused with mango puree and topped with mung beans and coconut for a subtle, balanced sweetness. It showcases the versatility of sticky rice, which can be enjoyed sweet, savory, or somewhere in between, just as Mae likes it.

Cook the sticky rice using your preferred method (see page 73). While it's cooking, prepare the mango shells, syrup, and mango puree.

Prepare the mango shells: Cut off about one-third of each mango from the narrow end. Carefully carve around the mango seed and slice the flesh carefully away from the skin without puncturing it. Gently twist and pull out the mango seed and, using a thin spoon, scoop out the mango flesh, keeping the skin intact to use as a shell. Set the mango flesh and the mango shells aside.

Make the syrup and the mango puree: In a small pot over medium heat, cook the sugar for 3 minutes, stirring a few times. Add the water and salt and stir until the sugar is fully dissolved. Pour the syrup into a bowl and let it cool for about 10 minutes. In a blender, combine the cooled syrup and the reserved mango flesh and blend until smooth.

Prepare the sticky rice: While the cooked rice is still warm, place it in a bowl and mix it with 1 cup of the mango puree. Stir well to allow the rice to absorb the mango mixture evenly.

Prepare the topping: In a small pan over medium heat, toast the mung beans and dried coconut shreds for 2 minutes, until fragrant. Transfer them to a deep mortar, add the peanuts and mix well.

Assemble and serve: Scoop the mango-infused sticky rice into the hollowed-out mango shells. Drizzle with additional mango puree and sprinkle the peanut, mung bean, and coconut topping over each stuffed mango. Serve at room temperature and enjoy!

Note

Champagne mangoes have a sweet, floral flavor and a smooth texture that makes them ideal for pureeing. They are smaller than other mangoes, making it easier to remove the pit without tearing the skin, creating a perfect single-serving portion for this dessert. You can also use Atkins mangoes, but since they're typically larger, one mango may not hold the right ratio of sticky rice for a single serving.

Khanom Nap ◆ Coconut-Stuffed Sticky Rice Dumplings

Serves 14; 1 per person

This dessert feels like a gift because it beautifully showcases the art of using banana leaves like origami paper, with the triangular fold shaping the sticky rice dumplings into elegant pyramids. People in the Lao community often make such desserts together, assigning a role to each person and enjoying creating something meaningful as a group.

Filling

3 cups frozen shredded coconut, thawed

½ cup brown sugar

¼ cup granulated sugar

¼ teaspoon coarse kosher salt

Dough and Wrapping

1½ cups (8 ounces) sticky rice flour (see page 18)

½ cup (3 ounces) jasmine rice flour

¼ cup granulated sugar

1¼ cups coconut milk

28 round banana leaves, each 8 inches in diameter (or use aluminum foil)

Make the filling: Place the shredded coconut in a food processor and pulse a few times until roughly ground. Heat a large skillet over medium-high heat and add the coconut; stir for 2 minutes until warm, then add the brown sugar, granulated sugar, and salt. Mix well until the sugar is fully melted. Remove from the heat and cool the mixture in the refrigerator for 15 minutes. Once the mixture has cooled, shape it into 14 balls by firmly pressing heaping tablespoons in your palm. Arrange them on a plate and set aside.

Make the dough: In a large bowl, combine both rice flours and the granulated sugar and whisk to blend evenly. Gradually add the coconut milk, stirring with a spoon until the liquid is absorbed. Knead the resulting dough by hand until it is smooth.

Assemble the dumplings: Take a heaping tablespoon of dough and flatten it in your palm. Place a coconut ball in the center of the flattened dough. Carefully form the dough around the filling so it is completely enveloped. Roll the dough ball in your hands to smooth and seal it. Repeat with the remaining dough and filling.

Wrap the dumplings: Layer two banana leaf circles one on top of the other with the lines of each leaf running perpendicular to the other. Wrap the leaves into a cone shape by folding them in half to create a crease, then gently pull the crease inward about 2 inches and place a dough ball inside. With the cone upside down, fold the thick end of the banana leaves that's closest to you toward the center, then fold in the left and right sides. Finally, fold the top piece down to form a triangular pyramid. Place on a plate to hold its shape, seam-side down, and repeat with the remaining dough balls.

Steam the dumplings: Bring a large pot of water to a boil. Arrange the wrapped dumplings in a single layer in a steamer basket, seam-side down. Cover and steam over medium-high heat for 20 minutes. Allow the dumplings to cool before peeling and serving.

Makes 12 bundles | Serves 6

Nap Salee ◆ Creamy Corn Sticky Rice Wraps

แซบสาลิ

7 cups water, divided

½ cup uncooked sticky rice

3 ears sweet corn in husks (to yield about 2 cups of kernels)

12 corn husks, for wrapping

2½ tablespoons coconut milk

3 tablespoons sugar

½ teaspoon coarse kosher salt

Working on farms was a common job for many refugee families at the time we arrived in the United States. During the summer, my family worked long days at a flower farm to earn extra money. Other families we knew worked on corn farms. They often brought home "ugly" corn that couldn't be sold, and we traded our imperfect flowers for their ugly corn. I knew how hard they'd worked to harvest each ear, which made enjoying recipes like this one using fresh corn from the farm all the more special. Nap salee combines the sticky texture of rice with the sweet flavors of coconut and corn, creating a comforting and satisfying dish. This humble dessert evokes the long, grueling days of hard work Mae and Paw put in to give our family a better future.

Prepare the sticky rice: In a medium pot, bring 4 cups of water to a boil. Place the sticky rice in a medium bowl, cover it with the boiling water, and let soak for 5 minutes. Drain the rice and set aside.

Prepare the corn and husks: Remove the corn husks from the cobs. Clean the corncobs and the husks thoroughly, and set the corncobs aside. Trim about ½ inch off the tops and bottoms of the husks to create tidier, more uniform wrappers. In a medium pot over medium-high heat, bring the remaining 3 cups of water to a boil. Boil the corn husks for 5 minutes to soften them, then drain and set them aside.

Make the filling: Using a sharp knife, cut the corn kernels off the cobs and place them in the jar of a blender. Add the soaked sticky rice, coconut milk, sugar, and salt and blend until a coarse mixture forms. Transfer the mixture to a small pot, set over medium heat, and bring to a simmer. Cook for 5 to 8 minutes, stirring occasionally, until it thickens slightly. Remove the pot from the heat and let the mixture cool for about 15 minutes.

Assemble the bundles: Lay one corn husk wrapper flat on a clean surface and scoop 2 tablespoons of the corn mixture into the center. Fold the sides of the husk inward over the filling, then fold each end downward to create a neat rectangular package. Repeat with the remaining mixture and husks to form 12 bundles.

Steam and serve: Bring a large pot of water to a boil. Place the bundles in a steamer basket in a single layer, with enough space between them for steam to circulate. Steam over medium heat for 20 minutes. Allow the bundles to cool for 30 minutes and remove the corn husks before eating.

Sankhagnaa Mak Uu ◆ Custard-Stuffed Kabocha Squash

ສັງຂະຫຍາໝາກອຶ

Serves 4

Kabocha squash has become a beloved ingredient in Lao cuisine. What began as a traditional custard dessert served in a whole coconut (known as sankhagnaa mak phao in Phia Sing's landmark 1981 cookbook) evolved into a popular custard-stuffed kabocha. This adaptation not only introduced the delightful pairing of creamy custard with the soft, sweet texture of kabocha squash, it also made a dessert that's much easier to cut and serve.

- 1 (1-pound) kabocha squash
- 5 eggs
- 1 (13½-ounce) can coconut milk
- ½ cup sugar
- Pinch of coarse kosher salt
- 1 pandan leaf (see page 23)

Carefully cut the top off the squash to create a lid. Use a thin spoon to scoop out the seeds and stringy parts from the center of the squash. Set the lid and the cleaned squash aside.

Make the custard: In a large bowl, crack the eggs and whisk them lightly until they have a uniform consistency but aren't frothy. In a small saucepan, combine the coconut milk, sugar, salt, and pandan leaf. Place over low heat for 5 minutes, stirring occasionally, until the sugar dissolves completely; don't let the mixture boil. Remove the mixture from the heat and slowly drizzle it into the whisked eggs, whisking continuously to temper the eggs and prevent curdling.

Strain the custard and fill and steam the squash: Place a fine-mesh sieve over a large bowl. Pour the custard mixture through the sieve to remove any clumps and ensure a smooth consistency.

Bring a large pot of water to a boil. Wrap the outside of the squash with aluminum foil to provide stability and prevent leaks. Place the squash into a steamer basket, and carefully pour the custard mixture into the hollow of the squash, filling it to ½ inch below the rim. Cover the opening of the squash with a flat piece of aluminum foil to prevent water from entering while it's steaming, and place the "lid" of the squash on the side to steam.

Put the lid on the steamer and steam for 60 minutes. To check if it's done, stick a toothpick into the custard and it should come out clean. After steaming, let the squash cool to room temperature. Wrap it loosely in paper towels and place it in a container with the squash lid on the side and refrigerate it overnight to allow the custard to fully set.

To serve, cut the squash in half. Slice each half into 4 equal pieces and ensure each person gets an equal share of squash and custard. Serve cold, and enjoy!

Makes about 30 balls | Serves 6 to 8

Khanom Maw Tod ◆ Crispy Banana-Stuffed Coconut Balls

ເຂົ້າໜົມໝໍ້ທອດ

Coconut Balls

1½ cups uncooked sticky rice

⅓ cup coconut milk

2 tablespoons granulated sugar

¼ cup dried shredded coconut

Pinch of coarse kosher salt

Batter

½ cup potato starch (see Note)

2 tablespoons granulated sugar

1 teaspoon baking powder

½ cup coconut milk

Filling, Frying, and Finishing

1 ripe 10-inch banana, cut into ½-inch cubes

Vegetable oil, for frying

¼ cup powdered sugar, or more as needed

Note

Potato starch is fine, light, and powdery and often used in creating a crispy coating. It can be found at many supermarkets and Asian markets, but make sure it's not potato flour, which is heavier and has a coarse consistency.

This is my take on the classic Luang Prabang dessert: round balls of sweetened sticky rice stuffed with ripe banana. If an American were to visit Laos, they might stumble upon these fried treats and mistake them for doughnut holes only to discover the delightful surprise inside. This dessert is a reflection of how different cultures create things that are unique yet familiar.

Prepare the sticky rice mixture and batter: Cook the sticky rice using your preferred method (see page 73). In a large bowl, combine the freshly cooked sticky rice, coconut milk, sugar, shredded coconut, and salt. Mix thoroughly until the ingredients are evenly incorporated and the mixture holds together. In a small bowl, whisk together the potato starch, sugar, baking powder, and coconut milk and whisk until smooth and the batter is lump-free. Set aside.

Assemble the dumplings: Set up an assembly station with a small bowl of water for wetting your hands, the diced banana pieces, and the prepared sticky rice mixture. Wet one finger on your dominant hand and the palm of your other hand. Scoop about 1 tablespoon of the sticky rice mixture into your moistened hand, flatten it into a disk, and place a banana cube in the center. Wrap the sticky rice around the banana, rolling it gently in your palm to seal it completely and form a ball. Repeat until all the sticky rice and banana pieces are used; you will have about 30 balls.

Fry the dumplings: In a medium pot, heat 4 inches of oil over medium heat until it reaches 350°F. Just before frying, dip eight sticky rice balls into the batter, rolling them so they are fully coated. With a slotted spoon, carefully place the coated balls into the hot oil. Reduce the heat slightly to maintain an oil temperature of around 330°F, and fry the dumplings for 8 to 10 minutes, stirring gently to keep them from sticking, until golden brown and crispy. Remove the dumplings with a slotted spoon and place them on a paper towel–lined plate to drain. Bring the oil back up to 350°F, and batter and fry the remainder of the sticky rice balls in three more batches.

Finish and serve: While each batch of dumplings is still hot, transfer them to a large bowl. Sprinkle over about 1 tablespoon of powdered sugar and toss gently, allowing the sugar to melt slightly and adhere to the surface of the dumplings. Transfer the sugared dumplings to a serving dish and enjoy them warm!

Khanom Mantone ◆ Steamed Cassava Cake

ເຂົ້າໜົມມັນຕົ້ມ

Serves 4 to 6

There's something truly special about buying steamed desserts from a vendor in Laos. You're presented with a vibrant selection of colors and flavors, beautifully on display among other irresistible Lao treats. Steamed desserts are known for their variously chewy textures; this particular dessert's stickiness helps the shredded coconut adhere to its surface, creating a harmonious blend of textures and flavors with each bite. Freshly grated coconut and fresh cassava root yield the best taste and texture. Cassava root is similar to tapioca in its bouncy nature; once shredded and steamed, if offers a mildly sweet and nutty flavor along with the satisfying chewiness and stickiness that make this dessert so and enjoyable.

1½ pounds sweet cassava root (see Notes)

2 tablespoons dried butterfly pea flowers (see Notes)

½ cup hot water

½ cup coconut milk

¾ cup sugar

¼ teaspoon coarse kosher salt

2 cups shredded fresh coconut meat

Prepare the cassava root: Peel the cassava root, rinse it thoroughly, and cut it into large chunks. Grate the cassava using an automatic grater or by hand, then pulse it in a food processor (this creates a smoother consistency in the cake). In a large bowl, submerge the grated cassava in water for 2 hours to remove the toxins. Drain the water and squeeze the excess liquid from the cassava.

Make butterfly pea flower water: In a small bowl, combine the dried butterfly pea flowers and hot water. Let it steep for 5 minutes until the water turns dark blue. Strain and set the water aside.

Mix the cassava mixture: In a large bowl, combine the grated cassava, coconut milk, butterfly pea flower water, sugar, and salt. Stir until it's a soft, even mixture.

Steam the cassava cake: Bring a large pot of water to a boil. Prepare your steamer by wrapping the lid with a clean kitchen towel to prevent condensation from dripping onto the cake. Pour the cassava mixture into an 8 by 8-inch pan, preferably silicone for easy removal, or use a nonstick or greased pan. Place the pan in the steamer basket, cover, and steam over medium-low heat for 30 minutes.

Cool and assemble: Let the steamed cassava cake cool for 1 hour. Cut the cooled cake into 2 by 1-inch pieces. Put the shredded fresh coconut meat on a wide shallow plate and turn the pieces of cassava cake in the coconut until they're fully coated and ready to serve.

Notes

If fresh cassava root, also known as yuca, is unavailable, frozen grated cassava can be substituted.

Butterfly pea flower is commonly used to make teas and as a natural dye. It's often found dried at Southeast Asian markets or specialty tea shops. For a brighter, more colorful appearance, add another tablespoon of butterfly pea flower water or a few drops of blue food coloring.

Makes 10 muffins

Khanom Jawk ◆ Garlic Rice Muffins

ເຂົ້າໜົມຈອກ

¼ cup uncooked mung beans

½ cup plus 1 tablespoon vegetable oil

4 garlic cloves, minced

¼ cup minced scallions

4 eggs

¼ cup coconut milk

2 cups jasmine rice flour

2 teaspoon baking powder

1 teaspoon coarse kosher salt

1 teaspoon MSG

½ teaspoon freshly ground black pepper

The first time I encountered khanom jawk was at a food stall in Laos, where the vendor seemed to make these effortlessly. He expertly pulled a metal cube mold from the hot oil, coated it with rice batter to create the base, then added a generous spoonful of mung beans to the center before topping it with more batter. The mold went straight into the deep-fryer, and he skillfully tapped the sides until the batter released from the mold, allowing the muffin to fry completely. Inspired by this traditional dish, I decided to re-create the recipe with a twist, using an oven instead of deep-frying. This baked version offers a different take on these flavorful muffins while keeping their essence intact. And note that though khanom jawk is here in the desserts chapter, it's a savory treat with an emphasis on "treat"!

Prepare the mung beans: Place the mung beans in a medium bowl and rinse them three times. Transfer the rinsed beans to a medium pot, cover with water to at least 1 inch above the beans, and bring to a boil over medium-high heat. Once the water is boiling, cover the pot, turn off the heat, and let the beans soak for 15 minutes, then drain and set them aside, reserving 2 tablespoons of the beans for the topping (the rest are for the filling).

Cook the mung bean filling: Heat a small sauté pan over medium heat. Add the 1 tablespoon of the oil. Sauté the minced garlic for 20 seconds, then add the minced scallions and sauté for 1 minute. Add the soaked mung beans and stir well, then remove from the heat and set aside.

Prepare the batter: In a stand mixer with the whisk attachment, beat the eggs on high speed for 4 to 5 minutes, until they're frothy with small bubbles. Add the ½ cup vegetable oil and the coconut milk and whisk for another minute. Turn the mixer to low speed and gradually add the jasmine rice flour and baking powder, whisking until just combined. Add in the mung bean filling, salt, MSG, and black pepper, mixing on low speed until evenly incorporated.

Assemble and bake: Preheat the oven to 350°F. Spray a cupcake pan with nonstick spray and pour ¼ cup of batter into each cupcake well. Sprinkle some of the reserved mung beans on top of each muffin and bake for 25 minutes, or until a thin chopstick or skewer inserted into the center comes out clean. Let the muffins cool slightly before removing them from the pan. Serve warm or at room temperature.

Jeun Mak Guay ◆ Fried Sweet Bananas

จื๋นหมากก้อย

Serves 4 to 6

The banana tree is the quintessence of Lao culinary culture, with nearly every part of it being put to use in the kitchen. Banana leaves, once they're fully grown, serve as natural wrappers and containers, used to hold dishes like mok pa (steamed fish) and khao tom (sticky rice parcels), while young, tender leaves are thinly sliced to enjoy in salads or noodle soups. Its large, showy flowers are a culinary treasure, their intricate folds requiring careful handling to remove the bitter buds. Once done, their subtly sweet versatility shines. Lastly, the bananas in Laos, smaller than their counterparts elsewhere, are firm yet sweet and perfect for frying to make jeun mak guay. Each bite combines gentle sweetness, creaminess, and a delightful crunch, a perfect companion to a freshly brewed cup of coffee. These were my favorite morning treats as a kid, especially on school mornings.

½ cup jasmine rice flour

¼ cup sticky rice flour (see page 18)

¼ cup cornstarch

½ teaspoon baking powder

¼ cup sugar

¼ teaspoon coarse kosher salt

¼ cup coconut milk

6 tablespoons water

2 tablespoons dried shredded coconut

1½ teaspoons white sesame seeds

1½ teaspoons black sesame seeds

8 firm, semiripe baby bananas (see Note)

Vegetable oil, for frying

Sweetened condensed milk, for dipping (optional)

Make the batter: In a large bowl, combine the jasmine rice flour, sticky rice flour, cornstarch, baking powder, sugar, and salt and whisk until evenly mixed. Add the coconut milk and water, and whisk until the mixture forms a thick, smooth batter. Stir in the dried coconut, white sesame seeds, and black sesame seeds until well combined.

Prepare the bananas and the frying station: Peel the baby bananas and cut them in half lengthwise; place in a bowl. Prepare a frying station. Set the bowl of bananas and the bowl of batter next to the stove. Fill a large frying pan with enough vegetable oil to cover the banana halves. Line a bowl or plate with paper towels for draining the fried bananas and set it near the stove.

Fry the bananas: Over high heat, heat the vegetable oil to 350°F. When the oil is hot, dip the banana slices into the batter one at a time, ensuring each is fully coated. Carefully place 4 to 6 banana halves into the hot oil at a time. Fry until the bananas are golden brown and crispy all over, 3 to 4 minutes. If the bananas stick to one another or to the pan, use chopsticks or tongs to gently separate them. As you fry the bananas, maintain the oil temperature at 350°F. If the oil gets too hot, the batter may burn before the bananas are fully cooked. Once they're fried, transfer the bananas to the paper towel–lined plate to drain excess oil.

Serve the fried bananas warm, either on their own or with sweetened condensed milk for dipping (if using). Enjoy!

Note

Use semi-ripe bananas for the best balance of sweetness and firmness. Overripe bananas may become too soft during frying.

9

LAO AMERICAN FUSION

The Funky Kid

Dearest Funky Kid,

I hope this letter finds you when you need it most. It is meant for you as a gesture of understanding and a reminder that your struggles, though they may feel different from those of the kids around you, are seen. This letter comes from a community that loves you fiercely and knows your potential to uplift our food and culture. It is written on behalf of all the Maes in the Lao diaspora, who will always feed you sticky rice, no matter where you go.

Once, "funky food" was not seen as a badge of honor. But today, second- and third-generation Lao food lovers have reclaimed it, embracing their heritage and challenging the idea that their culture's foods are somehow un-American. This bold stance comes from our determination to share Lao food exactly as it is enjoyed at home, without apology or compromise.

The story of Lao food in America began with refugees who bravely navigated an unfamiliar world, often hiding parts of themselves to fit in. Parents sacrificed their identities to protect their children and to help them succeed in a foreign land. Yet, a beautiful shift came when those children became adults and chose to show their parents that times had changed. They were finally ready to celebrate the food that once felt too foreign, embracing it and sharing it. The padaek hidden under the sink could now sit proudly on the table. Recipes tucked away in Mae's memory were preserved online and in books like this, honoring the legacy of Lao cuisine. Today, Lao culture, traditions, and celebrations, especially those around Lao New Year in April, shine brightly across America and beyond. For a community that arrived in our new lands with little more than dreams, this is nothing short of extraordinary.

The challenges faced by the Lao communities in the diaspora have only strengthened our resilience, matching the bold flavors in our food. These struggles fostered unity and pride, strengthening the Lao American dream. From small villages in Laos to crowded apartments in U.S. towns and cities, the journeys of the Lao diaspora are testaments to perseverance. Now, the children of refugees are opening Lao restaurants, food trucks, and fusion eateries, blending tradition with innovation while keeping sticky rice at the heart of it all.

This evolution extends far beyond the United States; it's true of Lao communities in Germany, Australia, Canada, Japan, the United Kingdom, France, Argentina, and beyond. The Lao story is a global puzzle, its pieces scattered but increasingly accessible thanks to the internet. Before social media, phone calls were the only way to connect. Now, recipes, photos, and videos shared online allow Lao people to rediscover our roots and reconnect with one another. What was once passed down through stories is now preserved in digital spaces where cooks proudly showcase their padaek. Social media has become a place where Lao cuisine thrives, celebrated by creators and cooks and preserved for future generations.

This chapter reflects on the journey of a refugee child who grew into a proud, funky Lao American. It explores how Lao food evolves while staying true to its roots, honoring both creativity and culture. Whether it is laab transformed into tacos in California, nam khao fused with musubi in Hawaii, or macaroni

Noodle Soup
Rice Noodle Soup
67

salad with fish sauce in the Midwest, the dishes in this chapter embody the spirit of the diaspora: They honor tradition while embracing new experiences, keeping Lao food at the core.

Although this is the final chapter of this book, it is the beginning of a new story for the Lao community. As more people share our food, whether at family potlucks or through online videos, our movement will continue to grow. The recipes and stories are an invitation to explore the world of funk and share it proudly with your neighbors and friends, just as Mae shared her padaek with the people in her village. Lao food has always been enough. It carries on the legacy of parents and ancestors who fought to give us the chance to share our yet-untold stories. Now, it's your turn to make the world a little more Lao.

I hope you find comfort in what this book offers, a gentle care woven into every spicy recipe and story it tells. With blessings tied around your wrist with white strings, take the spirit, the stories, and (especially) the food in this book as your superpower. Use it to fill every space, especially the kitchen and the table, with the spirit of Lao food. Let your inner funky kid shine.

With love and encouragement,
The Funky Lao American

Mochi Pancakes

Makes 8 pancakes | Serves 2 or 3

When my siblings and I wanted something different from Mae's comforting porridge for breakfast, we would turn to American options like pancakes. We were fascinated by how these thin cakes puffed up on the stove and were then drenched in syrup. But our excitement was always short-lived, since the overly sweet flavors never quite resonated with us. Reimagining this classic American breakfast food, I looked to one of Mae's pantry staples, sticky rice flour, for a way to create pancakes with the texture I loved: chewy and bouncy. Instead of maple syrup, I used coconut milk to create a rich coconut syrup. For fun, I used butterfly pea flower tea to add a light blue hue. These mochi pancakes became a way for us kids to enjoy a breakfast that felt authentic to who we were, blending inspiration from our culture with an American breakfast tradition.

Coconut Syrup

¾ cup coconut milk

1½ teaspoons cornstarch

2½ tablespoons sugar

Coarse kosher salt

⅔ cup water

¼ cup dried butterfly pea flowers (see Note, page 217)

1½ cups sticky rice flour (see page 18)

½ cup tapioca flour

¼ cup sugar

1 teaspoon baking powder

2 eggs

2 tablespoons melted butter

Nonstick spray or additional butter, for the pan

Sliced mango or other fruit, for topping (optional)

Make the syrup: In a small saucepan, combine the coconut milk, cornstarch, sugar, and a pinch of salt. Whisk until the mixture is smooth and well combined. Place the saucepan over medium heat and continue whisking as the sauce begins to thicken, about 5 minutes. As soon as the mixture starts to simmer, immediately remove it from the heat. Pour the syrup into a bowl and let it cool to room temperature before using.

Prepare the butterfly pea flower tea: In a small pot on medium heat, bring ⅔ cup of water to a boil. Place the butterfly pea flowers in a small bowl and pour the boiling water over them. Let the tea steep for 5 minutes, then strain and let the blue tea cool to room temperature.

Make the pancake batter: In a large bowl, whisk together the sticky rice flour, tapioca flour, sugar, baking powder, and ½ teaspoon of salt. Add the cooled tea, eggs, and the melted butter to the dry ingredients, whisking until the batter is smooth and well combined.

Cook the pancakes: Heat a medium frying pan over medium-high heat for 1 minute, then lightly coat it with nonstick spray or a small amount of butter. Reduce the heat to medium-low. Pour ¼ cup of batter into the center of the pan, spreading it slightly if needed to make a ¼-inch-thick pancake. Cook for 2 minutes, carefully flipping halfway through, until both sides have slightly golden-brown edges and the pancake is cooked through. Repeat the process, making sure to spray or butter the pan every time.

Enjoy the pancakes warm, with the coconut syrup and fruit (if using).

Fried Curly Banana Blossoms

Serves 4 to 6

One of the most unique and challenging ingredients in Lao cuisine is the banana blossom. Without proper preparation, things can go a bit wrong. For example, if the cut leaves aren't soaked in water with vinegar or lime, they quickly turn an unappealing dark color. Or, if the pistils inside the flowers aren't removed, they can make the dish bitter and add a stringy texture. This recipe addresses these challenges while also ensuring that every part of the banana blossom is used so that nothing goes to waste. More to the point, these curly banana blossoms are an irresistible snack.

3 cups sliced banana blossom leaves, ½-inch thick (see page 23)

2 cups banana blossom flowers, pistils removed (see page 23)

3 eggs

¼ cup thinly sliced on the bias lemongrass stalk (soft part)

15 fresh makrut lime leaves

2 cups fine potato starch

1 tablespoon garlic powder

1 tablespoon onion powder

2 teaspoons sweet paprika

2 teaspoons coarse kosher salt

1 teaspoon MSG

1 tablespoon roasted sticky rice powder (see page 17)

Vegetable oil, for frying

Jeow Bong Aioli

2 tablespoons Jeow Bong (page 26)

¼ cup mayonnaise

2 garlic cloves, minced

1 tablespoon tamarind paste

When you are ready to start, remove the banana blossom slices and flowers from their acidulated water and pat them dry.

Prepare the coating: In a large bowl, whisk the eggs. Add the banana blossom slices and mix until well coated. Repeat with the banana blossom flowers and sliced lemongrass. In another bowl, combine the potato starch, garlic powder, onion powder, paprika, salt, MSG, and roasted sticky rice powder. Mix thoroughly. Transfer the dry mixture to a large zip-top bag. Add the banana blossom shells and flowers, seal the bag, and shake until the pieces are evenly coated.

Fry the banana blossom: In a fryer or deep pan, heat 4 inches of oil to 350°F. Fry the coated banana blossom leaves and flowers in batches for 2 to 3 minutes, until golden brown and crispy. Fry the lemongrass for 2 minutes, or until crisp. Fry the lime leaves for 30 seconds and cover the pan with a lid to prevent splattering. Place the fried items in a large paper towel–lined bowl.

Make the jeow bong aioli and serve: In a small bowl, combine the jeow bong, mayonnaise, minced garlic, and tamarind paste and mix well until smooth. Arrange the fried banana blossom, lemongrass, and lime leaves on a platter. Serve with the jeow bong aioli for dipping.

Makes 6 tacos

Laab Tacos

Taco Shells

Vegetable oil, for frying

Twelve (6-inch) round sheets rice paper

Laab Filling

1 tablespoon vegetable oil

1½ teaspoons minced garlic

1 pound ground pork

½ teaspoon MSG

1½ teaspoons fish sauce (see page 18)

1 tablespoon lime juice

½ teaspoon coarse kosher salt

½ teaspoon ground dried bird's eye chile (see page 18)

1 tablespoon roasted sticky rice powder (see page 17)

1 tablespoon minced galangal

⅓ cup mint leaves

⅓ cup minced scallions, white and green parts

⅓ cup chopped cilantro, tender stems and leaves

¼ cup thinly diced shallot

Avocado Crema

2 medium avocados (about 9 ounces total weight)

¼ cup chopped cilantro, tender stems and leaves

½ teaspoon coarse kosher salt

2 tablespoons lime juice

1 garlic clove, minced

To Serve

2 cups shredded lettuce

1 large tomato, diced

6 lime wedges

In LA, you can't walk far without stumbling upon a taco stand that's offering some of the best tacos you've ever had. I was inspired to start my own food cart, Thum and Thum, in the heart of Koreatown. Instead of tacos, though, I sold the kind of street food you'd find in Laos, like spicy, pungent papaya salad bursting with bold flavors. LA's rich diversity is an exciting playground for culinary innovation, a place where foods from different cultures evolve naturally, and sometimes intermingle. A few years after I started Thum and Thum, this laab taco was born, a product of my love for both Lao food and LA's taco culture. The crispy rice paper shells are filled with flavorful pork laab and topped with a cooling avocado crema. Each bite perfectly captures my Lao-Cali experience.

Prepare the taco shells: Set a bowl of room-temperature water next to the stove. In a large pan, heat 2 inches of vegetable oil to 350°F. Quickly wet two rice paper sheets in the water and let most of the excess water drip off. Stack them together so they stick, then place the stacked rice papers on a taco mold and fry for 40 to 60 seconds, until crispy on all sides. If you don't have a taco mold, fry the layered rice paper flat for 30 seconds, until it begins to harden. Use a chopstick to lift up the middle of the rice paper round, creating a deep crease. Fry for another 20 seconds to set the shape. Set on a paper towel–lined tray to drain. Repeat with the remaining rice paper to shape 6 taco shells.

Cook the pork: Heat 1 tablespoon of vegetable oil in a large pan over medium-high heat. Add the minced garlic and sauté for 30 seconds. Add the ground pork, sprinkle with the MSG, and sauté for about 5 minutes, breaking up clumps, until fully cooked. Transfer the cooked pork to a large bowl and let it cool for about 10 minutes.

Season the filling: In a small bowl, mix the fish sauce and lime juice. Add this mixture to the cooled pork along with the salt, chile, and roasted sticky rice powder. Stir well to combine. Gently fold in the galangal, mint leaves, scallions, cilantro, and shallot.

Make the avocado crema: Halve and pit the avocados and scoop the flesh into a blender. Add the cilantro, salt, lime juice, and garlic, and blend until smooth and creamy.

Assemble the tacos: Fill each rice paper taco shell with ¼ cup of the laab pork mixture. Top with shredded lettuce, diced tomato, avocado crema, and a squeeze of lime. Serve immediately.

Som Moo Milk Bread Sandwich

Makes 2 sandwiches | Serves 4

Laos has a vibrant sandwich culture heavily influenced by its French colonial history; it's evident in the fresh baguettes sold at morning markets and the khao jee pâté sandwiches found at night markets. Though similar to neighboring Vietnam's báhn mì, the Lao-style baguette sandwich features local touches, including pork floss, thinly shredded papaya for crunch, drizzles of spicy fish sauce and pepper dip, pâté, Lao ham, and fresh herbs. This recipe draws inspiration from the traditional Lao baguette sandwich but reimagines it with a Midwestern twist, inspired by my childhood white bread sandwiches with bologna and Cheddar cheese. Instead of a baguette, fluffy milk bread is cooked in egg like French toast. The sandwich filling combines sour pork sausage with pork floss for balance. It's then spread with a creamy and spicy jeow bong aïoli to tie everything together. This sandwich is both comforting and bursting with flavor.

Eggs and Bread

6 eggs

1 teaspoon coarse kosher salt

1 teaspoon freshly ground black pepper

½ teaspoon MSG

2 tablespoons minced cilantro, soft stems and leaves

2 tablespoons minced scallions

4 tablespoons unsalted butter, divided

4 slices milk bread, or preferred white sandwich bread

Jeow Bong Aïoli

¼ cup Jeow Bong (page 26)

½ cup mayonnaise

4 garlic cloves, minced

2 tablespoons tamarind paste

Filling

¼ cup pork pâté

1 pound thinly sliced Som Moo (page 115)

⅔ cup pork floss (see Note)

½ cup chopped mustard greens

Prepare the eggs and bread: In a small bowl, whisk together the eggs, salt, black pepper, MSG, cilantro, and scallions. Heat a medium nonstick pan over medium-low heat, and melt 1 tablespoon of butter. Place one slice of bread in the pan and toast for 2 to 3 minutes on one side, allowing it to soak up the butter. Remove to a plate and repeat with the remaining 3 tablespoons of butter and 3 slices of bread.

Reduce the heat to low and pour a quarter of the egg mixture into the pan, spreading it evenly. Place a slice of bread on the egg, non-toasted side down, and cook until the egg is set, 1 to 2 minutes. Remove, and repeat with the remaining egg mixture and bread.

Make the jeow bong aïoli: In a small bowl, mix together the jeow bong, mayonnaise, minced garlic, and tamarind paste until smooth.

Assemble the sandwiches and serve: Arrange the four slices of bread egg side up. On two slices, spread your desired amount of jeow bong aïoli. On the other two slices, spread the pork pâté, then layer with som moo slices, pork floss, mustard greens, and a second layer of som moo. Place the slice with jeow bong aïoli on top to close the sandwich. Cut the sandwiches in half and serve immediately.

Note

Pork floss is fluffy and light Chinese-style shredded dried pork. It can be found at Asian grocery stories. Other than eating it in this sandwich, it makes a perfect accompaniment to sticky rice and a jeow.

Serves 6 to 8

Nam Khao Musubi

Rice Patties

2 cups uncooked jasmine rice

2½ cups water

1 egg

1 tablespoon Red Curry Paste (see page 21; or use store-bought)

1 teaspoon coarse kosher salt

½ teaspoon MSG

2 fresh makrut lime leaves, minced

¼ cup dried coconut shreds

Vegetable oil, for frying

Dressing

1 tablespoon lime juice

1 tablespoon fish sauce (see page 18)

¼ cup crushed roasted peanuts

½ cup diced cilantro soft stems and leaves

2 scallions, chopped, white and green parts

2 cups thinly sliced Som Moo (about 10 ounces; see page 115 and Note)

½ cup whole mint leaves

6 to 8 fried bird's eye chiles (see page 18)

5 sheets nori, cut into 2-inch-wide strips

This recipe gives nam khao tod a fresh twist, inspired by the tropical flavors of Hawaii. During my time living in Hilo, studying counseling psychology and, perhaps more passionately, immersing myself in the island's food and culture, I found inspiration in every bite of poi, laulau, and kalua pig. Hawaii's vibrant mix of cultures inspired me to create this Lao-Hawaiian fusion. Instead of the soft white rice traditionally used in musubi, I incorporated fragrant red curry–infused rice shaped into crispy patties to hold the tangy soured pork sausage. A sweetened fish sauce glaze balances the flavors, while the signature nori wrap pays homage to the essence of Spam musubi. My time in Hawaii was one of self-discovery and aloha, deeply enriched by the people I met and the food I experienced. That journey is reflected in this recipe, blending the flavors of my Lao heritage with the spirit of Hawaii.

Prepare the rice patties: In a large bowl, rinse the rice with cool water three times, then strain thoroughly. In a medium pot, combine the rinsed rice and the 2½ cups of water. Bring to a boil over high heat, then reduce the heat to low, cover, and cook for 15 minutes. Spread the cooked rice evenly onto a baking tray lined with parchment paper. Let it cool to room temperature, about 20 minutes.

In a small bowl, whisk together the egg, red curry paste, salt, and MSG. In a medium bowl, combine the cooled rice with the egg–red curry mixture, stirring until evenly coated. Add the minced lime leaves and shredded coconut to the rice mixture and mix well. Form ⅓ cup of the rice mixture into a patty using a musubi press (or shape by hand, wetting your hands with water to prevent sticking); repeat with the rest of the rice.

In a medium pan, heat about ½ inch of vegetable oil to 350°F. Fry each rice patty for 6 minutes, flipping halfway, until golden brown and crispy. Transfer the fried patties to a paper towel–lined plate to drain and cool.

Prepare the dressing and assemble the musubi: In a small bowl, mix the lime juice and fish sauce. Lightly brush one side of each fried rice patty with the dressing. Place a fried rice patty on a flat surface. Layer on crushed peanuts, cilantro, scallions, som moo slices, mint leaves, and a fried bird's eye chile, then wrap the stack with a strip of nori to secure it. Serve the musubi immediately, or wrap tightly in plastic wrap for later.

Note

Cut the Som Moo into 15 slices, each about ⅛ inch thick, 3½ inches long, and 2 inches wide. Each should weigh around 1 ounce.

Lao-Style Poke

Serves 2 or 3

Once you've mastered the art of making jeows, your fridge will likely be filled with jars and containers of these flavorful Lao dips. This recipe was born from my desire to experience those bold, spicy flavors in every bite of poke. Tuna is a versatile fish that easily absorbs flavors, making it the perfect canvas for tangy jeow som and smoky jeow bong. Together, they infuse the fish with incredible taste and give it a vibrant red hue. The toasted sesame oil ties all the flavors together, creating a harmonious balance. Whether you're enjoying it on a beach or in the comfort of home, this dish is a perfect lunch.

Poke

1 pound sushi-grade tuna

2 tablespoons Jeow Som (page 31)

1½ teaspoons Jeow Bong (page 26)

½ teaspoon seasoning sauce (see page 22)

1 teaspoon toasted sesame oil

1½ teaspoons gochugaru (Korean chile flakes)

2 fresh bird's eye chiles, stemmed and minced

¼ cup chopped cilantro, tender stems and leaves

¼ cup chopped scallions, green parts only

¼ cup thinly sliced shallot

To Serve

Cooked jasmine rice

Smelt roe

Sliced cucumber

Sliced radish

Sliced avocado

Fried riverweed (see page 140) or seaweed

Prepare the tuna and dressing: Cut the tuna into ½-inch cubes and set aside in a medium bowl. In a small bowl, whisk together jeow som, jeow bong, seasoning sauce, sesame oil, and gochugaru until evenly combined.

Assemble the poke and serve: Pour the dressing over the tuna cubes. Add the minced bird's eye chiles, cilantro, scallions, and shallot. Gently toss everything together until evenly coated, being careful not to mash the fish.

Plate the poke over jasmine rice and garnish with smelt roe, sliced cucumber, radish, avocado, and fried riverweed. Serve immediately and enjoy!

Serves 4 to 6

Roasted Rice Macaroni Salad

8 ounces elbow macaroni

Dressing

½ cup mayonnaise

1½ tablespoons fish sauce (see page 18)

1 tablespoon lime juice

½ teaspoon MSG

1 tablespoon roasted sticky rice powder (see page 17), plus more for garnish (optional)

To Serve

2 Persian cucumbers, thinly cut into ¼-inch-thick circles

½ cup seeded, thinly diced red Fresno chile

½ cup chopped cilantro, soft stems and leaves

¼ cup minced scallions

⅔ cup whole mint leaves

⅓ cup thinly sliced shallot

2 fresh bird's eye chiles, stemmed and thinly sliced

1 head lettuce, for serving (optional)

When many Lao refugee families first arrived in their new states, they often relied on government assistance and local support, including food pantries and food boxes. These boxes contained unfamiliar ingredients like macaroni. Families adapted by adding macaroni to chicken soup and making it extra spicy. Inspired by these creative adjustments, I created this fish sauce and toasted rice–infused macaroni salad. It's designed for easy sharing and can be enjoyed as a salad or as a lettuce wrap like many Lao dishes.

Cook the macaroni: In a medium pot, bring 3 quarts of water to a rolling boil. Add the elbow macaroni and cook until al dente, about 11 minutes. Set aside ½ cup of the pasta water, then drain the pasta and rinse it under cold water until it cools to room temperature. Drain well, and set aside in a medium bowl.

Make the dressing: In a medium bowl, combine the mayonnaise, fish sauce, lime juice, MSG, 1 tablespoon roasted sticky rice powder, and the reserved pasta water. Whisk until the mixture is smooth and well combined.

Assemble the salad and serve: In the bowl with the cooked macaroni, add the cucumbers, red chiles, and dressing. Toss to coat evenly. Add the cilantro, scallions, mint leaves, shallot, and bird's eye chile. If you like, sprinkle with additional roasted sticky rice powder for extra flavor. Serve as a lettuce wrap or enjoy as a side dish.

Khao Tom Het ◆ Morel Sticky Rice Parcels

Makes 11 parcels | Serves 4 to 6

Mae's mushroom foraging was a regular part of our spring weekends when I was a kid. While Mae wandered into the woods, searching near tree trunks for mushrooms, I'd ask to stay by the playground. After stopping at several parks in the morning, we'd head home to clean the mushrooms and portion them into small bags to share with friends. On the drive home, I'd sit in the back seat next to giant bags of mushrooms she had gathered, which were nearly as big as I was. I once asked Mae how she knew which mushrooms were safe to eat. Her answer was simple: community. She learned by going out with friends, who had learned from the generation before them. These mushrooms found their way into all kinds of dishes, but this morel sticky rice recipe is a tribute both to Mae's love of mushroom foraging and the creativity in the kitchen that she helped cultivate in me. It's something new, made just for her. Traditional khao tom is a sweet sticky rice parcel filled with banana, taro, or black beans. This version takes a savory approach to khao tom, highlighting the umami-rich flavor of morels and pairing it with the creaminess of coconut milk. The result is a perfect seasonal snack that's both unique and satisfying.

2 cups uncooked sticky rice

1 tablespoon vegetable oil

4 garlic cloves, minced

¼ cup minced scallions

½ cup thinly sliced fresh morels (see Note) or shiitake mushrooms (cut in circular pieces)

1 cup coconut milk

1 teaspoon coarse kosher salt

11 (5 by 5-inch) aluminum foil squares

Prepare the sticky rice: Place the uncooked sticky rice in a large bowl, and rinse and drain it three times. Then add hot water to the bowl to cover the rice by at least 1 inch. Soak for 1 hour. Drain the rice, transfer it to a rice steamer (see page 73), and steam for 30 minutes, flipping the rice halfway through cooking.

Cook the mushroom mixture: Heat a medium pot over medium heat, then add the vegetable oil and minced garlic and sauté for 30 seconds. Add the scallions and chopped morels and cook for 1 minute. Reduce the heat to low and stir in the coconut milk and salt. Mix well to combine. Add the warm sticky rice, stirring until all the liquid is absorbed and the rice is evenly coated, then remove from the heat.

Assemble and steam the parcels: Place a foil square on a flat surface. Scoop ⅓ cup of the rice mixture onto the side of the foil closest to you. Roll the foil tightly around the rice to form a tube, then fold both ends of the tube, securely enclosing the rice parcel. Repeat with the remaining rice mixture and foil squares. Bring a large pot of water to a boil. Arrange the foil-wrapped parcels in a steamer basket. Steam on high heat for 30 minutes. Allow the parcels to cool slightly before unwrapping and serving.

Note

If fresh morels are not available, you can use dried morels (find them at a specialty market). To rehydrate dried morels, place them in a medium bowl and pour enough boiling water over the mushrooms to cover them. Let them sit for 10 minutes. Drain, then slice and use to make the mushroom mixture.

Serves 4 to 6

Fish Sauce and Butter Seafood Boil

Seafood Boil

4 quarts water

3 tablespoons fish sauce (see page 18)

¼ cup chili garlic sauce (sambal)

1 yellow onion, halved

1 lemongrass bundle (see page 21)

¼ cup thinly cut peeled galangal (about 1 ounce)

4 fresh makrut lime leaves, crushed by hand

1 pound snow crab legs

1 pound corn on the cob, shucked and chopped into 2-inch lengths

1 pound shell-on jumbo shrimp

1 pound mussels, preferably PEI

4 to 6 peeled hard-boiled eggs

Garlic Butter Sauce

1 cup unsalted butter

2 tablespoons minced lemongrass (from the soft part of 1 stalk)

¼ cup minced garlic (about 10 cloves)

1 tablespoon garlic powder

1 tablespoon onion powder

1 tablespoon sweet paprika

1 teaspoon MSG

3 tablespoons lime juice

3 tablespoons chili garlic sauce (sambal)

1 teaspoon sugar

1 tablespoon roasted sticky rice powder (see page 17)

3 tablespoons fish sauce (see page 18)

To Serve

½ cup minced cilantro

⅓ cup chopped scallions, green parts only

1 cup chopped celery (¼-inch slices)

¼ cup minced fresh bird's eye chiles

Cooked sticky rice (see page 73)

I may be allergic to seafood, but I still eat it, just like Mae. I remember watching her savor shrimp, even after she had done so the week before and broken out in hives. Her attitude toward allergies seems to be: Do allergies even exist, and if they do, can't we just push through them? In my family, our deep love for seafood clearly outweighs the consequences. We persevere, enjoying the bounty of the ocean whenever possible, especially in dishes like this seafood boil, accompanied with a luxe, Lao-style garlic-butter sauce. The butter melds with the nutty aroma of roasted sticky rice powder, the tang of lemongrass, and the funk of fish sauce.

Cook the seafood boil: In a large pot, combine the water, fish sauce, chili garlic sauce, onion, lemongrass bundle, galangal, and lime leaves. Bring to a boil over medium heat, then simmer on low heat for 15 minutes to infuse the flavors into the water. Add the snow crab legs and corn and boil for 4 minutes. Add the shrimp and mussels, and boil for an additional 3 to 4 minutes, until all the seafood is cooked through. Drain well and transfer the seafood and corn to a large serving bowl. Once the seafood is cool, add the hard-boiled eggs.

Make the garlic butter sauce: In a small saucepan, melt the butter over medium heat. Add the minced lemongrass and garlic and cook for 2 minutes, until fragrant. Stir in the garlic powder, onion powder, paprika, and MSG. Cook for a few seconds and remove from the heat. Add the lime juice, chili garlic sauce, sugar, roasted sticky rice powder, and fish sauce and mix thoroughly.

Combine and garnish: Pour the garlic butter sauce over the seafood mixture in the serving bowl. Toss gently to coat everything evenly. Add the cilantro, scallions, and celery and mix gently. Garnish with minced bird's eye chile, and serve the seafood boil with sticky rice on the side.

Lao-Style Fried Chicken

Serves 6 to 8

In the busy city of Vientiane, there's a famous food stall that's said to serve the best fried chicken in Laos. The story goes that it was created by someone who once worked at a major fried chicken chain before returning to Laos to re-create the fried chicken experience with a twist. And I can confirm, it's incredible. The chicken is perfectly crispy, and they take it up a notch by offering it with spicy papaya salad and french fries, a pairing that's both bold and satisfying. This place made me reflect on my own identity. I often feel like I straddle two worlds, Lao and American. Inspired by the story of the stall in Vientiane, I decided to re-create their fried chicken, but with my own twist: making it gluten-free by using rice flour. The result? One of the crispiest fried chickens I've ever had, paired beautifully with a jeow bong–inspired sauce for drizzling or dunking. It's a perfect fusion of flavors and textures.

Marinade

1 tablespoon coarse kosher salt

¼ cup peeled, roughly chopped galangal (about 1 ounce)

¼ cup minced lemongrass (from the soft part of 1 stalk)

¼ cup whole garlic cloves

½ cup coconut milk

1 egg

Chicken

1 tablespoon salt

1 tablespoon MSG

1 tablespoon onion powder

1 tablespoon garlic powder

1 tablespoon sweet paprika

1 tablespoon white pepper powder

3 pounds chicken (4 thighs and 4 drumsticks)

Vegetable oil, for frying

1 cup sticky rice flour (see page 18)

1 cup cornstarch

1½ teaspoons baking powder

Jeow Bong Wet Sauce

½ cup Jeow Bong (page 26)

2 tablespoons fish sauce (see page 18)

3 tablespoons tamarind paste

3 tablespoons brown sugar

2 tablespoons white vinegar

¾ cup water

1½ teaspoons vegetable oil

Garnish

10 whole dried bird's eye chiles

3 tablespoons roasted peanuts

Prepare the marinade: In a deep mortar, pound the salt and galangal into a paste. Add the minced lemongrass and continue pounding until combined, then add the garlic and pound into a smooth paste. In a medium bowl, whisk the paste with the coconut milk and egg until well combined.

Season and marinate the chicken: To make the dry seasoning, mix the salt, MSG, onion powder, garlic powder, paprika, and white pepper in a small bowl. Set aside 3 tablespoons of the mixture. Add the remaining seasoning mixture to the marinade and mix thoroughly. Place the chicken pieces in a large bowl, pour the marinade over them, and turn to ensure all pieces are well coated. Cover, and marinate in the fridge for 2 to 3 hours or overnight for best results.

Prepare for frying: In a large pot over medium-high heat, add at least 4 inches of vegetable oil. Heat the oil until it reaches 350°F (use a thermometer for accuracy). In a medium bowl, combine the sticky rice flour, cornstarch, baking powder, and the reserved 3 tablespoons of dry seasoning mixture; whisk to combine well.

Next to the stove, gather the marinated chicken, the flour mixture, a plate for the coated chicken, and a rack for draining the fried chicken. Coat each piece of chicken in the flour mixture, pressing the mixture onto the surface of the chicken to ensure even coating, and shaking off the excess. Set the coated pieces on the plate.

Continued

Lao-Style Fried Chicken
continued

Fry the chicken: Once the oil reaches 350°F, fry four pieces of chicken at a time: Carefully lower the chicken into the oil, reduce the heat to medium, and fry for 15 minutes without stirring. The oil temperature may drop to around 300°F during frying, which is fine. Remove the fried chicken and place it on the rack to drain. Bring the oil back to 350°F before frying the next batch. Repeat with the remaining four pieces.

Bring the oil to 375°F, then reduce the heat under the pot to medium and fry each batch of chicken again, for 5 minutes this time. Place the double-fried chicken on the rack to rest for at least 10 minutes.

Make the jeow bong wet sauce and garnish: In a bowl, combine the jeow bong, fish sauce, tamarind paste, brown sugar, vinegar, and water; mix well. In a small sauté pan, heat the oil for 1 minute over medium-high heat. Add the dried chiles and cook, stirring frequently, for 1 minute, then remove and set aside. Discard most of the remaining oil, and pour the sauce mixture into the pan. Simmer, stirring continuously, for 3 to 4 minutes, until thickened.

Serve the fried chicken hot, tossed in the sauce to coat completely, or with the sauce on the side for dipping. Garnish with the sautéed chiles and roasted peanuts.

Sai Oua Wontons

Serves 4 to 6

Under the bright studio lights, with several cameras pointing at me and only thirty minutes left on the clock, I took sai oua, the beloved Lao sausage, and transformed it into bite-sized wontons, perfect to pair with sweet chili sauce. I was a contestant on the national TV show *Rat in the Kitchen,* and this was my moment to showcase what Lao food truly means to me. That dish won me the episode and a $25,000 cash prize. But while the prize was exciting, the truest joy came from representing, and from sharing with the world the pride and passion I have for Lao cuisine. Every time I make these wontons now, it feels like a celebration of that moment and a reminder of everything I love about Lao food and Lao culture.

2 tablespoons chopped lemongrass (from the soft part of 1 stalk)

1 tablespoon chopped galangal

1 tablespoon minced garlic

1 fresh bird's eye chile, stemmed

1 shallot, chopped

1 pound ground pork

¼ cup minced scallions

¼ cup minced cilantro

3 tablespoons oyster sauce

1 teaspoon freshly ground black pepper

Splash of fish sauce (see page 18)

25 wonton wrappers

Vegetable oil, for frying

Sweet chili sauce, for serving

Prepare the aromatic paste: In a food processor or deep mortar, blend or mash the lemongrass, galangal, garlic, chile, and shallot into a coarse paste.

Make the meatball filling: In a large bowl, combine the aromatic paste with the ground pork, scallions, cilantro, oyster sauce, black pepper, and fish sauce. Mix thoroughly until well combined.

Assemble the wontons: On a work surface, lay out the wonton wrappers (work in batches depending on how much space you have). Wet the edges of a wrapper with a small amount of water, and place about 1 tablespoon of the pork mixture in the center of the wrapper. Fold and seal the wrapper tightly around the filling to form a ball. Repeat with the rest of the wrappers and filling.

Cook the wontons: In a deep frying pan or pot, heat 4 inches of oil to 350°F. Fry the wontons in batches until golden brown and cooked through, about 3 to 5 minutes; turn them halfway through. As they finish frying, remove the wontons to a paper towel–lined plate to drain. Serve hot with sweet chili sauce for dipping.

Serves 2 or 3

Jeow Som Wings

My family has always loved pairing sticky rice with chicken wings and jeow som. Inspired by my family's love for these flavors, I decided to combine them in a new way by creating sticky rice–coated crispy wings smothered in a thickened jeow som sauce. These wings are perfect for gatherings, and they capture what I love most about food: how it can take on new and creative forms while still delivering familiar, comforting flavors.

Marinade

2 pounds whole chicken wings (about 8 wings)

4 garlic cloves, minced

3 tablespoons oyster sauce

1 tablespoon seasoning sauce (see page 22)

1 teaspoon MSG

Freshly ground black pepper, to taste

Sauce

½ cup sugar

¼ cup water

¼ cup lime juice

¼ cup fish sauce (see page 18)

6 fresh bird's eye chiles, stemmed and minced

Flour Mix

¼ cup cornstarch

¼ cup sticky rice flour (see page 18)

½ teaspoon baking powder

1 teaspoon coarse kosher salt

Vegetable oil, for frying

Garnish

1 tablespoon fried garlic (see page 21)

1 tablespoon whole cilantro leaves

Prepare the wings: Line a large baking tray with paper towels and set it next to a work surface. With a cleaver or chef's knife, cut each wing into two pieces at the joint between the meaty drumette and the rest of the wing. Place the wing pieces on the lined baking tray and pat them dry with another paper towel.

Marinate the wings: Transfer the wings to a large bowl. Add the garlic, oyster sauce, seasoning sauce, MSG, and black pepper and mix thoroughly, ensuring the wings are evenly coated. Cover, and refrigerate for at least 30 minutes, or overnight for best results.

Make the sauce: In a small saucepan over medium heat, cook the sugar until it melts to a smooth, golden liquid, about 3 minutes. Carefully pour in the water to stop the caramelization; stir. Add the lime juice, fish sauce, and minced chiles. Stir continuously until the sugar is dissolved and the sauce thickens. Let it gently simmer until small bubbles form and pop slowly, indicating the right consistency, about 5 minutes. Remove from the heat and set aside.

Prepare the flour mix and fry the wings: In a large bowl, combine the cornstarch, sticky rice flour, baking powder, and salt. Heat 4 inches of oil in a wok or deep-fryer to 350°. Dredge five wings at a time in the flour mix, ensuring they're fully coated. Shake off any excess flour and, using tongs, carefully lower the wings into the hot oil. Fry until the wings are golden brown and cooked through, 5 to 7 minutes. Remove the wings and place them in a bowl lined with paper towels to drain. Repeat with the remaining wings, making sure the oil is 350°F before you add each batch. (As an alternative, air-fry the wings at 400°F for 30 minutes, flipping halfway through.)

To serve, toss the wings in half of the sauce, ensuring they are evenly coated. Sprinkle with fried garlic and garnish with cilantro. Serve with the remaining sauce on the side.

ACKNOWLEDGMENTS

The Lao word *sahtu* is often spoken when a person receives blessings and well wishes from friends, family, and loved ones during life's significant moments. As I think about you, the reader, holding this book in your hands, I can't help but reflect on the journey that brought it to life. This book is filled with stories about my family, but even more so, it is about the greater Lao community where we are all one another's brothers, sisters, aunties, and uncles. The white blessing string that was tied around my wrist at birth has been with me through every chapter of my life, leading me to this moment of sharing our food and culture with you. This book exists because of the collective love and support I receive from the Lao community.

To Mae and Paw, who survived the Secret War and carried my two-year-old self on your shoulders to an unknown land in search of freedom: You left behind everything familiar and started over. Thank you for raising me with love woven into every basket of khao niew, every slurp of pho from a freshly slaughtered cow, and every fiery bite of thum mak hoong that made me sweat. It took me thirty-five years and the writing of this book to fully understand the depth of your love, poured into every meal. I can't imagine what it was like to raise children in a new world, where the language and customs were foreign, but you did it. You built a home, raised three kids, and found your Lao community, who stood by you through every trial and triumph. Watching you create that community shaped my own love for the Lao diaspora.

I never knew that being the middle child between my two beautiful sisters, Daeng and Amy, would save me. You have been monumental in my journey, always letting me spread my wings, knowing I would find my way back. Leaving home, I felt lost, unsure of where I would be fully accepted as a queer kid. But it was you two who helped me navigate our relationship with Mae and Paw, lifting boulders off my shoulders along the way. Thank you for helping me search through family photos, for recalling our childhood stories, and for always being there. You both continue to give so much to your growing families while remaining a constant support for our parents. I couldn't have asked for better sisters.

To my Euay and mentor, Kulap Vilaysack, thank you for the endless laughter, guidance, and tear-filled conversations we've shared since I moved to Los Angeles. We first met when I catered Lao food for your fundraiser, and I never could have imagined how our relationship would evolve. From game nights to deep conversations about our shared childhood traumas, you have created a space where I feel truly seen. You pushed me to build the life I wanted and always listened without judgment, except when you knew I needed a push. You are the heart of Laos Angeles, a mother figure to over three hundred people, creating a community we all longed for. I am forever grateful to be part of it.

To Vannapha Sisouphanthavong, I was once afraid to visit Laos, but you changed that for me. Thank you for helping me navigate my fears and for sharing your favorite places every time I visit. Your love for Lao food has deeply shaped this book, bridging the gap between Laos and the Lao diaspora. Our first meeting in Vientiane, and your help with connecting me to my aunt in Savannakhet, gave me a moment of pure love meeting extended family for the first time. Thank you for helping translate the recipe names, connecting me to Lao businesses, and suggesting recipes to make this book complete. Your friendship made me feel welcome in the motherland I once felt unsure of.

To my Lao food lovers, whether you've traveled with me to Laos or cooked along with me at home, thank you. Your willingness to test recipes and share feedback made this book better. I am grateful to each of you: Bill Bellair, Laura Dust, Kaisi Faithfull, Kerry Fongthavisay, Michelle Matte, Laura Praseutkoun, Derick Sananikone, Diana Savanh, Tiffany Sim, Anna Sorsenginh, Pathamaphone Stewart, and Alex Tsao.

To Sally Ekus, for being a bright light during every Zoom call and sharing your vast knowledge of the cookbook world; your unwavering support gave me the confidence to write this book. Your openness in sharing your personal journeys inspires me to share my stories and recipes with the world. I am so lucky to have you as my agent, and I can't wait for the day we finally meet in person.

To Kevin J. Miyazaki, thank you for helping me refine my photography skills, which allowed me to take my own photographs for this book. The process was both daunting and fulfilling, and I truly appreciate you taking the time to support a fellow Wisconsinite.

It was important to me to feature ceramics made in Laos, pieces I personally collected during my travels. Twelve of the photographs in this book showcase ceramics from Lao Pottery House and Mick Shippen of Doi Ka Noi, both of whom generously host travelers on my annual Lao Foodie Tour with delicious meals and stunning handmade pottery.

I am deeply thankful to the Ten Speed Press team for making my first cookbook such a joyful and meaningful experience. Zoey, I still remember the day you reached out after watching my social media posts about wanting to write a cookbook. Thank you for believing in my work and connecting me with the right people. You are a true advocate for stories that often go untold. Your talent with words and keen eye for detail have greatly improved this book. Emma, working with you has been effortless. You always created a space for open dialogue and encouraged my vision. Your praise for my photos and work ethic meant the world to me and reassured me that this was the right path. This book came to life because of our harmonious partnership, and I know the Lao community will be grateful for it.

I will never have enough words to express my gratitude to my partner, Roy. Thank you for always letting me dream and for supporting my passions every step of the way. You have been my rock helping me write and edit my stories, offering your thoughts on my food styling, and shaping this book into what it is. Your gift with words is something I admire, and I'm grateful this book holds your touch. From your creative food ideas to your skill in organizing the dozens of plates, your support allowed me to keep writing and working, helping bring this book to completion. Most of all, thank you for bringing Galabao into our lives. Our dog has taught me a love I never knew I would have. When we first started dating, you surprised me with a book about Laos. Now, I hope you see the magic we have created together in our very own Lao cookbook.

Through my travels, I have met so many of you, fellow members of the Lao diaspora, and it is because of you that I wrote this book. I wanted to create something that allows us to share our stories, speak up about who we are, and celebrate the deliciousness of our food. Every Lao household I have visited has welcomed me like family, just as Mae's kitchen always has. Whether we met through my visiting your Lao restaurant, celebrating Lao New Year with you, or seeing you proudly share your heritage online, know that this book is a representation of the blessing string so often given to me at community gatherings. Now, I give it to you, a string to tie around your wrist, wishing you a life of fulfillment and joy with every recipe you try. May the familiar and funky flavors remind you of home. Sahtu.

INDEX

T

V

W

Y

Some of the recipes in this book include raw fish and raw or sun-dried meat. When these foods are consumed raw, there is always the risk that bacteria, which is killed by proper cooking, may be present. Because of the health risks associated with the consumption of bacteria that can be present in raw meat and fish, these foods should not be consumed by infants, small children, pregnant women, the elderly, or any persons who may be immunocompromised.

TEN SPEED PRESS
An imprint of the Crown Publishing Group
A division of Penguin Random House LLC
1745 Broadway
New York, NY 10019
tenspeed.com
penguinrandomhouse.com

Typefaces: RDK Group's Lao font, Ed Benguiat's Barcelona, and Klim Type Foundry's Tiempos

Library of Congress Cataloging-in-Publication Data
Names: Douangdara, Saeng, 1989– author
Title: The Lao kitchen : Lao flavors and stories told through family recipes / by Saeng Douangdara.
Description: First edition. | New York, NY : Ten Speed Press, [2026] | Includes index.
Identifiers: LCCN 2025024510 (print) | LCCN 2025024511 (ebook) | ISBN 9780593836170 hardcover | ISBN 9780593836187 ebook
Subjects: LCSH: Cooking, Lao | LCGFT: Cookbooks
Classification: LCC TX724.5.L28 D683 2026 (print) | LCC TX724.5.L28 (ebook) | DDC 641.59/2959191—dc23/eng/20250702
LC record available at https://lccn.loc.gov/2025024510
LC ebook record available at https://lccn.loc.gov/2025024511

Hardcover ISBN: 978-0-593-83617-0
Ebook ISBN: 978-0-593-83618-7

Editor: Zoey Brandt | Production editor: Terry Deal
Designer: Emma Campion | Production designers: Mari Gill and Faith Hague
Production and prepress color manager: Jane Chinn
Writing assistant: Roy Sherwood Lee
Copy editor: Clancy Drake | Proofreaders: Patricia Dailey, Jason Rolan, Alissa Fitzgerald
Indexer: Heather Laskey
Publicist: David Hawk | Marketer: Emily Hotaling

Manufactured in China

10 9 8 7 6 5 4 3 2 1

First Edition